CAMBRIDGE LIBRARY COLLECTION

Books of enduring scholarly value

History

The books reissued in this series include accounts of historical events and movements by eye-witnesses and contemporaries, as well as landmark studies that assembled significant source materials or developed new historiographical methods. The series includes work in social, political and military history on a wide range of periods and regions, giving modern scholars ready access to influential publications of the past.

Home Letters Written from India

Between 1827 and 1841, Samuel Sneade Brown (1809–1875), a colonial administrator, was stationed in India. Published in 1878, this is a selection of the letters he sent home to his family during that period. Brown describes his correspondence as 'a journal of my heart, rather than a diary of my actions', and his letters are both poetic and humorous, telling a personal history of the British Empire. Brown reveals the high cost of colonial living, lamenting to his mother the fact that he could not afford to marry and support a family either in India or England. He communicates his strong bond of affection to his native country and to those he left behind. Making the connection between home and abroad, private and public, the domestic and the Empire, the letters present an insight into the economic changes and political challenges of the nineteenth century.

T0382515

Cambridge University Press has long been a pioneer in the reissuing of out-of-print titles from its own backlist, producing digital reprints of books that are still sought after by scholars and students but could not be reprinted economically using traditional technology. The Cambridge Library Collection extends this activity to a wider range of books which are still of importance to researchers and professionals, either for the source material they contain, or as landmarks in the history of their academic discipline.

Drawing from the world-renowned collections in the Cambridge University Library, and guided by the advice of experts in each subject area, Cambridge University Press is using state-of-the-art scanning machines in its own Printing House to capture the content of each book selected for inclusion. The files are processed to give a consistently clear, crisp image, and the books finished to the high quality standard for which the Press is recognised around the world. The latest print-on-demand technology ensures that the books will remain available indefinitely, and that orders for single or multiple copies can quickly be supplied.

The Cambridge Library Collection will bring back to life books of enduring scholarly value (including out-of-copyright works originally issued by other publishers) across a wide range of disciplines in the humanities and social sciences and in science and technology.

Home Letters
Written from India

Between the Years 1828 and 1841

Samuel Sneade Brown

CAMBRIDGE UNIVERSITY PRESS

Cambridge, New York, Melbourne, Madrid, Cape Town,
Singapore, São Paolo, Delhi, Tokyo, Mexico City

Published in the United States of America by Cambridge University Press, New York

www.cambridge.org
Information on this title: www.cambridge.org/9781108134170

© in this compilation Cambridge University Press 2011

This edition first published 1878
This digitally printed version 2011

ISBN 978-1-108-13417-0 Paperback

Home Letters,

WRITTEN FROM INDIA

between

THE YEARS 1828 & 1841,

BY

SAMUEL SNEADE BROWN,

OF THE BENGAL CIVIL SERVICE.

PRINTED FOR PRIVATE CIRCULATION.

London:

PRINTED BY C. F. ROWORTH, 1, BREAM'S BUILDINGS,
CHANCERY LANE.

1878.

PREFACE.

SAMUEL SNEADE BROWN, the writer of the following Letters, was born at Winifred House, Bath, in the year 1809. His father was for many years resident in Calcutta, and held the appointment of Reporter-General of External Commerce in Bengal, but on retirement returned to England, married Mary, daughter of the Reverend Samuel Sneade, of Ludlow, and for some years afterwards lived at Winifred House, where he died. The son was educated at Charterhouse, and was fortunate enough to obtain an appointment in the Civil Service of the then East India Company in the days when the patronage was in the hands of the Directors. On leaving Charterhouse he was placed with a private tutor, the Reverend Henry Mortlock, of Morcott, Rutlandshire (a period of his life to which he looked back with great satisfaction); and after passing through the college at Haileybury, where he gained the prize for Persian and other distinctions, he left England in the month of August, 1827, and landed in Calcutta in the following December. His course through the college at Fort William was accomplished in an unusually short space of time. He then entered the department of the service called the Collectorate, and, having been offered his choice of stations, selected Delhi as his first field for employment. From thence he was appointed Assistant to the Collector at Hissar, in the Upper Provinces, and then Assistant, and subsequently Officiating Collector and Magistrate, at the isolated and unattractive district of Sahuswan, returning to Hissar in 1837 as Collector and Magistrate. After passing upwards of twelve years of his life uninterruptedly at these stations, he returned to England for his furlough in the year 1841. During that period, namely, from his landing in India at the close of the year 1827 to his return to England in 1841, these letters were written. They by no means comprise all his correspondence. They are a selection only, and yet exhaust but a small part even of the selected letters. Looking upon his letters in the bulk, and bearing in mind the discouragement which existed in those days to letter writing, by reason of the tedious and uncertain postal communication by land and sea between the Upper Provinces of Bengal and England, it would be difficult to find more overpowering proof of the ceaseless and active affection which bound him to his native country and to those whom he had left behind. Such affection needed not quickening, but his mother and sisters in England did their part by never-failing letters to him—diaries rather than letters—which diligently narrated every incident calculated to interest him of their family life at home, and by sending him at intervals such books and periodical literature from England as they considered suited to his taste. How thoroughly he appreciated and requited this love on their part will to some extent be seen by the following letters; not to the full, or anything approaching to the full, extent, because the necessity of consulting the limits of the present volume, as well as of expunging frequent references to family matters, scarcely suited even to the private circle within which this volume is intended to be read, has led to the omission of large portions even of the selected letters. For instance, he delighted in transporting himself in thought from Hissar or Sahuswan into the midst of his family assembled at some well-remembered spot in England, and in writing down in a dramatic form, and often in the most humorous language, what he imagined each would do or say in the domestic scenes which he conjured up before him in the deserts and solitudes of India. As these graphic and interesting delineations of private character could not for many reasons be printed intact, it was thought better to include them in the category of omissions most reluctantly determined upon.

He exhibited the broadest sense of humour in his composition, combined with the deepest pathos; and though he often pretended to ignore and ridicule the latter, he never allowed any gloss or pretence to interfere with his avowed love and veneration for his mother.

Imperfect, however, and partial as the present compilation unavoidably is, it will be accepted by those who knew him personally, or are connected with him by blood or association, as a valuable record of one whose true character, although not borne on the surface or adapted to general society, contained a deep mine of devout thought and generous and poetical feeling.

C. R. W.

April, 1878.

EXPLANATORY NOTE.

THE family of the writer of these Letters consisted of a sister of the half-blood—Hannah (daughter of his father by a former marriage), who married Lieutenant-Colonel Monier Williams, Surveyor-General of Bombay; his own two sisters—Ellen, who married the Rev. John Olive, Rector of Ayott St. Lawrence, Herts; and Emma, who married George Wood Sheppard, Esq., of Frome, Somerset; and his two brothers, Frederick and Joseph, both in holy orders. Emma, whilst a little girl, used to aspirate her vowels, and when on a tour to the Lakes, set her heart on visiting Shap Abbey, pronouncing it Shap Habbey. The unlucky aspirate was never forgotten, and she is accordingly playfully personified throughout these Letters as "Shap Habbey." Peggy was the attached and faithful nurse who lived for fifty-two years in the family.

𝕷etters

OF

SAMUEL SNEADE BROWN,

Of the Bengal Civil Service.

———◆———

CALCUTTA,
February 27th, 1828.

Dearest Mother,

You will be pleased to hear that I have by dint of application got out of college within the period of two months from the day of my landing, a thing done by very few since the college was established. Had the examination come a week or too sooner even, I think I should have succeeded. Three weeks had elapsed from the time of my landing, when a Persian examination came on. I expressed my wish to try my chance (although, in Persian, I was pretty sure of succeeding), which was granted, and my name ranked first in the list, with four who had got out the same time as myself, after having been in college in Calcutta from nine months to two years, but two of them were very stupid and idle. In the Hindee examination, which followed four or five weeks after, I was the only one who succeeded, thus passing many who had the start of me by one or two years. In the college they also hold out two prizes for Persian, one a prize of 800 rupees (or 80*l.*), and a medal for high proficiency, and the other a prize of 3,000 rupees (or 300*l.*), and a medal, for an extraordinary knowledge of the language. In the first case, the candidate must read through two books in Persian,—one in prose, the other in verse,—in which he is examined; and he is required, also, to write good translations from Persian to English, and English to Persian, &c. The second prize is only to be obtained by a year or two of labour, as it requires a very great proficiency in the language, and a thorough knowledge of many abstruse books. One of the Persian professors strongly recommended me to try for the first prize, viz. the 800 rupees. I objected, saying that I had never looked into the books which they examined in. He said it did not signify, for that he thought my knowledge of Persian would carry me through any of the passages they examined me in. After reflecting a little, I consented, and the next morning offered myself for the examination, trembling for fear of failing, as I was influenced more with the fear of failure than hope of the reward. The examiners were aware I had not read the books, but their opinion was if I could do the parts they put before me, off-hand, I could do the whole, and therefore that it made no difference. In short, I acquitted myself so tolerably in both construing and translations, that two or three days after I learnt from the professor I had succeeded in this also. What the prize is I have not yet heard. At all events, the professors give me credit for a good knowledge of the language. What gives me a kind of wicked pleasure is, that I acquitted myself much better than young Grote, who came out six months before me, and who was examined a week or two before I was, after pegging four or five months at these two aforesaid books. I expect my prize to be 800 rupees, as usual. I certainly have been very lucky. At this distance, you know, I must needs be my own trumpeter. This prize affair is altogether an extra thing, and consequently optional; it has nothing to do with your getting out of college. The day after I heard of my success in the Hindee and second Persian examinations I went to Stirling, to consult him with respect to my future destination. He said, in answer to my inquiries, that the different branches of the Service ranked thus: the political; 2, judicial; 3, territorial, or revenue; 4, mercantile. The first ranks highest, as requiring men of talent in general. He said, also, that there was at this time a situation vacant at Delhi, to which a young man of talent, who had been a year and more in the country, had been appointed; but another situation being at the same time offered him in Calcutta, he preferred the latter. Of course, I saw nothing better than to take this appointment, and, in the course of a few days, shall be gazetted as assistant to Sir E. Colebrooke, commissioner at Delhi. Of course, one of the sub-assistants at first. My chief objection to entering this line was my inclination for the judicial, and my feeling myself not altogether fit for political matters. But this objection was removed, as I heard that it signifies but little the first two or three years what line I enter into, as I can change any time I think fit. Delhi holds out many advantages, and it is very important that a young man should at first go to some large station to learn his business well, instead of immuring himself in an up-country station with a few Europeans. For nine months of the year the climate is delightful, and it is so very near the hills, at the foot of the huge Himalaya Mountains which divide Hindostan from Thibet, and are said by some to be the highest in the world. In the three months of heat, many of the civilians in Delhi and thereabouts move, with their families, to the hills, and, pitching a tent, live there for that period. I have just been reading Fraser's "Tour to the Himalaya Mountains," and am so full of it, and of the prospect of viewing myself some of the stupendous scenes he describes, that I could run on for ever on that subject.

In the course of ten days or so I shall set off to Delhi, a distance of more than a thousand miles, in my palanquin. I am afraid I shall suffer very much by the way, as the heat is now every day becoming more and more intense, and the very idea of going this distance on men's shoulders, at the rate of three or four miles an hour, is horrible. Travelling incessantly, I should reach Delhi in twelve or fourteen days, but everybody tells me that if I were to attempt it, it would bring on a dangerous fever. I must, therefore, halt half-a-dozen times on the road, and as I pass through many interesting places shall find ample opportunity for amusing myself. There are no inns, of course, on the road; such a thing is unknown in India. I must, therefore, get introductions to gentlemen at the places I intend to stop at, which will be pleasant enough. My boxes, furniture, and, in fact, all my baggage, with the exception of the few things I take with me, together with three of my servants, go per boat. In the present state of the wind and river it will take four or five months for them to get to Delhi, a serious inconvenience, as it separates me from them for nearly four months. But I shall most likely live with some person during that time. Expenses increase upon me here daily. By my horses I am likely to lose 400 or 500 rupees, as I bought them when horses were dear, and I now sell them when they are cheap—but there is no help for it. Mackenzie lost by his nearly 1,000 rupees. I must take up stores in the boat, as everything of foreign produce is immensely dear up the country. A stock of wine, to the amount of 600 or 700 rupees, is also necessary. Tea, sugar, and numberless other et ceteras, I must procure previous to my departure, in tolerable large quantities. A gig is absolutely necessary; this will cost 1,000 rupees. All these things I was strongly urged to get by Archdeacon Corrie, who has lived much up the country, and knows the prices of things there. Boat-hire, also, will be expensive. My expenses in travelling by land are paid by government. To counterbalance these, and numerous other trifling expenses, I have about 600 or 700 rupees, the remnants of the 2,000 I drew from the college, and probably the 800 rupees as a prize, my pay for two months,—560 rupees,—and the money for my horses. This will not be sufficient, but it will not be necessary to pay for the gig immediately, and therefore I hope it will do. When I am to begin to save I know not. House rent, up the country, is not paid for us, as in Calcutta, by the government; we have to purchase or build a house of our own. We must have horses to carry us, &c. My mere eating expenses now, independent of wine, amount to 80 rupees a month, on an average. However, up the country I must do as well as I can in the saving line. I am afraid I have not mixed in society so much as you would have liked. Had I done so on my first arrival, most probably I should not have been out of college by this time; and afterwards so very brief a time remained, that I thought it useless to pick up new acquaintances for a week or two, in a place which I am not likely to see again for years.

Delhi,

May 9th, 1828.

My dear Mother,

It is time to send you another of my letters, although I have nothing particular to communicate. In two letters I addressed to my uncle, the 16th March, and one to Hannah Williams, the 28th April, I have mentioned whatever has occurred since I last wrote to you on my dawk journey, *i.e.*, in my palanquin, to Delhi, and my present situation. I cannot recapitulate, and will, therefore, proceed to tell you something more.

Imprimis, I like my present situation very much, nor, in my opinion, shall I ever regret the choice I made. It was chance, it is true, which threw me into my present temporary situation of 840*l.* per annum, nor could I have contemplated such luck whilst I was in Calcutta; but, independent of this advantage, which I am afraid I shall not hold more than three months, I like Delhi, its eastern scenes, manners and inhabitants. I am in a Mogul city, the capital formerly of the vast territory of Upper Hindostan, and the emporium for merchandize. It has sunk now from its ancient grandeur when it formed the metropolis of powerful kings, but it is still a noble place, and, in consequence of the few Europeans who are posted in this district, English manners and customs have not gained here. The king, though in reality completely under our power, keeps up a considerable degree of state, holds his levees, &c. We have acknowledged his right and title to the throne, and consequently pay him the honours due to his rank, but his provinces are governed by us and all the business is in our hands.

The civil service is a noble service in all parts of India, but particularly in this place. It is not that our salaries are larger than elsewhere, but in a few years a young man may look to become a principal assistant to the Commissioner, in which case he will have a whole province at his disposal. The duties of judge, magistrate and collector are united in him, and he has the finest field for the exertion of his abilities and a display of his justice and disinterestedness. As it is, even now I am invested with an importance in the eyes of the natives which rather amuses me than otherwise. The rajahs and nabobs pay me visits, and offer me their nazars or presents in money, &c., always presented by an inferior to a superior, which, by-the-bye, if my feelings of honour did not lead me to decline, my duty to the Company would, as the acceptance of these presents is strictly forbidden, although, I am sorry to say, their instructions on this point are frequently disregarded; and in the king's retinue we hold, as connected with the Commissioner, one of the foremost places amongst the princes. It is not that every Englishman has this honour paid him; it is confined to the Great Sahib, as they call the Resident, and his assistants alone. It is a fine sight to see more than two dozen elephants, with their splendid trappings and canopies, waiting at the huge gate of the palace for the appearance of the king, and on his appearing, mounted on the largest elephant which can be selected from those monstrous animals, the whole mass of elephants sink on their knees, whilst those upon them rise up and salam to his majesty. But you wish to know about me and not the King of Delhi, and I will return from this digression.

Notwithstanding the 1,600 rupees I got as prize-money from the college and my present handsome salary, I could not expect to get free from what I owe to government, viz., the 2,000 rupees which I told you in a former letter I had borrowed for a year and à-half from the present time. I must say the idea is an unpleasant one of not being able to lay up any money during that time for yourself, all my savings going to liquidate the debt to government. It palsies one's efforts, and deprives one of the peculiar zest which is natural to every person engaged in business when he feels that he is adding to his income by his praiseworthy exertions. I must then beg, if possible, that 200*l.*, if so much now remains of my 1,000*l.*, may be transmitted to Messrs. Alexander & Co., that I may get free from this debt as soon as possible. Pray mention this to my uncle. You have no conception how I long to be perfectly free from any incumbrance of the kind. Do not think me extravagant; I am not so, indeed, but I must have two or three horses for exercise and amusement, the expense of which at the first purchase completely clears my pockets. I do not grudge the money, for I find it essential to my health. I sustained a heavy loss on my horses in Calcutta, when I sold them again,—70*l.* at least. I bought them when horses were fetching a high price, and sold them when they were comparatively cheap. It was a great sum to lose after so short a time, but there was no help for it. On arriving here I was obliged to purchase another Arab, a sweet-paced horse, for 800 rupees, or 80*l.*, and have sent to Colonel Arnold to procure me one, if he can, for 500 rupees. If I can get the latter for that sum I may expect to be freed from the expense of buying horses for the next two years at least. There are many country horses here, very fine-looking animals, to be procured from 200 to 350 rupees, but they are so unpleasant to ride with an English saddle, chucking you over their head every minute, that after trying one or two I was obliged to give over the idea of purchasing one; they are also so incorrigibly vicious that I have seen a horse kneel down for the express purpose of tearing his rider off his back. I bought 700 rupees' worth of stores,—as tea, coffee, a little furniture, and all the English necessaries which are not to be procured here,—whilst I was in Calcutta; I had also to pay 300 rupees for boat hire from Calcutta to Delhi.

I am the only young man in the college who has drawn only 2,000 rupees,—even sober Mackenzie having drawn the whole 4,000. What is to be done? After spending the 2,000 rupees I brought out with me in horses, palanquin, servants' wages, &c., I had nothing to live upon, as the government most injudiciously keep all the civil servants in arrears two months, which was the time of my stay in Calcutta, so we are absolutely obliged to borrow from some one. I feel anxious to justify my conduct on this point, as apparently I had no excuse, being so well supplied in funds and equipment. My pay for January, my first month, was not paid into my agent's hands until the 28th of March, a fortnight after I had left Calcutta. My cooking apparatus, &c., &c., cost me 400 rupees, my horses 1,500, my palanquin 200; thus in one week went my 2,000 rupees. Pray get 200*l.* transmitted for me to Alexander; it will be a great relief to my mind. I cannot see why the whole of the remnant, whatever it may be, should not be placed in my agent's hands. You have no idea how rapidly money accumulates when you have a foundation of stock, however small, of your own to begin upon. The chief difficulty in this country is to persuade yourself to begin to lay up. I know many who, whilst they scrupulously avoid debt, always live to the extent of their pay, merely because they neglected to lay up a small sum at first. It seems almost useless to let 200 or 300 rupees remain in your agent's hands, and thus a man is led to draw the whole of the small sums which might otherwise accumulate.

One of the Miss Kerrs, my shipmates, a fine, handsome girl, died eight weeks after landing in Calcutta. They lived for two or three years in one of those houses above the turnpike leading to the Lansdown racecourse. You need not be afraid of my marrying here; I have become so ugly I don't think anybody would have me. I correspond constantly with Mackenzie, and we like one another as much as ever. He is a very gentlemanly young man, and liked very much in all the societies he has as yet been in. He writes me about the agreeable ladies at his station, and, as he is rather susceptible, I should not wonder if he was to become a married man. I am at no expense at present, except my servants' wages and extras. I always dine with Sir Edward Colebrooke; I have also a handsome house as secretary. I should have found it exceedingly inconvenient to have set up house whilst all my baggage was elsewhere. Remembering me with my pencil and slate at Lyme, on the important occasion of writing to Whitestone, you wonder, I suppose, how I get on in an office of this kind, as all the letters to the Commissioner are directed to me, and I answer them in his name, and in this way hold a correspondence with all the wise heads in the country; but the routine of letter-writing in a secretary's office is easily acquired, and all the more important letters are written by the Commissioner himself. Not that I sit down like a clerk at my desk to answer with my own hand to every trifling correspondence which comes per dozen in a day. A draft of these letters is drawn up by a respectable man under me, as head writer, according to my directions, and submitted afterwards for my approval and correction; a fair copy is then made out, and I sign my name. Pray do not imagine that my business is that of banker's clerk.

Melons, grapes, mangoes, &c., &c., are in abundance here. All the foreign fruits, as melons, pineapples, &c., are infinitely inferior to those reared in England in point of flavour. There are also many very nice little apples, which I devour as voraciously as I used to do. Strawberries of the finest quality were to be had in Benares when I was there. Peas, beans, cauliflowers, cabbages, and artichokes we get every day. In Calcutta every kind of English vegetable is cultivated with success. On visiting the Botanical Garden I had a piece of wild thyme put into my hands by the gardener. It had been brought from Scotland in a small flower-pot.

Tom Seaton is only thirty-five miles distant with his regiment. He is, I believe, a very fine young man.

I was presented to-day to the King of Delhi, descendant of the house of Timour, who have sat for many centuries on this throne, and numbered amongst their ancestors several of the wisest and most powerful kings that have ever held rule in the East. It was the anniversary of his accession, and the scene was a most magnificent one to European eyes. After presenting four gold pieces, to the amount of 7*l.* sterling, I was invested with a robe of honour, which looked odd enough on my English costume.

My health up to the present has been excellent. I had one violent attack of fever in Calcutta, but got over it in a few days by taking early precautions.

No letters from England yet. Remember to send me the Bath papers regularly. Communicate to me your views respecting Fred, and do not despise my opinion. I can now speak from observation on the different services in India. I would not have him go to a public or any large school; he is already too much of a man ever to become a sawney, which is the chief objection made to private education. If you destine him for the army in India, let him commence the study of the language as soon as possible; it is of great advantage to a military man.

This is not, I am aware, a kind of letter you like, but in writing from India to England it is difficult to carry in your mind the length of time intervening, and that scenes and sights which interest us here convey not the same interest to our English friends. I will make up for it by writing again soon. Pray write often. Postage no one *ever* thinks of. Unless the heart is kept alive by frequent communications from England, it is too apt to become dormant.

Delhi,
June 5th, 1828.

Dearest Mother,

I was equally astonished and delighted to receive a second letter from you to-day, dated 23rd January; the last which reached this place, three weeks ago, being a letter of Ellen's, the 17th August. Whatever letters may have been written by you in the interval will, I suppose, arrive in time.

I have at last the satisfaction, and a great one it is, to know that you have returned from your tour in health, and are settled once more at Lyme for a season.

My first impulse on receiving an English letter is to sit down and answer it instanter. I will, therefore, scrawl away a few lines to you. Ellen's letter broke off at Martigny, after you had been rambling amongst the superb scenery of Mont Blanc and its environs. Oh! how I envied you—how I longed to partake of the delights, and accompany you in the excursions of your tour, in the planning and management of which you have, at all times, a most felicitous invention. Expecting to find a continuation of your trip in the next letter which might grope its way to Delhi, I find you snugly ensconced at little, quiet Lyme. But to speak of myself. The hot weather is now in its glory; the only time in the day in which it is possible to stir out of one's house is between five and six in the morning, and at seven in the evening, when it is almost dark. All nature languishes. Imagine yourself placed in front of a huge oven, and a large bellows introduced at the opposite end, so as to puff the heated vapour in your face—imagine this, and you will have some idea of the hot winds. Disagreeable as these winds are, they are preferable to no wind at all, when the stagnation of air is horrible. I am obliged to have the punka, or large fan fixed to the ceiling, moving night and day. I find confinement to the house for twelve hours of the day irksome; and as I have no companion to while away the leaden hours, I am dull enough in general. I should have liked beyond everything to have gone to the same station as Mackenzie—and many were the castles which we used to build when in Calcutta together—but he got out of college and had set off to his station a few weeks before me; and we were both aware that by entering into the same line, at the same station, and about the same time, we were likely to interfere with one another's appointments in future. I long much for him in this place. We certainly always agreed delightfully, and entertained for one another that sterling kind of liking and steady friendship which will, I trust, surmount time and distance. Now that I look round me calmly, and have had time to weigh the advantages and disadvantages of my line of life, although I have not overrated in the least my estimate of the former, still there are several circumstances which lead me to abate the high satisfaction which I may have expressed in my former letters. The want of a friend or companion, the distance from Calcutta and the consequent inconveniences, the want of a church and fixed clergyman, so that my ears are never blessed on the Sabbath with the sound of the church-going bell—these, and a few other things, damp my spirits sometimes. On my departure from Delhi, whenever it will take place, I shall have to go out into the district and live a hermit's life for months, with, perhaps, one senior, in a house fifty miles distant from Europeans; or, perhaps, I may be ordered to perambulate the various portions of the district, living in tents, for the purpose of business. I feel certain, however, that I shall never repent of the choice I have made; and the numerous occupations and avocations, which occupy one's time for eight or nine hours together, will prove a sufficient bar to ennui or melancholy. At present I have not much to do. I have been very unwell for two or three weeks from an accidental injury, and, being confined to my couch the whole time, felt quite depressed in spirits from my loneliness. The other young civilian is so much occupied during the day that we never meet except at meals, and the weather is too hot to admit of our riding out. My health is excellent. I never drink beer; my beverage at this season of the year being claret and water and light wines. It is impossible to drink port or Madeira in this country; they are too strong; nothing is drank but claret, hock and other French wines. One great blessing in this country is, that there are no infectious disorders of any kind. The cholera morbus, the scourge of India, the various fevers, are quite harmless to all but the unhappy sufferer. I really believe that if a person takes proper precautions he will have no reason to complain of India as an unhealthy country. I always wear flannel next my skin, which is exceedingly disagreeable in this smoking weather, but is, at the same time, indispensable. Peaches and grapes are in abundance here; I devour them, as you may suppose, readily enough. I am anxious about my baggage boat, which cannot reach me until the end of August; it contains all my comforts and conveniences, my clothes, books, plate, purchases, &c. Nothing is so common as the sinking of a boat, in this confounded river, from the sudden squalls prevalent at this season, which rush on with incredible violence. I have stood on the banks of the Ganges and seen small native boats sinking in all directions; the natives swim like fish, and are seldom if ever drowned. I shall break my heart if I lose all my things; and, although I have insured them for 3,000 rupees (300*l.*), at the rate of 5 per cent., I shall never be recompensed for the infinite expense and trouble I shall be subject to in fitting myself out again ; but I will hope for the best. My books, alas! what a pang it will be to me to lose them. You have heard by this time, I presume, of Henry Brown's duel of three rounds—it was a wonder that no fatal accident happened. How war-like our family is becoming ! I have received two honourable testi-monials from Government on my success in college, with a compliment from the Governor-General. I will transmit you the letters soon. I am continually wishing now that I had been born first, in which case I should have had most probably the talents that Ellen undoubtedly possesses, whereas the little sense which I possess, improved as it is by application, would be ample for a woman. I am tremblingly alive to my own deficiencies, and as the young men in this part of the country are frequently acting for a time in very responsible situations, it is requisite to call every spark of talent, or grain of sense, into life. Ellen has a clearness of understanding which I would give any-thing for. It would be far more useful to me in my present situation than the most brilliant, or rather flashy, talents; and yet it is pleasant to have some responsibility attached to one's situation; the absence of it forms my only objection to my acting secretaryship, which will shortly, I fancy, expire. I am anxious to learn your various plans respecting Fred. What would I give for a writership for him ! The law our family have no turn for—it is a system of roguery and toil. Joe is to be the parson. The only choice which is left him is to handle wares in a counting-house, or drugs as a doctor—I don't know which is worse. If he turns soldier, he will run away on the field of battle, and get shot in his bottom. I wouldn't give much for our family valour, of which the tailor's shears is a good emblem. I expect to be a regular yellow-faced, sunburnt Indian in a year or two, and fear that no one will have me as a spouse. That picture of Slater's flatters me terribly. I am a great self-tormentor when unem-ployed. You have no idea of the rate at which we perspire in India in this weather—the least motion, the slightest exertion of mind or body, " makes the streams to flow." If one gets opposite to duck, turkey or goose at table, a good half-pint of perspiration may be considered as added to the gravy. I find it rather a pleasant change to dine with Sir Edward every evening after business is over; he is a frank and pleasant old gentleman; I like him much. We call his lady the *Bore* Constrictor. The state of Europe at present excites much interest in this country. The Russian army is no great distance from Bagdad, whence it is but a step to Bombay. But politics lose half their interest by the time they reach this place. Nothing, however, is so acceptable as an English newspaper. I long for something to amuse me during the intervals of business or study,—some source of interest, friendship or affection; there is a void which I would were filled; all my affections and friendships at present are nourished by the mind and memory—memory soothes but does not satisfy. I really believe that many a person is led by this cause to seek in the society of an Indian female some object of interest, in order to prevent the best feelings of his heart lying fallow until they are blighted by the damps of selfishness and wintry unconcern; but I am metaphorical, and you will think my opinion an odd one. I find my silk stockings and little feather pillow of great comfort; the latter is almost invaluable. They charge twelve rupees, or twenty-four shillings, for a very small English cheese in this part of the country. I do not grudge good wine, of which I have the best, but I grudge my stomach. I regret that the beautiful road to Lyme has been destroyed. I shall always think of that little town with pleasure. How nicely Ellen will be able to instruct in music, and other accomplishments, any little tawny nephews or nieces whom I may hereafter commend to your care!!! It is almost needless to say that my attempts on my unhappy flute have hitherto failed—such puffing and blowing! I have sent for Josephus, in Greek, from London, in order to keep up that language.

DELHI,
June 14th, 1828.

My dear Ellen,

I received with pleasure the other day two more letters, one from you, dated 20th October, and another from my mother, 23rd November. I read them with a delight and interest only to be felt by one who is separated thousands of miles from those who are near and dear to him, to whom many a deep feeling and sympathy is called once more into life, as he peruses the letters from a far-distant land, as he thinks on past scenes and impressions, and longs for the realization of the object of his wishes, which, when he enjoyed before, he prized too little. I cannot say that I pine for England, or that I find fault with this country, but there are certain times and moments when recollections overpower me. The periods of my life which I recur to with the greatest pleasure is the time I spent with you at Lyme, and with Mortlock at Morcott. I think frequently, with tears in my eyes, on our quiet summer evening walks by Pompey's Pillar and Titania's Green, with the trees and mounds and ferns, and the bright shining sea, and, forgetting my own captious temper, wonder that I viewed such objects with such indifference, and that I did not enjoy to the utmost such tranquil pleasures. This memory sheds a peaceful light over past scenes, brightening the dark shades, and tempering the bright parts of the picture. My constitution will not allow of my continuing long in low spirits, but I cannot help feeling somewhat depressed at present, —why or wherefore I know not. I sadly want a friend with whom I can communicate freely on all subjects; and still I feel more inclined to revert to those few with whom I lived formerly on terms of friendship, than to form new friends. I have no news to communicate, and yet I take pleasure in writing. Day after day passes away in the same uniform routine of breakfast, business, dinner and rest. Instead of looking forward to each day with pleasure when I rise in the morning, I feel rather glad when it is over. But I am unnecessarily querulous, and indeed the hot weather is enough to make me so. When my books arrive I shall be all right.

I contemplate with pleasure and delight a trip to the hills, two or three years hence,—hills before which Chimborazo and the lordly Andes hide their diminished heads, and Mont Blanc, the monarch of mountains, would dwindle to a molehill. What a blessing they are to those who live in this part of the country! Instead of being obliged to proceed 900 or 1,000 miles by land to Calcutta, and thence to ship themselves to the Isle of France, the Cape, or China, for their health, they run up in three days to lovely stations for invalids amongst the chains of hills which lie at the feet of these stupendous mountains, and invariably return new persons. The air, the exercise, the grand scenery, the peaked, snowy mountains for back ground, have a vivifying effect. Archdeacon Corrie used to speak of his short stay in these scenes with rapture. Those who go there for amusement take their tents and servants with them, and saunter about from day to day.

I have made, at different times, various inquiries relative to the different modes and places by which and where a young man may gain, or attempt to gain, a fortune in the East. If he goes to Botany Bay, a settler like Mr. Bertie Clay, he is associated with convicts who, with the exception of the governor, form the society of

New South Wales. The country, also, is ravaged by rebel, run-away felons. In short, it is not worth a thought even, as far as a gentleman is concerned. Few men ever realize even a pittance there. Whilst in the country they may live comfortably, but their wealth consisting in landed property and cattle, which everyone possesses in abundance, it is almost impossible to realize any stock in money to serve for their maintenance in England.

Indigo planters in India, though some are gentlemen, generally consist of Scotch adventurers. It is perfect chance and hazard, and many have been irretrievably ruined by the fluctuating demand for that article in the English markets, and the speculations in which they are necessarily involved. They are also considered as a middling class of society, very little above the shop-keepers, by the civil and military, who are quite glad to meet with any of their own country, their inferiors, in a country like this, where, in the absence of titles, and by uniformity of employment, all are equal.

As assistant in a banking house, or house of agency, unless a young man is connected or related with the heads of the house, and unless that house be one of the first in precedence, he can scarcely expect to be admitted into genteel society. I have stated this for my mother's information. Law and physic for Fred are out of the question. I am very averse to a counting-house, in which he will meet with inferior society, and innumerable temptations to wickedness. Fred will be a fine fellow. Do not stick him behind a counter. There is something in the prospect of India, of visiting a new country, of viewing new scenes, and visiting new tracts, far more pleasant and exciting to the young mind than being cooped up in a dirty counting-house, engaged in a spiritless round of business. This is my poor opinion.

There is not so much vice in the army here as in England. Many young men attach themselves to native women, no doubt. This, strange as it may appear, improves rather than destroys the morals of those who are constitutionally wild. It is, from many reasons, neither desirable or proper; but "to lay the heart on *one* shrine" is surely better than running a destructive round of dissipation—yes, and has proved so to many. Besides, where the society is more confined, the conduct of each individual is more open and liable to censure. The Civil Service is in a far more flourishing state now than it ever was before. India is in profound peace. Is it ordained by Providence or not that we should continue to hold our Eastern possessions? I confess I have my doubts sometimes. The natives of this part of India are as different as possible to the effeminate creatures in Bengal. They are fine, stout, handsome men, brave as lions, jealous of their honour, and resentful of affronts. They are, without exception, the handsomest race of men I ever saw.

I shall have to resign my office in a month, and lose 300 rupees per month in consequence, but 400 rupees here goes as far as 600 in Calcutta, as I have no expenses in the eating way, taking all my meals with the Resident. I am very well contented where I am, if I had but Mackenzie.

We hear of wars and rumours of wars in this remote part, but I cannot say that politics in England much interest me when they are five months old.

Excuse this stupid letter. My life is now so uniform that I have really nothing to tell you. There is a grand Mahomedan festival approaching. All the Delhi people of that faith assemble, to the number of many thousands. It is a most grand and imposing sight to see the performance of their prayers and prostrations.

Camels are here only 40 rupees (or 4*l*.) each, and are most useful animals. It is an interesting sight to see a long string of these animals, laden with merchandize from Cashmere or Persia, threading their way amongst the old ruins.

DELHI,

July 13*th*, 1828.

My dear Mother,

I take up my pen, I know not why, unless it be to give relief to my mind by committing those thoughts to paper which I am not able to communicate to any sympathizing friend. My heart is heavy within me; there is a vacuity in it which is painful in the extreme; my very nature requires,—perverse as I am, and strangely tempered as you used justly to consider me,—my very nature, I say, requires some object of interest or affection, some being from whom I may look for some kindly feelings to make the long, the far removed prospect of a ten years' absence, or rather exile, tolerable. When in England, a new scene and novel prospects were opening to me, and I felt not my separation from England and its pleasures. When in Calcutta, I was too much occupied between my studies and Mackenzie's society to dwell on the subject; but now, when I am left to myself and my own reflections,—now that my destination is fixed, and the novelty worn off, I begin to long intensely for home. I have been often told that this longing is more acute the first year, and it may be so, yet I never conceived that I should have experienced it so much, or so feelingly.

July 16*th*—

I have just received dear Ellen's letter of 13th February. You are, indeed, fortunate in the enjoyment of England, its delights and privileges; and I have seen few, or, rather, have never seen any, more formed by dispositions and habits to appreciate its tranquil recreations. Whether it is your peaceful mode of life, or your feelings, which are so alive to all the beauties of nature, or both combined, I know not, but you appear to me to live most happily, and, I may add, most harmoniously, except when a new pair of stays are to be put on, or the hair to be dressed for a dance in any particular style—the discordant key has now been removed, and the instrument, in consequence, plays sweetly. Let me regret—I cannot anticipate; anticipation cannot lead the mind to overlook the dreary waste of a ten years' exile, or fix its view on the dim semblance of the probability of a return after that period. But enough of this. Remember, I am not discontented. There is a wide difference between discontent and regret.

I am happy to say that I have received all my baggage safe from Calcutta, books and all. My stores are likely soon to prove useful to me; my armchair is inestimable. I bought, when in Calcutta, some more jean for trousers, some silk camlet, also some thicker jean, and collected a great many useful sundries. Several boats belonging to gentlemen were plundered by armed robbers as they were coming up the river, but mine escaped. My books are as neat and clean as when they left England. I bought a small edition of Scott's Novels in Calcutta, which included all with the exception of the four last, which I intend to procure in order to complete them. It is fortunate that they give us something to do, as there is not a book, scarcely, to be got in this place of any sort or kind. I wish you to send me out any really humorous publications that may make their appearance. I should like, "Thinks I to myself," two volumes of "Mornings in Bow Street." I should also like "Wordsworth's Poems." There is a plaintive simplicity in many of them which goes directly to the heart. I admire them more for the ideas and feelings than the poetry.

I intended to commence a regular course of history on my being freed from the Oriental studies, and had commenced Gibbon for that purpose. I read two volumes, but the third, being misplaced, I was obliged to give it up for the time. What an interesting style of writing his is; it is a perfect romance; but how constantly the cloven foot makes its appearance in his guarded yet sneering irony against the precepts of Christianity! I purpose pursuing it shortly, and following it up with "Milner's Church History," and afterwards skimming over "Russell's Modern Europe," but it will be some time before I shall be able to accomplish this; in fact, reading of that kind is so totally unconnected with my present occupations that I find some difficulty in persuading myself to give much time to a course of reading which might be better occupied by perusing publications relating to India.

I wonder what has become of Digby R—— I can gain no intelligence respecting him, nor do I know where he is. Do not think with so much horror of his living with a native woman. They are not the abandoned creatures, lost to all sense of shame, as in England. Treated with indifference, as they universally are, by their own countrymen, who have no higher idea of love than as a passion, they are delighted and flattered by the attention shown them by Europeans, and repay it in general with all the affection they are capable of feeling. They are always children in their minds, amused with the most trivial things, with almost infantile playfulness exerting all their little arts of fascination to please their master. I have observed that those who have lived with native women for any length of time never marry a European; they are so amusingly playful, so anxious to oblige and please, that a person, after being accustomed to their society, shrinks from the idea of encountering the whims or yielding to the fancies of an Englishwoman. I do not say that the connection is a desirable one, but it should not be considered so heinous as persons in England are inclined to think it. I have merely mentioned this subject in this letter and in a former one in order to palliate poor Digby's fault. Unless a man is enabled to keep constant watch over himself, it is difficult for him to abstain from connections of that nature, unless, indeed, he is aided from above. As for myself, I feel certain that I shall never marry in this country; and I shall be so ugly and so yellow after ten years' residence here, that no one but broken-down old maids will have me. In short, all idea of matrimony has left me long ago.

By-the-bye, has Mr. "Hattitude" renewed his addresses to "Shap Habbey"? Alas! alas! bye-past times, how they throng on my mind as I sit solitary here in Delhi. Of one thing I am certain, that whatever length of time I may remain in India, I shall always remain the same, unchanging and unchanged as to my longing for England.

DELHI,

August 14th, 1828.

My dear Mother,

I received yesterday a letter from Clerk, dated 9th July, from Bombay, where he arrived in May. He writes as if he were suffering much under depression of spirits, partly from indisposition, and partly from thoughts of home and the pleasures which he has been forced to exchange for exile. His letter, which was a sweet and affectionate one, was so melancholy that it brought tears into my eyes. I feel a deep interest in his fate, the more I know and hear of him. We shall, of course, correspond. I assure you, when I heard of his arrival in India, I felt as gladdened in heart as if the quiet personal intercourse which we enjoyed at Hayleybury were to be renewed again—little chance as we have of ever meeting again. His arrival is a source of delight to me, as I look forward to his correspondence as a channel by which I can give vent to the feelings and the thoughts which I have none at present to communicate to in India, and none to sympathize with. Mackenzie is also a most affectionate, warm-hearted fellow, but of a character so different that I can't feel the same extent of friendship to both, without a diminution on either side ; in fact, my feelings towards both, although bearing the same name, are of a wholly distinct character, being diversified by the habits, feelings, pursuits of the objects of that friendship ; but there are many things, thoughts and feelings which I should take a delight in communicating to, and expatiating upon, with the elegant-minded Clerk, which I should deem it mawkish to touch upon with the open-hearted Mackenzie. What a pity it is that in my present situation, where I can meet with no one to whom I can even give the title of an associate, I should be so wholly separated from the only two whom I ever felt as friends ! Clerk, in his letter, has poured out all his heart to me in confidence ; he is a young man, I should imagine, naturally of a melancholy temperament, which, worked upon by many causes which he has explained, has weighed upon his spirits occasionally for two or three years. He says, in his letter, " At the

time of my coming to Hayleybury, I was particularly depressed and
unhappy, and intended not to associate with any one. Yourself, as
you know, formed the only exception, and many a time has your
society relieved me, for a time, from the distress of mind under which
I suffered ; often have I sat in my chair listening for the sound of
your steps about the time of your diurnal visit to me." Poor fellow ;
he put me in mind of that passage in "Peveril of the Peak," where
Bridgenorth, in affliction, is described as seating himself in his armchair before the window, and looking forwards with so much interest
to Sir Geoffrey's passing salutation.

August 15th—

I have received to-day your letter dated 22nd March. Your letters
are a great comfort to me ; my heart leaps with joy when they are
brought in to me. So dull, so uniform, so changeless, is the tenor of
my life here, that the day on which I receive a letter forms a date
until another arrives. You say, "I hope you destroy our family
letters." Could you then expect me to be guilty of such a sacrilege ?
Could you expect me to cast away the olive leaf brought by the gentle
dove over the waste of waters, the memento which affection wafts to
the weary soul of kindlier regions, of kindlier hearts than those
amongst which it moves ? Many a time have I regretted, whilst
looking over my old letters, that so many have been thoughtlessly
destroyed in former times. I bought in Calcutta a box, in which I
deposit them, and when I wish to recur to past times and past impressions, I open that box and live over again the few happy moments
of my wayward life. They are my tablets of memory—why should
I deface them ? Time and absence have removed the bitterness of
the regrets which were once so painful, and changed them to a
holier, a better feeling. Poor Clerk! he told me in his last letter
that though I might be a man of regrets, I was also a man of
hopes ; and I was able to answer that I now indeed began to
cull the few soothing reminiscences of my past life, and that my
regrets were so softened down that I could now give them a place
amongst those reminiscences as a source for mild and quiet reflection. I told him, who had so little to regret, to think on times
past and gone, as the pleasurable sadness arising from such a train
of thought would dispel his gloomy fancies. But I make my letters
a journal of my heart, rather than a diary of my actions ; but, in
fact, I have nothing to communicate. I carry on business as usual,
write my letters, read my books, hear petitions, search the records,
crack jokes with myself for want of a listener, and crack nuts with
my monkey.

August 22nd—

Your birthday passed, and I knew it not. I was travelling at the time in my palanquin. Oh! my mother, it is only when my heart is full that I am prompted to seize my pen. Oh! do not forget my miniature of yourself, which you must send out to me. If it is done by an inferior artist, it will be a cause of grief to me instead of satisfaction. I have just finished a letter to my uncle Charles, and sent one a fortnight ago to my aunt Kilburn, so I hope you find every one satisfied. I feel particularly grateful to the Kilburns for the kindness of heart which their presents to me manifested—they are nice, kind people. My uncle Charles, too, is one for whom I have ever felt a great respect; besides, it is somewhat gratifying to think that one is now and then made a topic of conversation; and this may, perhaps, be one of my motives in writing occasionally to the different branches of my family, lest they should forget me altogether, or lose all interest in my fate. I have not forgotten Julia and Florence crying when I left Whitestone the last time. I regret now that I did not write oftener on my first arrival at Calcutta. I could have told many things relative to my landing which would have interested you. Mackenzie's kindness and warm-hearted attentions I shall never forget. I do not expect to save much this year—if anything. The chances are so great of my ever living to enjoy the fortune I may acquire in India, that I cannot deny myself the few pleasures or luxuries which tend to make this country endurable in prospect of so contingent an enjoyment. I feel particularly anxious that my brothers should remember me with affection. How I would tend them like a father, were either of them to come out here! I sadly, sadly want some being on whom I can bestow my surplus thoughts and affections.

DELHI,

October 9th, 1828.

My dear Ellen,

      I have just received your letter, dated April 12th, and, as usual, hasten to reply.

      Your plan for a pedestrian excursion amused me mightily, and, remembering the work we used to have to shove my mother up the steep Lyme Hills, I could not forbear making the enclosed sketch as illustrative of your intended tour. I hope I shall not forfeit your regards for investing you with such a ponderosity. Fred, I hope, will acknowledge his likeness. How beautiful looked the Isle of Wight that fine August day, when we coasted it in the "Palmyra" on our way to India. I could see distinctly the road along which I crept with mangled heels, the inns I put up at, and the scenery I admired during my short trip from Southampton. You have also seen by this time the tomb of sweet "Little Jane, the cottager," in the churchyard at Brading. I stood by it on a fresh January morning, when the sun was just breaking its way through the mists of the valley beneath, and the interest I felt in gazing at the narrow sod beneath which the mortal part of the young Christian reposed was such as I have never experienced since. I lingered in that beautiful churchyard half-an-hour in the stillness of the morning, and when I cast my great-coat over my back and surmounted the opposite hill on my way to Shanklin Chine, where I breakfasted, my thoughts were soft and sweet. Oh! what a glorious morning it was, and with what willingness I trudged along, with my eyes fixed on the ocean and the high hill above Shanklin! You will also have passed by the little country inn at Brading, where I took up my quarters for the night, drinking tea with the publican's wife and her children in the kitchen round the fire, the parlours being occupied by the country club. Then my breakfast at the pretty Shanklin Inn, where I gave the waiting-maid a shilling for doctoring my heels; then my walk to Bonchurch, and my weary trudge to the Whiterock Inn under the craigs, and my ride to Newport the next morning in a cart through the snow. But, alas! those joyous times have passed away, and when will they return? I have sometimes a sad misgiving that I shall lay my bones, after all, in India. I say a misgiving, for it is my most earnest wish that when I find the hour of my departure draw nigh, I may see myself in my native land.

      Remember my mother's picture; invaluable will it be to me. I should like much also a little sketch in crayons, with a touch of colour, of Fred and Joe. Every person in India has some miniatures of those they love. A young man was showing me the other day miniatures of his parents, and brothers and sisters, and I had none to show in return; no, not one to enable me to call up the features of the distant. I returned home, sorrowing at my negligence in having omitted bringing out with me similar mementos.

My mother seems to expect something very wonderful from me. Frequently have I in vain attempted to assure you and her that my abilities are limited, that I rather approach mediocrity than rise above par. Of my diligence and industry she cannot entertain a doubt, or of the anxiety I constantly feel to do my best in everything; but I know myself, and am able now to compare myself with others, and I find myself deficient in the scale. I do not tell you this to vex you, but merely to prevent you puffing me unnecessarily, and to obviate any disappointment you may feel at not seeing your overgrown hopes realized. It is, and always will be, my endeavour, when placed in a more extended line of duties, to render myself as useful to the public service as lies in my power. At present the range of my business. is cramped, and I am not able to exert myself so much as I otherwise would. As to my clothes, they last me tolerably well; the mode of washing in India, however, destroys one's clothing. The washerman, after soaking them in cold water, lays them on a flat board; he then takes a round club in his hand and thumps them for half-an-hour together; he then starches them, and dries them. I can get a suit of clothes washed and ready to put on in two hours. By this process— and it is vain to attempt to teach them any other—your clothes are hammered to pieces, buttons broken, seams rent, &c., &c. They are, however, made beautifully white. It is such a luxury to put on three clean shirts every day instead of every week, as in England. One very, very great blessing in this part of the country is, that we are not troubled with mosquitoes. Oh! the way in which I suffered from them in Calcutta! I was driven to perfect madness sometimes by the irritation of the bites. I never dared venture out of my narrow post-bed, in which I was tucked by mosquito curtains. If one even got in, I could get no rest all night, for they are such active little devils that you can't kill them like a fly. Here my bed consists of a couch, which I use in the day-time for a sofa, a small country bolster, my darling little feather pillow, and sheets. At night time I put on a large kind of drawers, sit in my easy ship-chair writing and reading, and when I feel tired fling myself on the bed and sleep soundly.

I caught a glimpse the other day of the snowy mountains of *Himalay*, which in Sanscrit means " the throne of snow." Splendid and beautiful they looked, rearing their peaked crests to the sky, tinged with the faintest red from the setting sun. I intend to sham ill in two years, and make a trip up to them. Persons, civil and military, resort there now from all the upper parts of India for the benefit of their health, and two or three little Montpeliers have already been built in different parts of the skirts of these giant mountains. Strawberries, apricots, cherries, gooseberries, currants grow there in abundance, but inferior to those in England. I have to-day been sitting ogling a plate of fine, large, rosy apples, brought from Cabul, with no small satisfaction; and presented to the young men in my office, of whom there are four, the spectacle of the secretary transacting his business with an apple in his mouth. Grapes, too, we get from Cabul, equal to the Portugal grapes in winter, and abundance of beautiful and jucy oranges from Agra. The oranges are really delicious.

My establishment, in servants, amounts to one man to dress me, tend my clothes, &c., one butler, two servants to wait at table behind my chair, one washerman, one water carrier, one sweeper or menial servant, six grooms or grass-cutters, six bearers for my palanquin; in all nineteen. Wages of all, per month, amount to 100 rupees, or 10*l.*

You may remember that I strongly recommended, in a former letter, an engineership for Fred, and even a cadetship, if nothing better could be got. I still think that the former is a very desirable appointment, but on maturer deliberation I would not recommend a mere cadetship. The service of the Engineers is a very fine one, and the nature of their duties leads them to be employed in civil capacities. All the surveys ordered by Government to be made are conducted by Engineers, and a steady-going man, who has acquired a knowledge of the languages, would get on rapidly. In the native army promotion is slow; and in a line where no inducements are held out, or no advantages accrue to a young man from his knowledge or studies, an appointment can scarcely be desired. I beg you will weigh this. You know how well Colonel Williams got on. It is, besides, a sensible and intellectual situation. An engineer's duties are not confined to brute fighting or the tediousness of the drill, but he has to plan, to devise, whilst the others operate.

I am well in health, but my good English appetite is forsaking me by degrees. I eat nothing with zest, and I frequently wish for the hearty relish with which I devoured the simple, neat dinners in the Pompeii-room at our house in Lyme.

Next to cholera, dysentery is the most prevalent complaint, and the most fatal, in a climate like this. I much fear that I shall not escape it, being subject to bowel complaints naturally. I will write again soon, when I receive another letter from you.

DELHI,

October 30th, 1828.

My dear Mother,

  One of the reasons which actuates me in keeping up a correspondence with the only two friends I have in India, Mackenzie and Clerk, is, I confess, the earnest wish I feel that should I be called the way of all flesh I may at least have two in this land of strangers who would lift up their voices and cry, "Alas! my brother."

  Mackenzie has returned no answer to the letter I told you in my last I had written to him about marrying ; so, feeling lest he might be offended, I wrote a punning letter in rhyme, in order to deprecate his displeasure, beginning with "My dear Mackenzie—I'm almost in a frenzy—I fear'd you would scold—at my being so bold—but with humblest submission—and deepest contrition—I implore your pardon —for being so hard on—your waltzing and dancing—and jumping and prancing—with all the young ladies—like the sweepers on May-days." I had told Mackenzie in a former letter the story of Miss Caldwell and her lover on the Clifton downs, in a most pathetic style, thinking it would interest him, being in love, to which he replied that the lover in tumbling on his knees before the lady must have dirtied his breeches ! So, after a page or two of my doggrels, I ended with, "And then in my letter—tho' you can't tell a better—you laugh at the distress—of the lover and mistress—and say, whilst he flirted,— his smallclothes he dirtied—If he did, the poor chap—'twas from fear or mishap—in his haste to beseech—that he dirtied his breech— But as an example—his misfortune is ample—and I therefore implore —that, behind or before,—when courting a dame—you may ne'er do the same ; now as for my rhyme—and poetical chime—why, you may depend on't,—that here there's an end on't."

  Thus sad and merry thoughts chase one another through my mind, leaving me at one time in my solitude with tears starting to my eye, at another time laughing with myself at old recollections, and at another groaning in that extraordinary way which used to attract your attention in England, and which confirmed you in the belief that I should be some day deranged,—an event, thank God! not very likely to happen. My recollections of past times are peculiarly vivid, and the feelings which impressed me at the time of their occurrence recur to me at the time when I recall them to mind.

November 8th—

Six months have now elapsed since the date of your last letter in April. It is a great misfortune to persons in India that such an immense time should intervene between the date and the receipt of letters from England.

The weather is becoming really cold; our summer clothing we have doffed, and assumed once more cloth coats and breeches. In the morning on riding out I am glad to button up my coat, the air is so sharp.

I enclose a letter to Miss Parry. I would not have made you pay for a double letter had I known where she was likely to be. You may read it, seal it, and dispatch it to her. You need not complain much of postage, for I pay the postage for 1,000 miles, viz., from Delhi to Calcutta. We always post-pay every letter we write, and, consequently, every letter we get is also post-paid, so it comes to the same thing in the end. I pay two shillings, or one rupee, for every single English letter to Calcutta, and four shillings and sixpence for a double one.

I do not find the climate disagree with me, nor do I consider it by any means an unhealthy one if persons will take care of themselves and keep out of the sun. Many in quest of sport or on shooting excursions expose themselves to the burning heat of the sun without suffering inconvenience; but if I were to stand, even covered, in the noonday sun for half-an-hour, or walk about under an umbrella, I should feel as sick as possible afterwards. Next to cholera, dysentery is the most common and most fatal disorder prevalent here. The natives die in numbers from the effects of it. They have a shocking practice here of half-burning their dead before they fling them into the river. Riding out the other day I was attracted by a peculiar kind of flame rising from a heap of sticks and firewood a short distance off; on approaching the spot I found two corpses slowly consuming over a fire, whilst the friends of the deceased were seated round, watching the progress of the burning. They burn their dead thus by dozens every day, and toss the half-consumed bodies afterwards into the river, where they can be seen floating down in numbers, the vultures and large fish regaling themselves on them.

What will you say when you hear that we pay twenty-four shillings for a small cheese in this part of the country, which, after all, is so dry and tasteless as to be scarcely worth eating; four shillings for a bottle of beer; and everything else in proportion? It is indeed no wonder that money flies out of one's pockets when, if you wish to live as a gentleman, you must give in to these extravagances. I paid the other day thirty-two shillings for a pot of raspberry jam, and thirty-six shillings for a jar of red herrings, which I could have got in London for two. One hundred and forty shillings is paid for a dozen of champagne, and one hundred is the average price for the other wines, sherry, Madeira, and claret. When I give a dinner to any friends it consists of soup, (which my head cook makes equal to Birch's, on Cornhill), a saddle of mutton with currant jelly, stewed meats or English preserved salmon, wild-fowl or poultry, tarts made from the apples imported from Cabul, and plum-pudding and jellies, cheese, and dessert of walnuts, oranges, Cabul grapes, plaintains, and sweet cakes of various sorts and descriptions which the natives have a knack of making. I never see my cook's face from one year's end to the other, and if I were to go into the cook-room I am certain I should never be able to eat any dinner for the next fortnight. All the meat is utterly useless and stinking the next day if it is in the hot weather.

Delhi,

January 17th, 1830.

My dear Mother,

Sir Edward Colebrooke has been removed from his situation as Resident, having been convicted of dishonourable practices. The orders, depriving him of his office and salary until the pleasure of the Court of Directors can be known, have just been received. Thus has a service of fifty years, during the whole course of which he was beloved for his amiable qualities and kindness of heart, as well as respected on account of his high talents and experience, terminated at last in disgrace, the deepest which could fall on a man who holds the rank of gentleman. But such should be the issue of such transactions if persons can so far forget themselves as to lend themselves to them. Example is good—and particularly in this country, where the means of peculation and dishonesty are numerous, and the chance of their being attended with discovery slight. How strange that a man, possessed of a most handsome competence—I should rather say a splendid fortune—of good birth, and of liberal education, should descend so low as to engage in transactions which, from their pettiness alone, would be sufficient to stigmatize him for ever after, independently of the breach

of honour, of gentlemanly feeling, and of the oath prescribed by the
regulations of Government which accompany them. I am glad to
say that instances of this nature are wholly confined to the number
of senior civil servants who came to India early in life, and at a time
when the most open corruption was tolerated—if not encouraged—by
those at the head of the Government; and that, even amongst them,
they are few and far between. I cannot help commiserating the poor
old man; and I visit him occasionally, from recollection of his kindness to me, of his amiable disposition, and the many pleasant days I
have spent in his society; but I cannot but feel disgusted at dishonesty,
and particularly when that dishonesty, instead of being confessed and
repented of, is attempted to be defended by libellous aspersions and
glaring falsehoods. Sir Edward will leave this place shortly, which
I am glad of. For the last eight months our situation here has been
anything but pleasant, owing to the progress of the late events preceding the investigation into his conduct, and pending it. Parties
were formed by the adherents of the accused, and the little society
which we were able to boast of was broken up by the bickerings and
altercations which followed every step in the proceedings. In the
meantime, the eyes of all the European community in this part of
India were turned on Delhi, for the whole business has excited an
interest and stir scarcely to be conceived, owing to the rank, age, and
abilities of the party accused. I was resolved to join myself to no
party; but I had a most difficult course to steer between my principles and my feelings, and it gives me no small satisfaction to reflect
that I have succeeded. As long as I continued to frequent Sir
Edward's table after the commencement of the business, I preserved
a strict silence on the points connected with it, which were too often
discussed at the dinner-table. My principles and my respect for the
character of my absent friend, added to my knowledge of the impro-
priety of Sir Edward's conduct, placed a seal on my lips whenever the subject was introduced; and when pointedly addressed,
either by Sir Edward himself or his wife, for the purpose of pro-
curing my assent to their assertions, I sat silent; or, if I spoke at
all, it was only to deprecate the introduction of so painful a subject
in the presence and at the table of the party immediately concerned.
By this I preserved my character as a steady, independent man; and
I observed, in a short time, that Sir Edward never ventured to address
me on the subject, but rather seemed anxious to change the topic
whenever this unfortunate one was introduced by his lady. When
the virulence of party spirit led me to believe my presence irksome to
the latter, who could not bear a neutral guest, I absented myself then,
but not till then; Sir Edward himself, who stood in awe of his

termagant wife, agreeing with me as to the propriety of my resolution. I thus screened myself from the charge of ingratitude, which might otherwise, with some show of reason to those unacquainted with the circumstances in which I was placed, have been brought against me for deserting Sir Edward whilst under a cloud, after having lived on the most intimate terms with him for a year and half before; and, by behaving more distantly towards his successor, I escaped the imputation of being a time-server, in having forsaken my old master for the purpose of paying my court to the imperious new one.

During the whole of this time my intercourse with my friend Trevelyan continued on the same footing as before. Since the day on which I left Sir Edward's table in August last I have visited him occasionally in a morning, but he knew me too well to invite me to dinner again, where I should have encountered her ladyship and exposed myself probably to a pointed insult. By this line of conduct, which I have steadily followed, I have preserved the respect of all parties, and have been the only person, young or old, connected with the Residency against whom Sir Edward, in the progress of the proceedings, has not launched some charge, either of ingratitude, meanness, or any other imputation which his excited feelings induced him to bring forward and even to invent. He spared me because—and without vanity I say it—he respected me. I need not recount all the attempts on his part to induce me to leave my avowed neutrality and enlist on his side in the early stage of the proceedings. He used to enlarge on the subject of his intimacy with my father, endeavour to bind me down by the proffer of favours, and dwelt on our former intimacy. You may therefore conceive the constant struggle which was going on within me between my feelings and my principles; but I am satisfied that I could not have acted better, nor would I have followed any other course had it been in my power to retrace my steps. I know not why I again trouble you with a detail of the grounds on which I thought proper to regulate my conduct throughout this trying business; but it has occupied so much of my thoughts, has been of so deeply interesting a nature, and from the importance of the case and the noise which it has excited in this country is so likely to reach the ears of such of the community in England as have connections in this part of India, that I cannot help reverting to it as a kind of episode in my dull life here.

I went to take leave of him previously to my departure, or rather of his, for he set off for Calcutta two days before I did. He received me most kindly, and on returning home I was rather surprised to find an invitation to dinner for the last evening of his stay in Delhi. I say surprised, because I had been given to understand that Lady

Colebrooke entertained no favourable sentiments towards me, having fostered an idea that I had gone hand-in-hand with Mr. Trevelyan in conspiring against Sir Edward, using the term which his party applied to my friend's conduct and motives throughout the business; but if she ever entertained such, she evinced no signs of them on our meeting at dinner. I had not seen her since August last, but she received and parted with me very kindly as well as Sir Edward, and I went home quite melancholy with the reflection of the downfall of the character and reputation which Sir Edward once possessed, but which are now in the eyes of every honest man irretrievably gone. On my friend Trevelyan's conduct the highest encomiums have been passed by the Government; and, although some still persist in picking holes in his character, it has been established on so sure a footing by the result of the proceedings that he may with confidence say, "I have done my duty; it was a painful and an invidious one, but I have discharged it with unflinching integrity and honour."

CAMP, PANIPUT,
March 5th, 1830.

Dearest Mother,

It is high time for me to commence my monthly epistle, though I confess I have seldom found myself so disinclined to studying or letter-writing, or any of my other customary occupations, owing to the uncertainty in which I am placed with regard to my future prospects and destination. I am still marching about the country; and after spending a fortnight with a friend stationed at a place called Nottack, moved northwards to Paniput on a similar visit, where I am at present waiting the result of my reference to Government. My present mode of life is, as you may suppose, far from agreeable to me, for I have no public business to transact; and, though anxious to the last degree to make myself useful, find myself deprived of all opportunities of exertion. But a month or six weeks will decide my destination, so there is no use in grumbling. The weather has proved peculiarly temperate during the last month, but the hot weather is fast coming on, and I begin to find the heat in my tent rather troublesome. I shall, however, be able to weather it out until the end of this month, by which time I shall have it in my power to determine my place for the hot season. At present I am wholly at a loss to divine what will become of me. My spirits, fortunately, resemble the tides ; they seldom keep for any length of time at a low ebb, and when I find them sinking a little I drown the recollection of the event which has caused the depression—not in wine, but in books. I begin, notwithstanding, to wish for a termination of my wandering life, and a settled situation and duties; business, in this country particularly, is rather a pleasure than a trouble. I do not know otherwise how we could contrive to pass those long, long days in the hot weather. Society is extinct during the four hottest months of the year, even at the largest and most sociable stations. Nobody thinks of paying a morning call; and a man who invited any of his friends to dinner or breakfast in May, June, July, or August, would be looked upon as a veritable salamander, as well as entail upon himself a plump refusal from the invited guest. The idle consume the day in eating, drinking, smoking, and sleeping. The ladies read novels when they can get them, stuff their children, scold their native servants, take siestas, sip beer, and languish for hours in a déshabille under a punka. The more intellectual male portion of the community attempt to spin out the day by diversifying their studies until the mind becomes wearied by the constant and unbroken stretch of attention required, after which he wanders about the room, taking care not to move out of the influence of the punka, in shirt and drawers, or else sits with his legs on the table gazing on vacancy, wishing himself in England perhaps, or listening to the melancholy, monotonous cry of the water-drawers at the adjoining well. A nap, produced by his tiffin, then follows; he snoozes uncomfortably for an hour or two, and then sallies out in his buggy, stupid, heavy, and unrefreshed, to inhale air like that of a lime-kiln. On his return he sits down to a dinner which he has neither stomach nor inclination to touch, and goes to a bed on which he knows that, however tired he may be, the heat will not permit him to compose himself to sleep until cock-crow.

If such is the life of an individual at a station where, if he choose to defy the heat, he may enjoy, or at least meet with, tolerable society—or, at all events, have the satisfaction of seeing a civilized face now and then in the evening drive—how miserable would the man be who is shut out from all society of every kind and sort during the greater part of the year at some remote station! It is really fortunate for such unfortunates that they have business to occupy them for a few hours in each day. I used to find it rather a pleasure than otherwise, and it is the want of that occupation now that makes me feel so unsettled and uncomfortable. One's reading, too, is generally—and, indeed, necessarily—very promiscuous. After reading most of our own books, we are forced to look to our friends for a fresh supply, and to content ourselves in consequence with his collection, whether trashy or otherwise.

To follow a regular and well-connected system is impossible, owing to the paucity of the means; and to sit down to Hume, Smollett, &c., &c., for four or five hours in the hot weather is equally impossible. I generally have some standard work in hand, which I lay down, resume and lay down again, according as chance may throw any hitherto unread volumes in my way; not that I approve of this style of study, but as the time allowed us for the perusal of the borrowed books is but short, we are obliged to make the most of it by getting through the work without any further delay. Then a man's brain becomes a receptacle for a jumble of the classics, modern novels, Asiatic researches, &c., &c., &c.

Again, yesterday, did I enjoy a glorious view of the snowy peaks. The distance of the mountains from Paniput is great, and I had felt disposed to discredit the accounts heard by me beforehand of their being visible; but, on rising in the morning (a shower of rain having previously fallen), I traced the whole line of snowy peaks extending from east to west. Their bases were hid in the midst of the plain, but their glittering peaks were distinctly visible, with their outlines traced clearly on the cold, bright sky. I embraced in one view the whole extent of the range of mountains included in our dominions, which, extensive and stupendous as it is, forms not one-eighth of the whole chain. Mountains of 21,000, and 22,000, and 24,000 feet rose in front to such a height that, although I immediately recognized the shape of each as seen by me in my travels, I could scarcely avoid fancying them clouds. But, if I touch again on the subject of the hills, I shall talk on for ever; and I have already given you a tolerable dose of them in my two last letters, which I hope you have received.

March 8th—

I have been laughing this morning, until I felt quite sick, over Don Quixote, which I have not read since I was at Dr. Knight's. It is most supremely ludicrous, and every time I take it up it sets me in convulsions. The adventure of the fulling-mills in the first volume, and Sancho's unfortunate call of nature, together with the ridiculous manner in which he satisfied it, almost made me roll off my chair. I am afraid that the fame which dear Ellen must necessarily have acquired as a blue-stocking has scared away all suitors, for how can a young lady who learns Hebrew expect to get married? From the superiority of her mind and her attainments over those of the every-day class of men, as well as on account of the happy and peaceful life which she leads amongst you, it is probable that she rather flouts the idea of marriage than otherwise,—but marriage is important on many grounds. I do not lay much stress on the unpleasantness (if we view it in the light that most misses do) of dying an old maid; but the home of a married elder sister always affords an asylum to the younger, and raises up friends for her brothers in the event of the head of the family being removed from this world. Do not, dearest mother, think me harsh or devoid of feeling in venturing to anticipate an event which must happen sooner or later. Long may you live, my beloved parent! May you live to see your children loving and beloved, pious and happy; and may I be permitted to form once more one of your little circle! But life is uncertain,—a saying trite but melancholy.

I think I told you in my last that Palmer's house in Calcutta had failed. The distress which it has occasioned is inconceivable. Some have lost the whole of their savings in India, others are irremediably beggared, and at the age of forty obliged to commence life again. An event of this kind in India is attended always with peculiarly distressing consequences. Home is the beacon to which all turn, however dissimilar they may be in their pursuits and modes of acquiring means to return there. The loss of their all is the crash of all their hopes; the grave to their pleasures. It separates fond families for life, the unfortunate father being forced to toil on in the re-acquisition of a subsistence. I pity from my soul the poor sufferers, who are very numerous. Many have been compelled to have recourse to the strictest economy, after living in comparative affluence; and as the house has been long established, the losses have fallen on the seniors principally, many of whom have been arrested in their intention of returning to England on a competence by this unhappy circumstance. The dividends, too, will be small. When I shall have it in my power to begin to save money I know not; at present there is but small prospect of it. The civil service has exhibited a sad figure during the last year, owing to the several instances of peculation, and other dishonourable practices, which have come to light, on the part of several of the senior servants and others. Two or three have been removed from the service. The junior portion of the civilians are all honourable men; it is only the old stagers who have proved themselves black sheep,—a circumstance which I trust will be noticed for the sake of our credit and character. I am anxious to have your opinion of my conduct throughout the whole of that trying business of Sir Edward's at Delhi.

March 13th—

I have left Paniput, and am now once more on my march to the westward. The gentleman who was appointed to Hissar has arrived there, and my former objections to the situation of assistant there are, in consequence, removed; but I am still uncertain whether the young man, who has acted there for the last year, will remain himself as assistant to the new comer, or return to Delhi; in the latter case, I shall proceed to Hissar from Rhotuk, where I expect to hear of his determination, on which my destination must depend. I hope, however, to have completed my arrangements, and fixed my plans for the hot weather, in the course of a fortnight. I have now lived under canvas since the 14th November, and, from the two years' trial of a marching life, like it so much that I shall move out into tents at the commencement of every cold season. No one, who has not sweltered for six or seven months in one house, can form any idea of the pleasantness of the change, although with your English ideas of hot and cold you must suppose it very miserable work. If my life be spared, it is my intention to make an excursion somewhere or other every cold season. At present, I have no specific duties to prevent me, and I am, consequently, anxious to make the most of my time, and see as much of this part of India as possible, before I get tied by the leg to some appointment, which, whenever I may be fortunate enough to get one, will effectually put a stop to the trips of this kind by not admitting of a week's absence from my charge. I am encamped to-day near a remote village, amongst a clump of trees; around me are many pretty woodland glades, interspersed with sheets of water; the scene is enlivened by herds of antelopes, which, from the secluded situation of the village, appear unconscious of mischief, and are browsing quietly on the rich vegetation; monkeys, in dozens, are hopping and grimacing on the branches, and a tribe of parrots are yelling in concert on a tree in the distance. I am fully fifty miles from any European, and, though solitary, felt so delighted with the calm repose of the scene, that I had just commenced the song, " Merry it is in the good green wood," when I checked myself, on recollecting that these were not the good green woods of merry England. How prettily Heber terminates a poetical sketch of the scenery on the banks of the Ganges, by the following natural reflection:—

> " Yet who in Indian glades hath stood,
> But thought on England's good green wood,
> And breath'd a sigh, how oft in vain,
> To gaze upon its oaks again."

Near my tent is the village well, crowded with the native females, whose peculiar duty is to fill the waterpots for the day's consumption; and the numbers, old and young, of that sex coming and going with their waterpots balanced on their heads, and the jingling of the ornaments with which their arms and legs are covered, complete this truly oriental scene. The natives never harm any wild animal, either bird or quadruped, which accounts for the tameness of the antelopes and peacocks; hundreds of the latter I have frequently seen about a village, unmolested even by the children. The monkey is a sacred animal, and it would be a hazardous business for an European even to kill one. The cow is also a sacred animal, and the sin of killing one, in their estimation, ranks amongst the most heinous offences that man can commit. They are, however, allowed to treat cows as they please, and to thump them to their heart's content, provided death does not ensue. I remember seeing, at Hurdwar, a Hercules of a zemindar who had walked from his native village, five hundred miles distant, on a pilgrimage to that sacred spot, for the purpose of washing away the deep stain of guilt incurred by the accidental death of one of his cows from the blow of a stick. He was standing up to his neck in the water, and the officiating Brahmin was seated on the bank reciting, in a loud tone, verses out of their Sanscrit books, while the fellow was scouring and rubbing himself most lustily; but instead of attending to his priest, his mind seemed to be dwelling on the amount of the fee exacted from him by his spiritual guide, for as soon as he saw me, he began to bawl a vociferous appeal to me against the unreasonableness of the Brahmin, whom I questioned for the purpose of discovering the usual amount given on such expiatory occasions. The priest, who seemed quite indifferent to the man's expostulations, having already pocketed the money, replied that "the sin was an enormous one, being no less than the murder of a cow, and that the fee which he demanded was very moderate, only one rupee eight annas, whereas the penitent was only disposed to give him five pice, and he a zemindar too!" I thought it advisable not to interfere, and, accordingly left the clamorous disciple shouting and roaring in the middle of the water. I observed many humorous traits of Hindoo character during my march, and gained a considerable insight into their superstitions. After my frugal dinner in the evening, I used to sally forth with a thick bamboo in my hand, and direct my steps wherever I saw anything to attract my attention, and, by this means, I have lighted on many a humorous adventure, as well as learnt much regarding the manners and amusements of the native population. I enjoyed a delicious bath, in the cool of the evening, in the canal which flows not far from the village, and was delighted at the opportunity of having a good long swim in the running water. Bathing in any of the large rivers is entirely out of the question, owing to the large fish with which they are filled; and few tanks are large or inviting enough to tempt the swimmer; so I tumbled about and rolled over and over in the water with all the enjoyment of a stranded porpoise who has regained his native element.

HISSAR,

May 2nd, 1830.

My dear Mother,

Behold me, seated in my bungalow, at Hissar, on the borders of the sandy desert, the most westerly of any of our possessions in this part of India. Picture the country,—treeless, barren, and comfortless, with an old tomb, or the ruins of a dilapidated mosque rearing themselves in the distance, the memorials of past ages. Hissar was once a large city, and formed one of the favourite resorts of the luxurious emperors of Hindostan. The country around it was considered the garden of this part of India, and thence termed Hussiana, "the verdant tract;" but war, famine and neglect have effected a change, not only in the works of man, but also in the aspect of the country, and the quality of the soil, such as is only to be met with in these Eastern countries, where the smile of approbation of the monarch in former times was sufficient to form a paradise out of a bleak wilderness, or his frown to turn the most flourishing cities into a howling desert. Such has been the fate of Hissar, once called the "Fortunate," where little is to be seen now save sand-heaps, ruins and desolation. With such a prospect before me, and with the hot west wind fresh from the Rikaneer desert howling round the house, how can I avoid recurring to the mild, soft, balmy days in the commencement of our May in England, or help condemning my existence as cheerless and monotonous? The little society I enjoyed at Delhi I am debarred from here, and my only prospect until the return of the cold weather is a dreary round of duties, which are so heavy and numerous as almost to bear me to the earth. This press of business is unavoidable, and the business, heavy and complicated as it is, must be got through during the hot weather; and, had I not been gifted with a tolerable portion of perseverance, I should have fled a station where every duty devolves on my shoulders, owing to the indifference of my superior, and where all my toils pass unrecompensed.

I arrived here on the 25th of March, and conducted business for three or four weeks during the absence of my superior. On his return, my labours rather doubled than diminished. Though exceedingly good natured and good tempered, I found him singularly careless as to how matters went on; he left everything in my hands, as his assistant, and in that capacity I toil from morning to night, engaged in the transaction of his business, so that the credit, if any, attaches to him, whilst my only satisfaction rests in the enjoyment of a power not legitimately my own, and in the performance of duties which, from their nature alone, are sufficient to daunt the boldest and the most indefatigable. The sole charge of a district 150 miles in length, and 60 in breadth, is no trifling matter; the responsibility is great, and the very circumstance of its not falling on my own shoulders, but on those of my superior, renders me ten times more careful and anxious than if I were the only person concerned. Had the ordinary routine of revenue, magisterial or custom duties occurred this year, my labour, with a little management, might have been made comparatively light; but an immense accession of business in the revenue department has taken place, which scarcely allows me time to pay proper attention to the ordinary business. In short, I am occupied from morning to night, unceasingly, and should not have missed sending my usual monthly letter last month had it not been for the press of occupations. My only leisure moment is half an hour after dinner, when I am so exhausted and worn out that I can scarcely hold a pen. Although I have no objection to business, principally because it relieves the mind from the tedium and listlessness produced by want of employment during these interminable days, and partly, too, because I feel a pride in the management of the district placed under me, it is not very satisfactory, I confess, to be exposed to such unremitting toil unrecompensed, and apparently unthanked, whilst my superior, who lives in the same house with me, passes his time in idleness. But I am far from discontented; I transact my multifarious duties with cheerfulness and readiness, and shall continue to exert myself to the utmost of my ability for the ensuing five months. We get on very well together,—as well, that is to say, as two men can get on who have not one feeling, taste, habit or pursuit in common. He is very good-tempered and obliging, and it would be strange if we did not agree together, for I would work myself off my legs to assist a man who acted towards me with civility, and evinced a disposition to be obliging.

After an interval of three and a-half months I received, yesterday, your letter, dated in November, or rather Ellen's. The last but one that reached me was dated in July. If any letters, therefore, were despatched in the intervening months, I fear they must have miscarried. But where is the miniature? I cannot induce myself to believe that it has been lost, but I ought to have received it many months ago, and as yet I have heard nothing of its arrival. How very provoking! This is the mischief of sending valuable articles out to India by private hands. I do trust that I may receive it ere long, for the loss of it would sadly vex me.

I could not help smiling when I read the account of the murder and suicide committed in your vicinity,—at the vivid picture which my recollection of your Thurtellian horrors enabled me to draw of your fright and alarm at the occurrence in an abode so near Park Street. Well do I recollect your raw-head-and-bloody-bones terrors in that business of Thurtell's,—when you used to scamper, paper in hand, to Mrs. Oates, and read the "fee-fo-fum details" to the shivering conclave,—and when I used to accompany you, partly to eat toasted cheese, partly to see Miss Hibbert, trembling from top to toe, in night-cap and dressing-gown, and partly as an escort. Here, now, indeed, is speculation and rumination for you, and in your next letter I fully expect to find an account of the whole transaction,— from the perpetration of the deed up to the coroner's inquest on the unhappy baker. By-the-bye, thinking of the dark walk in Winifred House garden, do you remember my fit of naughtiness just opposite to it on one Sunday during Mr. Hales' tutorship, when you charged me, parasol in rest, with the felonious intent of propelling me into the ditch of the adjoining field, Miss what-d'ye-call-em's servant John looking on all the time? Miss George, by-the-bye, was his mistress' name. I have often reflected on the cause of those differences, produced by myself, which rendered me so irksome an inmate of the house during my childhood; aye, and I am ashamed to say, in my riper years; and I have often wondered how it was that families, composed of far more discordant and turbulent spirits than, to do myself justice, I can lay to my own door, lived in amity, whilst my brief residences at home were too frequently marred by petty disagreements. I attribute them to that determined self-will, that wish to have everything my own way, which, had it not been for the counteracting influence of other better feelings, would have made me a tyrant. That seed of self-will took its growth in my heart in my earliest childhood, and will, I fear, remain implanted there to the end of my life. It was this which gained me the epithet of "spoiled child" in my uncle Charles' u-ni-ver-sal-ly letter of famous memory, which occasionally bothered my uncle Benjamin and Hannah Williams, and which has ever rendered me restive when thrown with seniors. India, as I said in a former letter, is not exactly the country fitted, from the relative situations in which one is thrown in it, to weaken this feeling, or rather this principle, of my nature, and I often wonder what kind of a person I shall appear to you, if ever I live to see you again.

Many, many thanks for your present of twenty pounds to assist me in the purchase of a horse, but you must have mis-read my letter, or I must, unintentionally, have told you a fib, as my horse, though injured a little in his back sinew, is now as well as ever, and carries me on his back daily. But the twenty pounds, on its arrival, together with fifty pounds more of my own, shall go towards the purchase of a couple of shawls, which I have long determined on sending you. My horse was laid up for a time, and I apprehended that he would have been injured by the accident, but he has now wholly recovered from the effects of it.

I never knew what it was to be overwhelmed with business before I came here. My correspondence is all at a stand-still, and I have been a whole week writing the above three pages. This is far from agreeable to me, for I like a little leisure for recreation as much as anybody, and my reading is entirely put a stop to, my books lying unopened and dusty on the shelves. But let me not appear to complain, for I amused myself and idled away a few months in the cold weather, and have, therefore, no reason to cry out against the multiplicity of my present occupations.

May 15th—

I received your charming, long, affectionate letters of November and December three days ago, and reproach myself much for adopting small sheets in reply, instead of the more legitimate foolscap. But what can I do? Even now I have risen from a sick bed, with a shaking hand and confused head, to finish this one, which I commenced so long ago, in order that I may not delay its despatch any longer. Twice already have I been attacked with fever, at an interval of three weeks, which I ascribe to the effects produced on my constitution by unremitting toil in business, added to the heat of the atmosphere. The attacks of fever, indeed, are slight, but the discipline necessary to be adopted in order to prevent its assuming a serious form, though simple, is terribly severe, and pulls down the sufferer in a way not to be described. It ran through the whole of Upper India as an epidemic last year, and killed thousands of the ignorant natives, who would not undergo the English doctoring, but did not prove fatal to one amongst the hundreds of Europeans who were attacked by it, although it reduced them to skeletons, in consequence of its frequent periodical occurrence, and forced them to betake themselves to the hills for change of air. What can be worse, what can be more terrifying to the imagination, as well as dreadful to the feeling, than lying with blankets heaped over one to produce perspiration, when the thermometer is above ninety. The tremendous heat, the painful thirst, the inward heat of the body, cased in flannels, and when, after a time, the attempts to produce perspiration have succeeded, the tremendous, the overwhelming dissolving of the frame into floods of cold sweat which follows,—all these form an awful combination, sufficient to render a giant, in the course of two days, powerless as an infant. I said before that the fever is never dangerous when the commonest caution is taken, so you need not alarm yourself. I should not, indeed, have mentioned it at all, only I find it difficult to keep my griefs to myself so shortly after their occurrence, for I had a second consecutive attack yesterday.

Hissar is far from a healthy place, and a very little will induce me to turn my back upon it, as it does not suit my inclinations in any one respect. This heavy press of business will cease after two or three months' time, and when I have a little leisure to look about me, I shall be better able to form an opinion of my present station. I am gloomy, ten times more gloomy than I was at Delhi, for here I have not a soul to speak to hardly, except on the commonest topics. My companion, who is a mighty good-natured fellow, sits opposite to me, with his legs on the table, smoking his hoocca every day, evidently thinking within himself,—"though a tolerable man of business, this gentleman is one of the dullest companions I ever met with." And I cannot help cogitating, "who, on the face of the earth, educated thee, thou good-natured, bustling, idle one, who givest all thine energies to speculations on the mysteries of jockeyship, the sporting calendar, and the canine species, without infusing into thy breast one atom of curiosity or love of polite literature, or, in short, taught thee anything beyond what is necessary to render a man a complete adept in small talk?" And thus we jog on, very seldom taking the trouble to exert ourselves in introducing any topics, which must fall, dead and spent to the ground, after a five minutes' discussion, since they generally turn on the qualities of a favourite horse, or the virtues of some wondrous puppy-dog. In short, to tell the truth, I am very far from being happy. Is this, I sometimes exclaim, to be the sum total of the occupations, and the sole scene of the joys or woes, of my earthly existence? Are my hopes, my pleasures, my recreations, to be confined to a small and obscure and unhealthy station on the Rikaneer desert? Is this the existence I looked forward to in my youthful days, when, though well aware that India was a land of exile, I scarcely pictured it as the grave of one's hopes, or deemed Indian life a dull, cheerless flat, with no object to delight the eye or charm the sense of an individual constituted like I am? I read your charming account of your domestic felicity, your employments and your recreations with a bursting heart. But my die is cast; let me not seem to complain in a situation where complaint, if real, would be absurd and inexcusable. But mourn I must over the memory of past times and events; nor, whilst inwardly contrasting the tenor of my present life with my past, can I avoid sighing with bitterness over the prospects now held out to me,—not gilded prospects, such as you too sanguine folks in England are apt to hold up before the eyes of your young adventurers proceeding to the distant and ideally romantic shores of Ind,—but years of toil, years of solitariness, and that solitude mental,—a total absence of the few trifling pleasures which, for a short time at least, throw a gleam across the dull gloom of one's existence,—a state of seclusion from all society, and the sickening of Hope, which cannot long survive such an accumulation of adverse circumstances. I should not say that I was utterly cut off from society here, for two families live at the place, and a regiment is stationed at Hansi, which is only sixteen miles distant; but the weariness which I experience in the evening renders me perfectly unable to visit or dine out with pleasure, and I prefer staying at home with my book, eating a frugal meal, smoking my hoocca for a quarter of an hour, and then off to bed, to going out, or dining and straining all my inventive faculties to find small talk for the amusement of the ladies. In fact, they think me a very stupid fellow, and I have neither care nor inclination, at present, to induce them to alter their opinion. At Hansi there are two spinsters, moreover—wondrous belles! who have made sad havoc amongst the hearts of the penniless officers in the corps. But it is not in the company of spinsters that I seek recreation, after being overwhelmed and stupefied with business. I look back to the society at Delhi, where I used to complain to you of my solitude, and am disposed now to view it as a very Paradise compared with my present situation. Such, you say, will it always be with me, as it has always been : but this is the acme of cheerlessness, and I feel certain that nothing could go beyond it in discomfort. But enough of these sick man's reveries.

I have not yet received any tidings of any kind relative to your trip to Ludlow. There is at present a hiatus in your correspondence which more subsequent letters will, I hope, shortly fill up, as I am anxious to learn how my Ludlow acquaintances are, and what kind of a reception you experienced from them.

And so the miniature is lost! So I gather from a single sentence in your December letter. But how or where I cannot divine. How singularly unfortunate! How very provoking!

Your extracts from Fred's letters amuse me much ; they evince an understanding superior to his years and an excellence of heart which will comfort you in future years. Strange, passing strange it is that my disposition should have been formed in so wayward a mould whilst my brothers are perfectly exempt from that unamiable spirit which embitters the recollections of my childhood. The cause I have before stated; but it is a ruling passion which seems to have been confined to me alone, and from which the rest are so happily exempted. I find by your last letter that you begin to estimate the standard of talent in our immediate family with a little more accuracy than you were wont. I certainly have little scruple in asserting for us five a high place amongst our contemporary relatives in point of judgment and understanding, but the boast of talent is what none of us ought ever to put forth or can ever put forth with justice; and it can be but small matter of exultation to Ellen, or myself, or the rest of us, that we hold the highest rank for understanding amongst an assemblage of noodles. If the lives of my brothers and myself are spared, we may be considered as somewhat superior men to the generality, by the intellectual part of the community, as amiable or as agreeable men, but we shall never be shining characters or conspicuous for any great intellectual acquirements. I feel a kind of malicious pleasure in reducing your highflown ideas of family genius to their proper and becoming level, such as I know them likely to be rated by the world. There is fortunately but a small stock of vanity amongst us, otherwise we certainly should be inclined to consider ourselves paragons of excellence, however much the world might be disposed to think to the contrary, merely citing as our authority the oft-repeated assurances of our good mother to that effect.

HISSAR,
May 20th, 1830.

My dear Mother,

I despatched a letter to you a week ago; but as my time now is so limited by press of business that I have only leisure to finish my letters by scraps, I commence another without delay. Your last letter of December is spread open before me with all its interesting details relative to our Bath friends and acquaintances. Glad am I that you are again settled there. The recollection of that unpaid riding-school lesson has often made me feel uneasy, and my sensations on the subject are as if, were I to visit Bath ten years hence, I should prefer going in a circumbendibus round by the York

House to passing by that self-same school, lest I might be detected and abused as a swindler. So ease my fears, and if the school be in existence and the same man (not Schriner) in possession of it, send him the five shillings, for honesty's sake.

Your idea of Archdeacon Corrie being able to forward my interests in Calcutta amuses me much. I have as yet no statement of services to offer, and the Government knows as much of Kamschatka as of these upper regions. These are not prosperous times for the civil service, and I shall be well content if, in the ensuing eight years, I shall be able to scrape together sufficient to support me as a gentleman for three years in England. Being free from debt is one great advantage; and though only just able to square my accounts with my agents, I feel an independence of spirit unknown to the unhappy young man who has involved himself owing to his extravagance on his outset. I keep about 100*l.* in hand, and transmit any extra sums to my agents, which, however, seldom find their way to my side of their books, being generally absorbed in booksellers' bills and agents' charges and percentages. This sum in hand enables me to carry into execution any excursions which I may undertake for amusement and recreation during the cold weather; and if I have leisure I intend to devote a month or two every cold season to some kind of excursion which may brace up my spirits and give me some knowledge of the country. Next cold weather I intend to march to the westward, within the borders of the sandy desert, and shall probably extend my trip as far as Bhutneer, which is situated in a foreign territory, and which, though a city of some importance, only two or three Englishmen have yet visited. But this excursion will be an excursion on business, as part of the territory under our control lies in that direction, and I shall have to visit it next cold season. I am planning also an excursion dawk to Jyepore, which I am very anxious to see, but I shall not be able to carry this into execution until I return from my westward route.

I have an insatiable curiosity as far as regards the country, its inhabitants and their religion and manners; and I see so many instances of persons who have lived many years in the country being utterly ignorant of everything unconnected with their own limited sphere of action, that I am anxious to save myself from the reproach, which they so richly deserve, of sluggish apathy. Much I saw last cold season, but I have still much to see, and I find these trips so amusing, and so excellent a restorative of one's shattered health and spirits, that I shall avail myself of every opportunity of employing myself in leisure time in a similar manner. Even now I find a retrospection to my solitary but most interesting trip during last cold weather to have a soothing effect on my spirits. Vivid are my recollections of those sublime scenes, more vivid even than was my delight at the moment of beholding them.

I am anxious to know what you thought of Heber's Journal. I hope you followed his route in Arrowsmith's large map. Many a time have I stood on those grand flights of steps ascending to the Juma Musjid, of which a small wood-cut is annexed to his description of Delhi; and many a morning have I scaled those lofty minarets and looked down on the vast slumbering city beneath, or turned my eyes in the direction of the gigantic ruins which cover the face of the country to the southward. Many an evening, too, have I ascended those minarets for the purpose of obtaining a panoramic view of the crowds of Mussulmans prostrating themselves with their foreheads to the pavement at the time of evening prayer. It is indeed a noble structure, nobly situated. The external form of worship of the Moslems is beautiful and impressive to a degree, not to be imagined by one who judges of their external observances by the internal spirit of their faith. To me the posture, the prostrations, &c., are perfect, as exhibiting the deepest abasement and humility, alas! never experienced or even thought of by the unconscious worshipper.

May 26th—

I received to-day Ellen's letter of 21st December. What a pity it is that letters do not arrive more regularly from England! I am quite vexed at being obliged, for want of time, to revert to these small sheets and lay aside my foolscap, but were I to adopt the latter now two months or more would elapse before I could fill it. It is not a mere routine of business in which I am at present engaged, but a task perhaps the most difficult of any of the collector's duties, requiring judgment, penetration and local experience. The latter quality,—which, as both of us have lately arrived here, we cannot be expected to possess,—I am obliged to supply the place of by constant inquiries and investigations; and all this toil, to which I am forced to devote all the leisure hours formerly enjoyed by me after leaving court, is independent of the regular routine, so that I am well-nigh knocked up; but two months, I hope, will see me at the end of it all, and a happy day it will prove to me. I regret it mostly on account of the stop it has put to my correspondence. On leaving court late in the evening, after eight or nine hours' labour, the mind is too unhinged to apply itself to anything. Some persons find it easy to shake off all thoughts or plans connected with their official station as they would divest themselves of their robe of office; but I am a young hand in business, and the details which have occupied my attention for so many hours fix there and leave me unable to sit down quietly and commune with you all in the way I love.

I find Hissar much cooler and pleasanter as a residence during the hot winds than Delhi, where we were enclosed within the city walls, and again within the large enclosure in the centre of which our bungalows stood, so that the heat was excessive. Here we are open to the breezes on all sides. The hot winds, hot as they are, I prefer to the climate during the rains; the heat is a dry, healthy heat, whereas the oppressive damps and sultriness of the rains almost dissolve the frame. Our society here consists of a married captain and a doctor. The former is an excellent-hearted little man, and lives in very comfortable style; the latter is a native of Clifton, of the name of Child, who is on the point of returning to England, and intends to take up his residence at Bath. I receive constant invitations to their houses, and we live on very good terms with one another.

Now and then I mount my horse and gallop over to Hansi, about seventeen miles off, for change of scene, but my time is too fully occupied at present to allow of my frequently indulging in these trips. The society there, as I believe I mentioned before, consists of the subs and captains of an infantry regiment, a few families, and a brace of spinsters, independent of other equally rare and extraordinary productions of the animal world in the shape of ensigns, doctors, &c., wondrous to behold. I was born with an invincible shyness, and I shall never overcome it. To this shyness I attribute my inherent dislike to large dinner parties and mixed societies, and in this country I find no inducement to repress the feeling. After a long day's toil I cannot sit down all of a sudden, screw up my features, and lisp small talk to amuse the ladies; my mind is apt to recur to the weightier business of the day, and I cannot avoid introducing topics which, in the opinion of my gallant companion, smell of the shop, and are, consequently, unfit to be produced in a lady's presence. I, of course, laugh at him for his excessive devotedness to the ladies; but the fact is, that although I do not by any means deem myself deficient in conversational powers amongst a small party of friends, my tongue is paralyzed into silence in a large party, and I find it far too great an exertion to talk small talk. In short, I never was and never shall be a lady's man, a title to which so many in this country aspire, though the objects of their constant attentions would be thought in England only a degree above a country wench. I shall never marry in India; the probability of my marrying in England rests on my chance of ever seeing my native country again, or, rather, on the will of Providence. I have a sensitiveness of feeling regarding some points in matrimony which would render me very uncomfortable in this country, where persons marry, without the least mutual esteem, from interest or from passion. Nowhere, perhaps, in the whole globe could be found a region where every feeling approaching to romance is so completely banished. Love, too, loses its romance; I mean not by romance the fancied ecstasies of lovers in fashionable novels, but that high feeling, that spirit of devotedness to the beloved object which in these sober days supply the place of more enthusiastic sensations, and which, though for a time bordering on romance, are experienced by most lovers in England, or, at least, ought to be so. Here marriage is either considered and treated as a regular jog-trot business, and the preliminaries adjusted with all the forms and sedateness of diplomacy or hurried over in so indecorous a style as to satisfy the disinterested that possession was the object and the sole object of the admirer.

But to return to Ellen's letter of December. Let me see. On the 21st of last December, the date of the letter, I was encamped in one of the most beautiful valleys that ever fell in the way of a lover of the picturesque,—a purling stream full of fish, the richest vegetation, and a view to the northward of range above range of mountains. Delightful was the bath which I took in the cool of the morning in that limpid stream, and no less delightful was the stroll along its banks under the shade of the slender bamboo or wide-spreading banyan tree, and this when you were all crouching over a fire, frost-bitten and miserable. But you ought to have been with me in a Mont St. Bernard scene a fortnight before, when I passed the night in a solitary low hut, built on a small square piece of table-land on the peak of a mountain 9,000 feet high. I had set out in the morning from Suntah, and had partly ridden and partly been conveyed in one of their nondescript vehicles, nearly thirty-five miles along the continuous ridge of hills, averaging 10,000 feet in height, clothed with vast forests of pines impervious to the sunbeams. The path at one time plunged into the deepest recesses of these splendid forests, and at another emerging into some sunny spot, presented me with a view of the range of the Himalayas reposing in their majesty. Such language may appear ridiculous when applied, as it is by scribbling tourists, to the scenery of the Wye or the mole-hills of Cumberland; even Mont Blanc, "the monarch of mountains," has been trampled on by the foot of man, but nature has protected the crests of the snowy mountains from such a profanation, and amongst all the objects ever presented to my eye it is to them only that I can apply the epithet of "sublime."

I had taken the precaution of despatching servants beforehand to my halting-place, in order that some dinner might be in readiness for me on my arrival; but I had miscalculated the distance, and night closed upon me whilst my tired bearers were still tottering on over ascents and down descents which appeared interminable. A sharp, cold wind blew over the ridge, and I was perfectly numbed with cold, so much so that when I told my bearers to set me down, and attempted to revive circulation by walking, my legs refused their wonted office, and I fell prone on my nose, to the great amusement of my mountaineer companions, who asked me "if that was the way master walk up hill?" Great was my joy, after a wearisome tug of an hour longer, to catch a glimpse of a flickering light on an eminence above me, which I knew to be the fire kindled in the hut destined for my lodging. Shapes of mutton, cold pork, and hill pheasants danced before my eyes; I redoubled my exertions, reached the snug little hut, and found all my hungry expectations realized in the form of an excellent dinner, with a bottle of beer and sherry, prepared in an adjoining hut.

After paying full justice to the prog I stept out of the hut on to the small spot of table-land on which it had been built. The moon had risen, and I sauntered backwards and forwards on my mountain platform, admiring the splendid prospect on all sides of me. I was between 9,000 and 10,000 feet above the level of the sea, in the centre of the Himalayas, surrounded with the sublimest scenery. The feeling of loneliness imparted by a glance towards the solitudes around me heightened the pleasure of the moment. I could scarcely believe myself in India. The probability of my ever seeing such scenes as these in this country had never entered into my imagination on my first arrival, and the advantages possessed by me over those who resided in the hot, burning plains of Lower India led me to rejoice at having fixed on Delhi as my station. Independently of these feelings, the vastness and solitariness of the scene before me, the mountains untouched by mortal feet of tourists or sketchers, and the pine forests, unexplored save by the pheasant or the squirrel, added to the interest, and made me feel almost like an inhabitant of a new world. I have often, when a boy, thought of the primeval solitudes of North America with deep interest, and certainly there is a grandeur added to scenery when it can boast this quality, such as you folks in England—every corner in which some prying traveller has poked his nose into—can never feel. But a truce to description.

You hold out to me the feasibility of staying for good in England on my return, marrying a woman with fortune, and taking pupils. No, dearest mother, no. My lot has been cast in this country, and here I must remain. Is it, then, that I repine at my lot when I occasionally indulge in reflections in my letters? No. Is it the canker of discontent? No. It is merely the result of a habit which I naturally fell into of comparing one's life in India, together with its joys and sorrows, with that of those who remain at home; of calling up past reminiscences, and now and then of sighing over the picture afforded by the comparison. Your little fit of castle-building, as it ends in rich heiresses and bottom-whipping, is not very congruous or very likely to be realized; only pray keep pupils and everything approaching to teaching in the back-ground, if you are anxious to mould me to your views. Banging boys' bumfiddles is not a very romantic occupation, and I question not that under such circumstances I should heartily wish myself in India again. Poor Mortlock is a warning to me on that head, as I never saw a man more formed for domestic enjoyment, and never one more thwarted by duty from following the bent of his mind. Only conceive me, with the ferrule in my hand, engaged in the highly intellectual task of thumping Hic, hæc, hoc, into the addled pates of a pack of urchins in the school-room, whilst the *heiress* in the laundry is superintending the usual museum of foul shirts, patched and parti-colored breeches, &c., &c., exhibited on the turn-out of the last week's linen of a parcel of schoolboys in every school in the world; or whilst I am parsing some refractory pupil, and scoring his bottom with the pitiless birch, picture the *heiress* in the kitchen occupied in the mysteries of the manufacture of "scrap pie," "stick-jaw pudding," "sweaty dampers," or any other of the articles in the well-known bill of fare of a country school! Why, this is an airy vision, indeed; a vision of romance and happiness, of seclusion and elegance, of refinement and enjoyment! Oh, murder!

May 29th—

Another letter from you, dated October. Thus three months' letters have arrived all in a heap, after my remaining letterless from January to the middle of May. I am grieved that I have not leisure to write at my usual length in reply to your delightful long letters, but I must make up for the deficiency in quantity by despatching an extra letter or two now and then until my present labours shall have terminated.

The account you give me of dear "Shap Habbey" delights me much. How happy must the accomplished and elegant "Hattitude" feel at the prospect of their union. Little Cock Robin, of course, will publish the banns and perform the ceremony. Blissful match! But, "Shap Habbey," one word with you, and don't be angry, as I will allow you to give me as many lectures in return as you please. My mother speaks of your indifference to general society, and of your inclinations and pursuits being confined within the limits of the little family circle. Beware that this love of retirement does not end in a causeless shyness of company and society in general, supposing, even, that this habit of seclusion does not take its rise from that source. I am well fitted for a monitor on that head, as I experience myself the great inconveniences and disadvantages attending shyness, at the same time that I feel the habit to be an invincible one on my part, and would accordingly prevent its growth on yours. In this country the society is too confined to admit of its development; but my dislike of a large society, such as is to be met with in a few large stations, is inherent, and my present secluded life is not calculated to remove a feeling which was never wholly shaken off in my *gayest* time—viz., at Ludlow. Positively, "Shap Habbey," I forbid Euclid, or any publication connected with the learned languages. I feel as all men feel on that subject, and I tell you candidly that I should shun a woman who added a knowledge of the classics or mathematics to the rest of her acquirements. The uselessness and unsatisfactoriness of a mere smattering need not be pointed out; and what acquaintance with the classics can a young lady acquire beyond a Hic, hæc, hoc knowledge? I have always observed—and you will, I think, find the observation to be a correct one—that women of masculine minds, and weak affections, take to pursuits of this kind, which are horribly anomalous in the eyes of all sensible people. Bless my heart! what a learned family you must be—a second edition of the seven wise men of Greece, including Peggy and Thomas in the number—a bright personification of scholastic learning: law, physic, and divinity! Hebrew going on in the back parlour, and Euclid in the drawing-room; cook and Thomas reading "Locke on the Human Understanding" in the kitchen; and *missus* holding physiological lectures in the bedroom! Well may Park Street rear her head high, in exultation at her having harboured and protected so many Admirable Crichtons in bummycoats and petticoats.

We have sand storms here, in all their variety, very frequently. A small speck is seen on the horizon, and in the course of five minutes afterwards we are enveloped in a sand storm—howling, blowing, blustering. Objects at the distance of a yard are wholly obscured, and a twilight succeeds which does not admit of a person's reading without lights. Then the rush and scutter to shut the windows and bang to the doors, otherwise we should find all our rooms ankle-deep in sand.

Your maternal anxieties relative to my buggy-driving excites, I am sorry to say, a smile. You may depend upon one thing, viz., that I have too much regard to my own carcass to place it in any unnecessary predicaments. As to tigers, they are scarce enough now;

so be easy on that head. The wild beasts in this part of India—or, rather, from the westward of Hissar—are lions, not tigers, if that consideration can afford you any relief. Truly, my dear mother, your alarms on this subject resemble your anti-Catholic terrors, which seem to have raised in your mind visions of stakes, and fagots, and what not.

I am glad that you think my letters true transcripts of my feelings and dispositions. It is, and it ever will be, my wish to lay my whole heart open before you, and to receive such hints and admonitions as the survey of it may call forth. Do not let your affection raise me to a standard of excellence to which I can never aspire, lest, if I live to see you again, you might be disappointed at finding faults and blemishes which absence may have obliterated from your mind. It has been my wish, from the beginning, to impress on you the degree at which my abilities—such as they are—should be estimated. It pains me, therefore, when I read—the "highly celebrated in Oriental learning," which your letters contain. But let the subject rest for the present.

We are all in hot water here as to what will become of us on the termination of the company's charter in 1833—whether we shall become his Majesty's subjects, and transmuted into colonial officers, or revert once more to the old regimen, and continue in our allegiance to the wiseheads in Leadenhall Street.

I wish my age could have permitted of my coming out to India three years earlier; my prospects, in that case, would have been far better than they are now.

HISSAR,
May 30th, 1830.

Dearest Mother,

A letter to you which I have just finished lies before me on the table ready to be despatched, but as I have a moment of leisure to-day I lose no time in commencing another, being afraid to cross the one already written, lest it should prove illegible. You need not call my judgment in question in coming to Hissar; my life at Delhi was too idle to suit me, and I could not have tolerated my former situation, under the vain, shallow man who now fills temporarily the place of Resident, vacant by Sir Edward's removal. There, too, I learnt merely the theory of business; here I am engaged in active duties from morning to night, and in consequence of the amalgamation of offices in one individual held in the provinces to the east of the Jumna by three, I acquire an insight into every branch of the service, and shall qualify myself for an appointment either in the magisterial, judicial, or revenue line. This is a considerable advantage; and it was with a view to acquire some knowledge of the more active duties of my service that I changed from Delhi to Hissar. I am virtually the sole manager of this district, as my companion reposes the most entire confidence in me, and he is too idle to attend much to business himself. This, you may say, is a very unsatisfactory arrangement for you, as you get all the toil and none of the credit, but I came here for the very purpose of toil; and the very responsible duties which I have had to discharge since my arrival here will, I question not, prove useful to me afterwards. At all events, I am content, though by no means devoid of proper ambition. I am by no means giving up my Oriental literature. Whenever I am at leisure I resume my Persian volumes ; but to expect me to pursue my studies at the present time with the same assiduity as when I was in college, with the prospect of a definite advantage before my eyes, is preposterous. You may rely on my not forgetting the little I may have already acquired; but, as I said in my last letter, the instruction of youth—in other words, banging boy's bumfiddles—is a task for which I am wholly disqualified by disposition as well as by inclination ; and I have seen enough of the life of Oriental professors to lead me to shun the occupation. No, no; for heaven's sake, strike out some new device for my future profession instead of this abortive one, since you seem predetermined that I am to come home at the end of ten years, marry an heiress,—as if heiresses were as plentiful as the Winifred House apples—and settle in England, the only one of which likely to be realized is my return home,—and how uncertain even is that one!

Your terrors about wild beasts are so great, that the slight sketch of my trip to the Himalayas must have put you in a fever; but really, dear mother, you must drop such frights, as they are wholly groundless. You sent me a very pretty poetical Call of the Wanderer, by Mrs. Hemans, in your October letter. I send you his reply :—

O'er the far blue mountains,
  O'er the salt sea foam,
Fain would the wand'rer flee
  Back to his home.
Here no kindly glances greet him,
  No fond mother's smile;
Strange forms and cold hearts meet him,
  Cheerless the while.
          O'er the far blue mountains,
            O'er the salt sea foam,
          Fain would the wand'rer flee
            Back to his home.

Gone are India's promis'd pleasures—
  Fleeting all and vain;
Can its boasted treasures
  Soothe the exile's pain?
Memory fondly clingeth
  To scenes long flown,
Whilst airy fancy wingeth
  Back to his own.
          O'er the far blue mountains,
            O'er the salt sea foam,
          Oft doth the spirit flee
            Back to its home.

Hark! they chide the wand'rer's stay,
  And his features trace,
Softly whispering him away
  To their lov'd embrace.
His heart is with the absent ones,
  But soon the vision's flown;
And he wakes to bitterness—
  Friendless—alone.
          O'er the far blue mountains,
            O'er the salt sea foam,
          Fain would the wearied turn
            Back to his home.

And will he round the wintry blaze
  Fill the long-vacant place,
And sing the song of other days,
  And gaze on each fond face?
O'er hope's bright vision thoughts of gloom
  Their mantling shadows pour,
Whilst dreary echoes from the tomb
  Whisper "No more!"
          O'er the far blue mountains,
            O'er the salt sea foam,
          Ne'er may the wand'rer turn
            Back to his home.

" Back to his home ! "—when treading
  The verge of life's brief day,
When memory's lamp is shedding
  The last faint ray,
Through the boundless realms of space
  Never more to roam,
Then may Hope his pathway trace
  Back to his home.
            O'er the far blue mountains,
            O'er the salt sea foam,
            Then may the weary spirit flee
            Back to its home.

Indifferent as the lines are, do not be over-critical on their subject-matter, which has cost me many a sigh on my reflecting on by-past times. I wish I could write good verses for you, but you have these, such as they are, written in haste and in the midst of business ; but, nevertheless, felt by the writer. I am afraid it will be some time before I hear from you again, as your last letters came by the latest arrivals from England ; but we must put up with the uncertainties of the length of passage as well as we can. I would not recommend both Fred and Joe to turn their thoughts to the Church ; two clergymen in a family of five will fare badly. I have enjoyed a better opportunity of discovering what country curacies really are than any of you during my residence with Mortlock ; and were not the country curate's duties sacred, I should pronounce his life, as far as outward comforts go, to be utterly comfortless. How many a man have I seen in my peregrinations in Rutlandshire, with an elegant mind and refined education, struggling painfully against poverty and striving to bound his wishes within the miserable pittance afforded him by his pay. I have always thought that curates are, even of all others, to be pitied ; and that narrowness of means is felt by them more acutely than by the village paupers. For twenty years, at school and at college, they lead the life of gentlemen, when on a sudden they are cast on their own resources with £100 a-year, and left to languish in that most pitiable state, viz., genteel poverty.

I have not drawn too strong a picture, and it would be well for you to survey it attentively on both sides before coming to any definite determination. All who enter on the sacred office are not quite so fortunate in the extent of their means as my uncle Charles or Mr. Pardoe, or many other country clergymen whom you have met. Hitherto you have only seen the bright side ; but I, who have witnessed the accomplished gentleman and scholar sitting in a brick-floored room, with scarcely a servant to attend upon him or a decent suit of clothes to put on his back, am better competent to speak of the discomforts attending a life which, however satisfactory the duties may be, holds out no prospect of advantage or amelioration, but leaves the young man to vegetate in a state nearly approaching to destitution. Women are too visionary in general,—too fond of drawing a charming picture of the profession in life which they would wish their friends to adopt,—of dwelling on a train of fancied advantages which exist only in their own imagination, and of holding up the profession to the eyes of their pupils not as it really is, but as they would have it. You have read the life of that interesting young man, Wolfe, the author of the lines on the death of Sir John Moore, written by his friend. Do you remember the description of the utter comfortlessness—not to say absolute misery—of his situation when he first assumed the clerical profession and entered on the active duties of a country curate when fresh from college, in the hey-day of life, and after mingling for years in the elegant society of Dublin? Do not think that I mean to start objections to your choice. I would only wish the lights and shadows, the comforts and discomforts attending it, to be fully laid before Fred when he arrives at years of discretion. As to a boy of thirteen's choice of a profession, the idea is almost ridiculous; and yet I know you lay a great stress on the importance of consulting a lad's wishes on the point as soon as he is breeched. Do you remember the grave prognostics as to the bent of Fred's mind towards the military line in which you used to indulge at Winifred House, merely because he and Corporal Joe used to strut about playing soldiers, with daggers of lath, carpenter's paper-caps, and cockades composed of some of Peggy's cast-off ribbons? How many have I seen in this country who were pining on subalterns' allowances and feeling weary of existence—whose ideas of India and of an Indian life were drawn from the airy hopes formed by a few ignorant but sanguine friends in England, and coloured by the hand of affection! But I have said enough on this subject.

Hissar is a surprisingly cool place, contrary to my expectations, or else the season is a surprisingly temperate one, as I have not experienced one-third of the inconvenience from heat which I did at Delhi; but Hissar is certainly not a healthy place, and I shall not be sorry to leave a station so pestered with fevers. The discipline, however, produces one good result, viz., of reducing the full habit of body to which I am disposed by constitution; and as the fever itself is merely troublesome, not dangerous, it may have ultimately a beneficial effect. What I most lament at present is want of time to pursue my reading, but I am looking anxiously forward to the termination of our present occupation, which I hope will be got over in the course of a month or six weeks. I am a collector of petitions in English from the natives, as curious specimens of their progress in our language—and I cannot avoid transcribing one verbatim—which I received when at Delhi, where I used to attend the school in which English was taught.

"To Mr. Brown, Esq., &c., three time [three times three, I suppose, he means];

"The humble and respectable petition of Hurchund Mitter, humbly sheweth,

"Your poor petitioner, drown in poverty's gulf, because patron not one give service and bread since this miserable slave go expatriate from his own Bengal, but he creep small pismire on English tongue's lofty mountain and white gentleman's learning, and I hear your majesty grow munificent schoolmaster in Mudrisa [college at Delhi] to teach native also, and foster belly by sustentation. O, my lord, I request you let poor petitioner wipe dust from shoe with eyes' lash, that ardour coming to breast may quench in plenty of Persian study. Mr. Ranken know my goodness; he vouchsafe me two, four occasion, little rupee when I damned poor, but say after not got too much business, therefore excuse what other gentleman want you; therefore I implore your honor to make compassion and benevolence, and your petitioner will every pray.   "HURCHUND MITTER."

But Hurchund Mitter is flowery and scholastic in his style; here is another, simpler—

"The petition of Hussun Khan, in the cantonment of Delhi,
"Most humbly sheweth,
"That your poor petitioner most humble begs leave to represent his deplorable case before your honor, and same time solicits pardon of troubling your honor.
"That your petitioner has a wife named Bagun, in the cantonment of Suddur Bazar; that your petitioner, having been married with the said her about seven years ago, since the time gave her about hundred rupees, and which was all states, when she leaves on command to your petitioner. Afterwards, she having so vicious conduct, want another young man, and do not care her own husband. O, Lord God, it is very magnificent! However, also, your petitioner has a sword to the said vicious woman, being not given, and not give, and not come to your petitioner's house; therefore entreats your great goodness will be so grace-ously pleased call her at your mercy's sake, and try this few matter if it be so; your petitioner will be bound to pray for your health and prosperity for ever and ever."

Such is our Indo-English. I thought they would amuse you, and inserted them accordingly; I know, when Hurchund Mitter presented his, I burst into such an uncontrollable fit of laughter, that I well nigh rolled on the ground. Hearing Englishmen using the word "damn" continuously, both as a prefix and affix, he, I suppose, thought it merely a synonym for "very," and wrote it down as such, without any intention to offend.

The gravity with which Fred mentions, in one of his letters, as a matter of blame, a little boy at the school "reading Shakespeare," rather amused me. To be sure, the offence, coupled with it of omitting his prayers, is rather more serious; but it is the coupling of the two which raised a smile. Why, my dear Fred, an' thou hasn't read some of Shakespeare's plays—such as his Hamlet, his Romeo and Juliet—thou art a great booby, for I had read them all at the age of eleven years, and I read them now with increased delight at each successive perusal.

Your remarks relative to the treatment of servants in this country are just. Too often have I seen them cruelly treated by young men who have lately arrived in the country. I need not mention my abhorrence of the practice, as betokening cruelty and cowardice in the man who beats an unresisting and uncomplaining native. On my first arrival in Calcutta, I was quite tender to mine, never thinking of striking them, or even of abusing them unnecessarily; but at Delhi, my temper was much broken by the rascality of the servants there, and, being pestered with the stupidity of an immediate attendant, whom I did not like to turn off causelessly, I was tempted, on one or two occasions, to follow up my admonitions by a manual application of my fist to the shoulder of the offender. I never struck elsewhere, and never struck hard, so as to hurt him in the least, and my anger used so immediately afterwards to evaporate, that I believe both parties cared not much, trusting in the shoulder as a kind of safety-valve. Remember, this was not frequent, not more than ten or twelve times in the course of two years. The only servant I ever hurt was a poor native groom, whom I struck at with the buggy whip one day for some act of negligence; the poor fellow put his hand up to his eye, near which the end of the lash had lighted, and appeared to suffer pain, though he bore it uncomplainingly. I was cut to the heart, and felt exceedingly fidgetty and uncomfortable at breakfast afterwards, humanity telling me to make the man some amends, and pride forbidding me to lower myself by acknowledging a fault to an inferior, to a common groom, too, one so immeasurably below me; but humanity gained the day, so I sent for him, before my other servants, and said, "Buxoo, I struck you unjustly," giving him, at the same time, a small present in money. The poor fellow, though by no means indisposed to pocket the affront, seemed so surprised at master's confession, that he stood with the money in his extended palm, staring at me in astonishment. I saw him afterwards, for I was in camp at the time, seated under a peepul tree and telling his adventure to his fellow grooms in high glee. This occurred about six months ago, and I need not say that since that time I have given up the admonitory tap even, as tending to encourage a practice which I loathe from the bottom of my heart. I pay them their wages regularly once a month, and, as it is the usual custom to keep them sadly in arrears, I have reason to believe they like me much.

HISSAR,

June 13th, 1830.

My dearest Mother,

I was sitting in bedgown and slippers before my writing desk (once yours) this morning, scribbling a few lines to my uncle Benjamin, when my servant brought me the letters, and my heart leaped at recognizing one which, as I said before, in shape and superscription, resembled a direction card on a tun of wine, or a pianoforte, going per waggon from London to Bath; such, at least, it might have seemed in the eyes of a casual observer, but I knew it to be *another* volume of affection, another leaf from the olive branch at home, destined to gladden the heart of the one in a far country. Many in this country hear frequently from their friends in England; many a poor lad, ere he has become familiarized with the change of scene, and almost of existence, which meets him here, sits down to satisfy the longings of his correspondents at home by a periodical letter; and many a mother, doubtless, pours out her heart on paper in reply; but I have seen the warmest affections, the fondest feelings, on the part of my fellow-exiles, wither under the influences of an Indian life, and of a prolonged absence from the objects of them. Time will blunt even the keen edge of a mother's affection; the absent one may be spoken of as "my son," or "my brother," in India, and the former periodical records of a love and interest existing in the breasts of a few at home for their absent kinsman, may contract into dry family details, or a log-book of the weather, and other equally important occurrences; but I feel, at present, as if *we* were exempted from the chill of affection so often consequent on continued absence; as if our hearts would grow closer daily, and draw nearer and nearer to each other over the intervening waste of waters. That I should revert to home, and, in my present cheerless routine of life, experience a peculiar pleasure in communicating with my only confidants in this world, is not surprising; but that you, who have other objects of affection and interest around you, and other duties to engross your attention, should devote so much of your time to penning monthly letters of so delightful a length to me, is a sweet and convincing proof of your unabated love; as such, believe me, I esteem them, independently of the cheering assurances contained in them, and their interesting details, and I am almost ashamed of transmitting in reply such meagre tokens of my affection; but I have mentioned, in my last letter, the cause; and grieved as I am to lay aside the foolscap, I find the smaller-sized sheets much more convenient. You will not find me grow lax or negligent in my correspondence; I feel, on the contrary, an increased pleasure every month in writing to you, and certain am I that our feelings on this point are reciprocal. Yes, dearest mother, let us continue to correspond in the same delightful manner to the latest moments of our lives, that it may not be said, as is too often the case, that whatever my feelings, and errors, and sins might have been, my heart was ever for an instant estranged, or my feelings cooled, by absence. I consider you a happy family. I recall to mind occasionally all the family groups amongst our relatives and friends, and I remember none so really happy,—none so formed for the peaceful enjoyment of a tranquil existence, hallowed even in this world by mutual affection. Happiness,—I speak of the happiness of this earth, —is generally estimated by comparison; and how seldom do we see those who are in the actual enjoyment of it able to prize it at the time as highly as reflection and recollection in after years leads them to do! But then it is passed, and though looked back to as a sweet dream, regrets must mix with the reminiscences of past pleasure. Such has been my lot hitherto; and I, who have never known the value of opportunities till they have passed away, would, therefore, entreat you all to feel your present happiness, and to pursue your tranquil enjoyments under the impression that they cannot last for ever. Often have I heard you say that we should never prize you as we ought to do, until you were laid in Weston church-yard, and you said truly; for however much we may love and esteem you now, it will not be in our power to estimate, as we ought to do, all that you have done for us until you are removed for ever. Oh! distant be that period, dearest parent! May you live to see your earnest wishes in regard to us all realized, and let not the consciousness of not being prized, as you ought to be, until that period sadden you. Such is human nature, that deep as my affections are, and called forth, as they must be, by separation, when no events occur to disturb for an instant the train of feeling, so little trust have I in my temper, that I should almost dread our meeting lest its peculiarities might again cause you pain. I am impatient,—a fault which time may cure, and I am self-willed constitutionally, and, I fear, practically. The difficulty I experience in yielding my own views or wishes to the explanations or expostulations of another is great, and this, I fear, is an evil which experience and intercourse with society will not mend, as in my present, and probably in my future, situation society will have no calls on me for forbearance, and the tenor of one's life and occupations scarcely tend to improve me in this respect. It does not arise from vanity, or from self-love or self-estimation, but from an inherent dislike of being thwarted, which I can only account for by supposing it constitutional. But I have frequently alluded to these, my besetting sins, in former letters; let me then drop my monitory strain, and turn to your late letter of different dates, the last date being the 5th of February. I received to-day, also, a letter from my uncle Charles—the third or fourth which he has written me. I take his notice of me to be kind, inasmuch as I did not expect it, and you may be sure that I fail not to transmit in return an appropriate reply. He writes to me on the occasion of any marriage or death, or any other family occurrence, which I might wish to know—really I feel quite grateful to him in consequence, although his letters are mighty dry, and for all the world like a chance extract out of a parish register.

The average temperature of Hissar this year has been nearly fifteen degrees cooler than I experienced it at Delhi this time last year. You need not be afraid of reptiles or wild beasts at Hissar, or of my poking about in old ruins, as there are no old ruins worth poking in. My recreations are confined to a constitutional ride in the evening, and to an attempt to convert a barren, sandy patch of land near the house into a garden. The soil, however, is so wretched, and so incapable of improvement in the usual modes, that I almost despair of effecting my purpose. In many parts of this district the soil is too sandy to admit of grass even growing, and I have ridden over tracts treeless and shrubless, as glazed, dry and hard as a plate, which did not present even an appearance of verdure or vegetation, unless the rank tufts, which crown the summits of the sandy undulations, be allowed to pass under the latter. Water is from 130 to 160 feet below the surface of the earth, and the wells deepen as they advance towards the westward. In short, the aspect of Hissar is as cheerless as it could well be, and I miss much the many objects of interest which abound near Delhi, as well as the fruits of the country, none of which are to be got here. This is the mango season, and, as I am fond of the fruit, I feel quite disconsolate at not being able to lay my paws even on one.

June 25th—

The character of the natives in this country is a perfect anomaly. Patient, fawning, and parasitical, they will bear much without uttering a complaint; but rouse their passions, and they are more cruel and ferocious than a tiger. Intelligence was brought me late at night, three days ago, of a murder committed by a very respectable man in the town of Hissar, who, they said, after having cut three women into pieces in a fit of rage, had fled naked and barefoot into the jungles. I mounted my horse forthwith and rode into the town, when I learnt that the unhappy man had not been actuated even by jealousy. A kind of demoniac fury seemed to have seized upon him at the moment, and led to the commission of the cruelty. He had had a trifling dispute with his wife's sister, during which she had annoyed him by some expressions used by her. He took no notice at the time, but leaving the room returned with a sword, with which he attacked the wretched and helpless woman. At the first blow, he smote her arm off below the elbow, and, after inflicting two more frightful wounds on her neck and back, he rushed at her mother, who was crying out for assistance, and wounded her mortally with repeated blows. Even this would not satisfy this blood-hound, for he completed this horrid scene by cutting in pieces an unfortunate slave-girl who happened to enter the room at the time, no reason being assigned by him, on his subsequent examination, for the murder of the two last, except the brutal and frantic rage into which he had worked himself. I returned to the house, and, as the man could not have fled far, determined to accompany the public officers the next day on their pursuit of the criminal. We accordingly set out early in the morning, and gaining intelligence of the direction in which he had gone from a native labourer, we followed on the track of his footsteps in the sand, and at last discovered him standing with his back to a tree near a tank. His legs and feet had been torn by the brambles of the jungle, and were covered with blood. He had no clothing except a cloth round his loins, and, as he brandished his bloody sword, threatening death to any who approached him, he looked as horrible a figure as can well be imagined. I dismounted, and went as near as I considered it prudent to advance towards such a madman, and whilst reasoning with him, with a cocked pistol in my hand, which I assured him I should have no hesitation to shoot him on the spot with, in case he attempted any further violence, two soldiers approached noiselessly behind, and suddenly seizing his arms pinned them behind the tree. He was handcuffed immediately, and conducted back to Hissar. Such instances of brutal cruelty and fiendish rage are by no means uncommon, and excite little surprise here—witness that most atrocious and diabolical act of a petty Raja, to the northward of our frontier, who, for some trifling offence, cut off the hands, breasts and feet of one of his wives, and threw her into a dry well, where, strange to say, the mutilated creature was found alive two days afterwards. This horrid event occurred but lately.

June 27th—

The sky is overspread with clouds, and a plentiful shower of rain yesterday relieved us from the oppressive heat which always precedes the commencement of the rainy season. Certainly the change is a pleasant one, although I have not found the hot season disagreeable, comparatively speaking. After two more months the weather will become temperate, and then, in two months more, will come the cold weather, with its amusements and recreations. In a month more, I hope to have finished my present business, so as to enjoy a little leisure, which I intend to employ in taking a trip over to Hansi to see the two spinsters. But farewell! I fear to cross my pages, but my next shall be a foolscap sheet.

———————

CAMP, NEAR HISSAR,

January 25th, 1831.

Dearest Mother,

Judge of my surprise when, opening an English parcel, which reached me the day before yesterday, I found the identical miniature, the equally valued locket, and the other little mementos which I had supposed were at the bottom of the sea near the Isle of Wight, in the wreck of the "Carnbery." How it found its way to me I cannot guess; but as my Aunt Pardoe's handkerchief felt rather dampish, I presume that it had been of a verity under the waves, and was cut out of the belly of some shark which had swallowed it. It is altogether incomprehensible how it reached me. If, however, I was surprised, I was also tenfold more delighted by the recovery of such precious articles, and I have the little locket now in my waistcoat pocket, and have opened it a dozen times to gaze on the fold of hair, which is greyish, and not as I remember it when you unwigged yourself.

Dear mother, you cannot imagine how I value that precious little memento; I shall wear it round my neck with the watch-string which Ellen sent me some time ago, and it will be with me at all times, and in all places—in the hill and the desert, the city and the solitude. The miniature, too, is all I could wish—a neat and faithful picture.

I have completed the business which has occupied me incessantly for the last four months, and I am overjoyed to escape from the villany and corruption against which I have had to struggle. My report on the subject has also been despatched to head-quarters, and I hope it will gain me the approbation of Government, as showing me to be an honourable and faithful servant of theirs in a situation particularly trying and delicate, which has already proved fatal to the character of older and cleverer men than poor Suet Dumpling.

I received an order about a month ago to proceed to Cawnpore and assume charge of a situation there of deputy-collector of Government customs, which had fallen vacant, until another gentleman could be appointed. It left it, however, at my option to accept it or not, directing that another young man was to be sent there in case my services could not be made available at the time. I had no hesitation in declining the appointment, and wrote to the Resident to apprise him of my resolution. Cawnpore is 500 miles from this place. It is a large, gay, noisy, disagreeable station, and the climate is most insalubrious. I felt certain I should not feel happy there,—if happiness, which is merely negative in this country, can be found anywhere; and the nature of the duties did not suit my inclination. Besides, I knew not how long I might continue there; and as the appointment was merely a temporary one, I did not feel disposed to hazard my loss of local rank in the Delhi territory to which my three years of service here entitle me, or to undergo the toil and expense of moving bag and baggage 500 miles, and establishing myself in a strange station, amongst strangers, in the uncertain prospect of advantage held out to me in the appointment. My wishes are confined to the Delhi territory and its vicinity, and I shall remain here until I find a situation likely to suit me. I am far from being wanting in ambition; and, after the three years' schooling I have had, should not shrink from any duties which the service affords, but I could not reconcile my mind to such a transportation of 500 miles. The head of the present Government, though a determined clipper and retrencher, is a just man. He has few partialities, and looks minutely into everything, favouring those only who do their duty and exert themselves. This is gratifying to the zealous few, and stimulates them to exertion in the certainty that their labours will not pass unnoticed or unrewarded. I would fain hope that the present offer was produced by something favourable which he had heard of me, as I have no friends at court to bring me otherwise to his notice. He comes up to this part of the country in a month or two, and I expect to meet him. He will remain in the hills during the hot weather, and descend to the plains afterwards.

I spent my Christmas at Hansi, at a friend's house, and proceeded afterwards to Hissar, where I stayed three weeks, and am now once more in the jungles. I like a change occasionally, and the solitude of the deserts is by no means unpleasing to my mind. Health is only to be retained by making the most of the cold weather months, instead of remaining in a state of vegetation in the house. This winter—for I may really almost call it by that name—has been unusually cold. For the space of two months we had ice an inch thick every morning, and the air was piercing and refreshing. All these incalculable advantages are lost by the sojourners to the southward, between whose summer and winter there is but a slight variation. I shall remain in tents two months longer, and then for the house, and the tatties, and the howling hot wind, and the miseries of a temperature of 95 degrees.

We had a smart shock of an earthquake here a few days ago, which awoke me from a sound sleep, and sent the inmates of the house a running out of the doors and windows; but no damage was sustained by us.

I am now encamped on the borders of the great sandy desert, which stretches westward to the banks of the Sudry. Nothing is to be seen but waves upon waves of sandy ridges, with a few huts scattered here and there in the spots most favourable for cultivation. What a contrast does this seem to the fertile valleys and murmuring rills of England! Only think of my having succeeded in rearing cauliflowers in my little patch of garden-ground at Hissar! My success makes me as proud as a peacock. I told my old gardener, about two months ago, that I was fond of onions, and on my return to Hissar from the jungles I found that he had sown no less than eight onion beds, sufficient to serve a whole army of Welshmen. You may remember my having been reported missing one day at Winifred House, and being found, after a long search by Thomas Pinnock, seated in the midst of an onion bed, eating my fill—dirt, tops, roots and all. I found, also, cabbages, beetroot—yes, and a few rows of peas, stuck there for show, I suppose, for I could find no symptoms of a pod. Add to these some Indian vegetables, and you may form some idea of my garden in the sands. Cucumbers and melons, which are natural productions of the soil, I expect in abundance in a few months' time. I have made many attempts to get some young trees to grow, but the locusts eat them up root and branch. I have frequently shaken two or three hundred of these insects off a small sapling.

January 27th—

I have just returned from a long ride amongst the sand hills. Whilst scouring over the sands on my fleet little Arab, I could almost fancy myself transmogrified into a Mameluke. Nothing is to be seen save sand—sand—sand. Not a tree or bush meets the eye. The villages are mere collections of mud huts, covered with a little straw. Camels are the common beasts of burden here, and every villager of any substance keeps one or two for his own riding; and it is picturesque enough to see half-a-dozen of them racing over the sand on them at the rate of sixteen miles an hour. I always have a number of them with me to show me the country, and they keep pace with my horse's canter. I thought at one time of keeping a riding camel myself, as the best only cost 200 rupees, and they are most useful animals, but their motion is terrible, and knocks me to pieces. A long, hard, rapid kind of trot forms their only pace, and the jolt is terrific to those unaccustomed to it. Once I tried it to my cost, and having unluckily forgotten to provide myself with diachylon, suffered horribly in my nether man.

On arriving at the villages the principal men come out to meet me with some little offering—a rupee, or any other present, such as a goat or sheep, which, of course, I decline. I then go to the open space in the middle of their village, and listen to the individual petitions of the inhabitants, who are sure to have something to ask. After hearing all their wants, and promising satisfaction and redress, I ride off to another village. My mornings are thus employed, and the daytime is spent in transacting business. In the evening I either again ride or stroll about, and amuse myself with reading until bedtime. Early in the morning a cup of hot coffee, made after your prescription, is ready for me before my ride, and on my return I sit down to a substantial breakfast. Such is my life just at present. It is not wholly devoid of interest, and, though solitary, never leaves me a moment unemployed. The poor natives, I will venture to say, never had a master who looked more carefully into all their wants, and *Brown Sahib* is already known by name far and wide amongst these half-savages; in short, though not given to praise myself, I will venture to say that Government never had a servant more anxious to do his duty to them and their subjects, although they may have scores of more able and talented men.

The people of this part of the country are sad scoundrels. Their character is in general an odious one—ungrateful, deceitful, lying, treacherous, thieving. Business is grating to one's feelings under these circumstances, as one always finds the display of their very worst passions in intercourse with them. A philanthropist might well sigh over the deeply depraved character of the natives of this country, which years of British control have been unable in the least to improve. Other natives of other countries have a little good mixed up with much bad, but in Hindostan the evil part is unalloyed. I never could have believed that a nation existed on the earth so utterly destitute of all the better, and nobler, and honester feelings of our nature. Their character, however, has been formed by thousands of years of despotism and oppression. The momentary bursts of the love of liberty, and of the display of the better qualities which the history of every other people exhibits, is nowhere to be found in the annals of Hindostan. Hence the substitution of fraud and deceit for power and freedom.

CAMP IN THE DESERT,
February 12th, 1831.

Dearest Mother,

I had just sat down to a round of spiced beef which the little fat Captain had kindly sent me, when I received your long letter of the 26th of July, dated from Teignmouth. I forthwith called for some foolscap paper; but none being forthcoming, I was forced to commence my letter in reply on small-sized sheets. I know not which to admire most, the charming length or the punctuality of your letters. Certainly, no young man in this country ever had such a correspondent. I do my best to equal yours in length in my replies, but I am a solitary individual, with little to communicate likely to interest, with the exception of my own feelings. Change of scene or of place in this part of the country affords no novelty, and I have no details of personal adventure to swell my pages; yet the history of my affections, though so oft recapitulated, affords a theme which I feel certain will not tire you. Every letter which arrives from you opens the flood-gates of memory on my mind, and hopes, wishes, fears, and regrets, which had slept for a while, sweep once more over my recollection, and my spectacles are dimmed with falling tears whilst I recur to past times. The present is a barren void, and I seldom venture to indulge in hopes and anticipations for the future. The past is my theme, that on which my thoughts rest, the theme to which I recur on all occasions whenever I give scope to my fancy, and it proves a fruitful source for reflection. But to return to your letter. In the first place, set your mind at rest with regard to bears, tigers, &c., &c., &c. You may be assured that Suet Dumpling has too great a respect for his own carcass to expose it at any time to their fury. You seem to consider me a second hero of antiquity, or as forming an eighth to the number of the Seven Champions of Christendom, ready to peril my life on all occasions and in all adventures. Such, I assure you, is not my character ; I have too much of prudence in my composition, to call it by no worse term, ever to face even a pig, unless I am thrown unexpectedly in contact with him, as in the picture of Johnny Raw, the griffin's first attempt at boar-spearing, far less to expose myself to the hug of a bear or the ugly claws of a tiger. Your account of your little excursion at Teignmouth interests me much. I can almost fancy myself one of your party in your pic-nics. The mention of an Irish jaunting car always recalls to my mind our trip to Portland Island with poor little Miss Vieullemin, when we made the driver laugh so heartily at our jokes and fun. I believe I happened to be in a good humour on that day, and how pleasantly it passed in consequence ! and how many, many other days would have passed equally happily, and formed at the present time a pleasing source of recollection, had it not been for my wayward temper which embittered our simple pleasures so often and so causelessly ! Do you remember the poor little woman's shawl being caught in the door of the vehicle and the man driving off ignorant of the mishap, dragging her in triumph along the downs, whilst her shrieks were wafted by the wind over the cliffs quite in a contrary direction ? How we should prize these little interludes in our existence did we but know how often we should revert to them in after years, and how deeply we should regret the passing clouds which our own dispositions threw across those tracts of sunshine ! Alas ! alas ! we mourn when it is too late ; we picture to our own minds what our lives might have been had we exercised a little self-control and a little self-denial ; and we sigh vainly and regretfully when we compare these pictures with the reality.

The account you give me of the admirable temper and disposition of my brothers, and of the harmony in which they live with one

w.   F another and with all, delights at the same time that it saddens me. It delights me on your and their account, and it saddens me on my own. Why was not I such as they ? Why did I wilfully prefer the thorns to the roses which your love strewed in my path ? Why did I suffer myself to give scope to the worst parts of my disposition in your society, so as to render you doubtful of that deeper affection which lay beneath, and which absent or present in my earlier and my later years, even at the moments when I gave way to my temper, I have always borne towards you ? Why did I bear a smooth brow to all the world beside and a rugged one to you alone ? Why did I stifle those feelings of love, duty and respect which I have always recognized in absence or solitude, and which have now taken so fast a hold on my mind and thoughts ? I was formed to be a regretful being, and I deserve the punishment which my own thoughts supply, or a retrospect of the sweetnesses of my former life turned by me into gall and bitterness. It operates on my mind as a warning, and it has led me since my entrance upon life to shun too close an intimacy with those whom I have most liked, lest the inequalities of my disposition might mar the intercourse. It leads me to shun the idea of marriage, lest a fresh source for regret might be opened to me. If I made you unhappy during the brief periods of our meetings, even at the time when I knew that in a short time we should be separated perhaps for ever, what would be the consequence when I found myself bound for life to a being dependent on me, with whom I must be thrown daily and hourly throughout my existence ? It must not be, I frequently exclaim. If I wish to be free from anguish myself—if I wish to avoid entailing unhappiness on others—I must pass through this world as a single, independent, solitary individual. I must not be bound by an indissoluble tie to another, formerly a stranger, and pain her heart by my waywardness, or force her to keep those rare qualities of forbearance and forgiveness in constant exercise. If hitherto I have only bruised those hearts which bore with me so meekly and gently,—if I have only thwarted those wishes which were directed solely to soothe, conciliate, and gratify me,—why should I subject another to so severe and lasting a trial where the same feelings of long-suffering cannot be expected ?

Answer my questions if you can, for the little knowledge I possess of myself renders me unable to furnish a reply to them. You need not fear, my dear mother, that your little sermons on faith and temperance, and judgments to come, can ever prove tedious to me. They remain with me to be reverted to again and again. I never lock up a letter from you until it has remained by my side for months. Only let them be your own ; extracts from books which can be procured by me are recurred to by me with less interest when they occupy large portions of your letters which should be exclusively your own composition.

With regard to my handwriting, I regret that it is not distinct; but you must bear in mind that the nice formation of every letter would occupy a vast portion of my time as well as of my paper. Besides, I think that a little indistinctness is not unpleasant in a letter from England, as the delay which takes place in the deciphering of it enhances the pleasure by protracting it. I am occupied in business during the whole of the day, and the only leisure I have to take up my pen is after my dinner by candlelight, which adds to the difficulties of writing a letterpress hand. The ink of your letters does not fade in the least, but mine is execrable stuff, and I cannot get better. It is fortunate that you find them at all legible after their journey to England.

I condole with Fred on the unlucky excrescence on his nether man, which must have rendered him sadly uneasy during his interview with his new tutor, Mr. Hopkins, particularly as I am at present pretty much in the same condition, which has surprised me not a little after my total freedom from my former tormentors since my arrival in this country. It makes me sit awry on my saddle, like an "auld wife" going to market with her butter and eggs; but not being very severe, is not of much consequence. It is the effect of the abundant exercise to which I am exposed from the nature of my duties which obliges me to be on horseback half the day. I live frugally, not purposely nor from economy, but from want of inclination to pamper myself with niceties; and although the weather is fine and the air fresh and healthy, in spite of my exercise I only have two meals a day—breakfast and dinner—the one at nine, and the other at six o'clock, when I find my appetite but scanty. I am, however, in excellent health and in good bodily condition, thanks to the climate of these regions.

Why does not "Shap Habbey" write occasionally a few lines on the wrappers? I often laugh over the recollection of how carefully the big doll, in her children's days, and *the* journal in the latter, were hidden in holes and corners whenever I was expected from school or Hayleybury; and the shrieks when she saw me hurling the hideous present of Miss Gibbons up among the branches of the chestnut tree by the upper garden-gate, which still bears my name; and how she wept like Niobe when she saw her idol perched, by a lucky throw, a-straddle on one of the branches; and how the gardener was summoned with the great cobweb-brush to rescue it; and how I was deprived of my gooseberry-fool on that day as a punishment for teazing the embryo old maid; and how I purloined the journal in after years by the connivance of Peggy, whom I coaxed to point it out to me, hidden under cushions and feather-beds; and how triumphantly I brought forth that wonderful production, which ran a chance of being lost to the world by the diffidence of the author. But farewell for the present; I dare not cross the letter.

HISSAR,

May 20th, 1831.

Dearest Mother,

I received your November letter an hour ago whilst seated at my solitary meal. I am indeed, in every point of view, a solitary being,—solitary in my amusements, my thoughts, my feelings, and my affections. With a mind awake to the beautiful in poetry, the tender in sentiment, the noble in history, I meet with 'no one with whom I can communicate my thoughts on subjects so refining, and, at the same time, so instructive; with a heart open to the entrance of the affections I look around me in vain for a participator in its feelings; cut off by my situation from the Indian world, I am equally separated by my inclinations and pursuits from the few individuals of my own country whom I encounter occasionally in this desert solitude; deprived by death of the only two friends to whom I could have ventured to detail those thoughts and feelings, in the hope of being relieved in my turn by a reciprocation of confidence, by the charms of sympathy, or by the consolation of advice, I seem to be bound up in myself by an invisible chain of physical and moral circumstances. To use the words of a Persian poet, "When my friends withdrew their faces from me I said unto myself I will flee to the groves and fields, and nature shall be my companion and my comforter. So I went to the rose in the grey of the morning, and I found a thorn, for its leaves were scattered; and I listened for the song of the nightingale at eve, but I heard it no more." No wonder, then, that a letter from England is the highest enjoyment which I am capable of experiencing. The "undistinguishable throng" of hopes, fears and wishes pent up before in my own bosom seem to find a vent whilst I peruse it or pen my reply.

I feel then that in the absence of those external and mental enjoyments which sweeten our pilgrimage in this Valley of Baca, I possess a rich though a distant treasury for my affections where I can lay up the store of thoughts which swell in my breast in the certainty of a return. Every passing year binds me more strongly to my native land and all it contains, and my disappointments, or, rather, the absence of hope, which meets me here, leads me to abstract myself from the present scenes and to dwell more vividly on the past, since my doubtings scarcely permit me to look forwards with any degree of fond confidence to the future. Yet I am resigned to my lot, which, had it entailed on me poverty in my native land, would have been comparatively easy to be borne; but few can tell without experience how bitter a thing it is to be an exile, to vegetate on and on in a dull course of existence, and to feel that the thoughts we cherish and the pursuits we engage in, in the hope of investing our life with some sources of interest, tend of themselves to draw a still broader line of separation between us and those whom we may happen to hold intercourse with. My habitual and incorrigible reserve, or, rather, I should say, my shyness,—a failing which I shall never shake off,—disqualifies me for general society, even if I had it in my power to mix in it; my taste and judgment force me to lock up feelings which I find no one capable of sharing with me. My studies even are confined to myself, and become in consequence vapid and uninteresting. I read, it is true, from a wish for mental improvement, but when we have no object in our pursuits we naturally lose our zest in them, and follow from principle what we should be incited to from motives of pleasure.

These thoughts crowded on my mind this morning previously to the receipt of your letter, when I found myself seated with a volume of Josephus on one side and some works of our early English dramatists on the other. I rose and looked out on the grassless and treeless waste spread before me; I listened to the howl of the furnace-like wind of the desert around me, and the impenetrable clouds of dust and sand whirled before the blast or resting in darkness and gloom on the horizon; I looked up to the sky and saw it involved in the same yellow and dusky mantle, obscuring even the light of the sun; I looked within myself, and found dissatisfaction, undefinable wishes and regret, destined, doubtless, to be a means of improvement and amendment for the future by teaching us what we are to avoid and how, but too often turned by our perverse dispositions into a bane of the present. Your letter, therefore, was doubly welcome. You may think from what I have written above that I am desirous of leaving this country, but it is not so. I cannot deny that India yields little in the way of happiness and comfort even to those who are most eager to avail themselves of every source of amusement or interest which it can hold out; but I am sensible that my lot has been cast here, and though I may be permitted now and then to form a few indistinct wishes, which are as quickly expelled from my thoughts, from my consciousness of the inutility and folly of indulging in them, I never give way or even feel any disposition to repine.

HISSAR,
June 20th, 1831.

Dearest Mother,

The time for my monthly letter has come round, but as I am scant of news, and have received no fresh letters from England to furnish subject-matter for the one now due from me, I must be held excused for filling up the first page with a few lines of my own, which you must take for better, for worse. I shall never be a poet, nor am I able to tag rhymes on any subject save those nearest my heart, so you must pass over the faults for the sake of the feelings expressed in them. They are meant as a continuation of a beautiful little poem, entitled "The Spells of Home," in Mrs. Hemans' "Records of Woman."

1.

By the mother's accents, so sweetly wild,
As she breath'd a prayer o'er her parting child;
By the trembling eye-lid upraised to bless,
By the hand's warm pressure, the fond caress,
By the bosom's swell, and the kindling sigh,
And the love which beam'd in the sister's eye,
And the music sad of the farewell tone,
The charm is deepen'd,—the wanderer gone,
Whilst in lingering echoes around him fell
The last, soft notes of that holy spell.

2.

O'er the far blue hills, through the ocean spray,
He hath pass'd from the scenes of his youth away;
He hath left the calm joys of his fatherland
For the hues of a richer and brighter strand;
For a richer soil is beneath his tread,
And a brighter sun shines o'er his head,
And costlier odours perfume the breeze
From the balmy isles in those glistening seas;
Yet, still his heart in its inmost cell
Owns the mild force of that holy spell.

3.

Oh, sweet is the lotus flower-cup spread
In radiant folds o'er the water's bed,
And sweet in the depth of the leafy dell
Are the joyous bounds of the wild gazelle;
And soft is the dark eye of Indian maid
As she glides to the tank thro' the green arcade,
And the glittering fire-fly's starlike gleam
Glancing in twilight o'er shore and stream;
But softer and sweeter the thoughts that swell
At the mystic touch of that holy spell.

4.

Clime of enchantment, whose witching ties
Have fetter'd the soul's best sympathies!
Land of green forests and sunny main!
The wanderer's spirit hath burst thy chain,
By that homely charm he hath wav'd aside
Thy dear-bought treasures, thy robes of pride,
For a mightier, holier power than thine
Hath kindled its flame on his heart's lone shrine;
And the smile of Hope and the tear-drop tell
He hath guarded nobly that sacred spell.

5.

For a vision of home on his spirit beams,—
He hears the voice of its thousand streams,
He sees the pearl-drops of its summer showers
Flinging a bloom o'er the woodland bowers,
And the wavy gleam of the feathery grass,
And the spring birds twittering as they pass,
And the primrose bank, more dear to his eye
Than the citron blossoms of Araby,
Whilst Memory pours from her fairy shell
The oft-heard tones of that holy spell.

6.

And still, when Friendship's silvery cord
Is loos'd by the breath of some wintry word,—
When the brow's deep shadow and clouded eye
Tell of fading pleasures, and hopes that die,
In the spicy forest or desert rude,
In silence or dreamy solitude,
That sparkling vision resumes its power,
As a blessing and joy in the darksome hour,
Wakening the echoes of home that dwell
In the magic links of that holy spell.

7.

O Thou, to whose searchings unfolded lies
The page of the fond heart's mysteries,
Tho' the exile sink to his cheerless rest
On the sands of the billowy desert's breast,
Or live to revisit his island shore
And tread the lov'd hills of his youth once more,
Yet blest be ever Thy shielding power
Which hallowed the charm of the parting hour;
And happy the wanderer who guarded well,
As his heart's best treasure, that holy spell.

I am glad to hear that you have procured the books for Emma
and the boys, and at the same time I regret that you should have

thought it necessary to weaken the effect of the present by going to
a second-hand book shop for a cheap, but an inferior, copy. I am
aware that this originates in your wish to save my money, and
I thank you for the tender feeling,—a branch of the same utter
sacrifice of self when the pleasure and advantage of your children
are concerned, which elevates you, dearest mother, above all other
parents. I do not allude merely to sacrifices on occasions of moment,
which are seldom refused by any parent, but to the system voluntarily
laid down and pursued by you in the minutest matters of postponing
or yielding up your own gratification on behalf of that of your
children, of which so many little instances are still treasured in my
memory. Still, when we reach years of discretion, and have not
been convicted of any act or acts which might lead to a general
charge of imprudence, the half-execution of wishes of this kind
throws a reflection on the prudence of them, besides nullifying the
pleasure we might feel in giving, and that of the other in receiving.
Independently of this, your precepts with regard to the non-bestowal
of presents of this nature, and your advice, so often reiterated, of
laying up the money for our own purposes and wants, tend to give
encouragement to the hateful feeling of self, which is the idol
worshipped by all, more or less, in this country. If our circumstances and situation are taken into consideration, it is natural enough
that it should be so; yet this seeming necessity does not justify us
in making it the rule of our actions. I am not in a spot where calls
can be made on me for expensive entertainments, dinners, &c., &c.,
by the society, in return for similar attentions shown to me. I have
no friend near at hand whom I could aid, if circumstances required
it, in any way in my power. I have no black children to support,
nor a native mistress to spend my money for me. I consider it,
therefore, to be my duty, as much as I find it to be my inclination,
to remind myself, occasionally, of my friends in England, by sending
such little presents and mementos as I can at present afford. Few
imagine, when they commence on a plan of saving, that their
economy will at last terminate in miserly parsimony or selfish
gratification; and yet, the line drawn between economy and sordid
selfishness, in a country like this, in which the object of the former
must be *self*, and becomes, in consequence, too often a vice,—not our
children or friends, in which case it is a virtue,—is so impalpable, that
it is often crossed unawares, and the change is not perceived until the
individual is made aware of it by failing in his attempt to return to
a prudent liberality. Economy is a habit, and habit is a second
nature, ergo when the main-spring and motive of that economy is
self,—pure self,—selfishness becomes, also, a second nature with us,

and, whether it end in low parsimony or exclusive enjoyment, renders the owner equally despicable. Can the better feelings, or even the domestic affections, exist within the influence of this insidious but overpowering passion, in itself natural, and confirmed by habit? Or think you that, after having set it before my eyes as my sole object,— as the end of all my labours for ten or twelve years,—that I should be able to shake it off on my return to England, and open my pockets and my heart to those who have a claim on both? No, certainly not,—at least, I feel that, by indulging it on all occasions, it would become, with me, a ruling passion,—and you well know my bias for self in my early years, and have witnessed its effects in my headstrong preference of my own ways, measures and inclinations to those of other people. Was it not this which produced uncle Charles' memorable u-ni-ver-sal-ly letter? Trust my prudence, and believe me, that in sending these very trifling and insignificant tokens of my affection to my brothers and sisters, in return for your yearly presents of books, &c., I act as I would have my own child act in a similar situation.

———————

Cootub, near Delhi,
August 28th, 1831.

Dearest Ellen,

To you is due the first mention of the receipt of my mother's letter of March 29th, and my earliest congratulations on an event which has for so long a time formed the theme of my anxious thoughts and fervent wishes. But congratulations, dearest sister, is too cold a term for me to use who have loved you so tenderly from the days of our childhood. I wish you *happiness* in its fullest sense. Happiness, spiritual and temporal; and I rejoice to think that from your mutual affection and the unison which appear to exist in your tastes and feelings on all subjects, my wish is so likely to be realized. To me the intelligence is a source of unmixed pleasure. *I* shall not feel the loss of your society like Emma, or of your sisterly advice like the boys. The delight, therefore, which I feel in thinking of the change which has ere this time probably been effected in the whole tenor of your life, is with me unalloyed by any selfish consideration of the loss to which your marriage might expose me. *I* cannot be sensible of the vacancy which your absence will create in the small assembled family circle of which you were the ornament and pride. To me, indeed, who look on from a distance, that circle seems

widened by a new interest in life having sprung up,—a new tie to
bind me to home. Nor do I pity my mother or Emma, for I can tell
them from experience that the temporary absence of a beloved object
is necessary to enable us to appreciate it as it deserves; and I can
tell them, too, that there are pleasures in a re-union which are not to
be met with in the routine of an unbroken intercourse. I can also
hold out to them the happy prospect of that re-union taking place at
no distant period, and not unfrequently in your parsonage near St.
Alban's; and much would I give to see you there in the character
which you are so well calculated to adorn, that of a wife and a
mother. How happy will those meetings be, and how much have you
to look forward to! Your romance of life has now commenced. You
have happiness in retrospect, in enjoyment, and in anticipation, and
long, long may you enjoy it. Other cares, other duties and affections,
dearest Ellen, will now occupy your heart; but I feel still secure of
a nook in it, and I shall still write, as I have been accustomed to do,
family letters to all, and to you amongst the rest. This, I feel convinced, will be the best plan. It will still lead me to value you as
one of my immediate family circle, although a few miles may happen
to separate you from my mother; and it will keep up that unity of
heart and thoughts which I should wish to be maintained amongst
us all, even if we were scattered in the several parts of the globe.

I am very seldom violently affected at the moment either by good
news or bad news; but the contents of my mother's letters struck my
heart at once, and I have experienced a lightness of the spirit since to
which I had long before been a stranger. I can now build many
castles in the air and frame many plans of future pleasure. In
short, dearest Ellen, I am happy, very happy; but adieu for the present, as I have much to say to my mother.

Dearest Mother,—I cannot thank you enough for your letter
written between the 29th March and the 26th April, which has relieved
my mind beyond measure, and made me a different being. If there was
ever any alloy to the feelings of pleasure with which I used to regard
you all, it was in the regret I felt that Ellen's warm heart and noble
disposition had not been united with one who might be calculated by
a similarity in taste, sentiment, and the higher and nobler feelings of
our nature, to draw forth all the latent features of her character. I
regretted that one who had performed so beautifully on our quiet
domestic stage the part of a sister, a child, and a friend, should have
been deprived of the opportunity of appearing in the still gentler and
holier character of a wife and a mother. I regretted that a mind
and accomplishments so well fitted to make any man happy, and to
shed a mild and softening lustre on his home, should be merely called

into action in the task of instructing and improving the younger part of our family; but I grieved still more at the prospect of my sister passing through life with a void in her heart and affections,—a void which maternal or paternal love, cherished though it be, cannot fill; which all have felt and all must feel who live in ignorance of the thousand mysterious sympathies connected with the want of a wife or husband. I am happy, therefore, most happy in hearing that the earnest wishes which have occupied my thoughts for many a day in society or solitude, in the city and the desert, since my arrival in India, are on the point of being realized. I shall be proud of Olive as a brother, and I shall look up to him as a friend. An interest unknown before has been created in my heart, and a fresh link has been added to the " silver cord " which bound me to my family. I congratulate you all in the most heartfelt way on this joyous event, the tidings of which sung in my ear more sweetly than the attainment of any of my other wishes relating to myself or to my family could have sounded.

Your letter I received at dinner beneath the dome of this splendid old mausoleum. Some newspapers also, containing some of the most interesting of the late public news from England, arrived at the same time, and I was compelled to put your letter in my pocket unopened, whilst Mr. Trevelyan was reading out aloud the details of the present contests in England, after the cloth had been removed. Though deeply interested in the progress of public events at home, I listened to them with an aching ear and a palpitating heart,—eager, and at the same time half-afraid, to open the letter which I was well assured would decide the fate of one so dear to me as Ellen. Still Mr. Trevelyan continued to read in a sonorous tone of exultation the newspaper details about the successes of the Poles and the progress of the Reform Bills till my other companion chimed in with " bravo " and " excellent," so that even I caught a portion of their enthusiasm; and still I kept fingering the letter in my pocket, wishing them and the newspapers at Jericho. At last we broke up. I hastened to my bed, called for the candles and my spectacles, and after preparing myself for my night's rest, opened the letter carefully with a pen-knife, and commenced. The first line served to disperse my doubts, and to show the realization of my long-cherished wishes—my wishes, I may add with truth, my *prevailing* wishes for the last ten years of my life. Many, many thanks, my dear mother, for your affectionate remembrance of me in penning so long a letter at a time when your mind must be occupied by so many engrossing subjects. I feel your affections more strongly than I ever did at this moment, and would repay it, if I could with words, by many and ardent expressions of my never-ceasing love, gratitude, and filial respect.

DELHI,

November 8th, 1831.

My dear Mother,

I sent off a letter to you yesterday, but, at it was a short one, I commence another without delay. Amongst the letters which accompanied the books I find a note from Mrs. Ames containing a memorandum regarding slavery in Hindostan, and requesting you to ask your son a few questions on the subject. As by " your son " I, I suppose, am meant, I will mention all that I know on the point. That slavery exists in Hindostan, and that it prevails to a very great extent in the territories possessed by native princes, there can be no doubt, but in its nature it widely differs from that which is in practice in the West Indies and the southern states of North America. No kind of manual, that is to say, out-of-door labour, is ever performed by the slaves in this country; they are always confined within the precincts of the seraglios of the wealthier natives, and their usual employment is attendance on its inmates. The natives have a great objection to the secrets of their harams being known, which would be the case if the attendants and menial servants were hired; they there-fore purchase young boys and girls, who are generally kidnapped at an early age, and, immuring them within the walls of their private apartments, deprive them of their liberty for the rest of their life. This practice prevails amongst the Mahometan classes, the same strict system of seclusion not extending to the Hindoo females, with the exception of those of superior rank. Loss of liberty must be slavery, but in other respects the term is too harsh to be applied to this custom, which has existed ever since the Mahomedans first obtained possession of Hindostan. Their condition is, indeed, frequently bettered by the change, and, as they are not restricted from marrying any one within the precincts of the haram, their lot differs but little from that of the Moosliman females in general, who are themselves slaves in reality, although the system of seclusion universal in this country to all the Mahomedans, rich or poor, renders them incapable of estimating the privilege of a freedom from restraint. The Mahomedan female is as happy and contented in her haram as the English lady in her circle of society. They are wholly uneducated, their pleasures and amuse-ments are as infantine as their minds, and they remain children to the day of their death. To suppose it otherwise is a mistaken idea which almost every traveller in the East has fallen into, for were all the doors of every haram in Hindostan thrown open to-morrow I firmly believe that not one of the inmates would forsake its walls. Male slaves are very uncommon now, for, as I said before, slavery only exists within the walls of the seraglio. They were very numerous formerly under the native governments, but their employments even then were far different from those imposed upon the wretched and degraded Africans. They attended on, and frequently formed the body-guard of, their masters, to whom they were attached by the strongest ties. Many who were originally slaves rose to empires. The first Mahomedan monarch of Delhi was a slave, a circumstance which, for the sake of the contrast, gave rise to the saying, at the time the Mogul power was in its most flourishing state, that " the empire of Delhi was founded by a slave." In this respect the male slaves closely resembled the Mamelukes of Egypt, the word Mameluke signifying " a slave." A few male slaves are to be seen now and then in the houses of the rich natives, but they are always Caffres. It is scarcely necessary to add, that, in the parts of Hindostan subject to the British, kidnapping is visited by severe punishment, and that every woman slave is instantly freed on appealing to the authorities for protection, either when she contrives to escape from the kidnapper or from the seraglio, or, on an application being made in her behalf by her relatives who may happen to discover the place of her confine-ment. This is all that we can do, and all that we are called upon to do, with a view to the prevention of this practice. To search the harams of the natives in quest of slaves would cause the instant insurrection of the millions of native inhabitants subject to us, and would bring our eastern empire to a termination in a day. You are, perhaps, aware that the massacre of all the members of the Russian mission at Ispahan two years ago was entirely owing to the rash and indiscreet zeal of the ambassador, Greybadoff, who, hearing of several Russian and Georgian females being kept as slaves and mistresses in the houses of some Persians, demanded their instant liberation and transmission to their native country. In two instances he succeeded in effecting his object, but when the people gained intelligence of his intentions, they rose at once and murdered him and his suite almost under the walls of the king's palace, and in defiance of his troops, viewing Greybadoff's proceedings as a national insult, which, on account of his interference with the harams of their countrymen, could only be wiped out with his blood.

Such is the slavery in this part of India. What the practice may be in the Madras presidency or in the southern states I am ignorant. Probably they do not differ from the customs here, for Indians are the slaves of custom, and there is, perhaps, no country in the world of equal extent which presents so few distinguishing features in the habits, characters, or customs of its inhabitants. The memorandum, therefore, I consider exaggerated in its statements, whoever the authors of them may be. Lord Cornwallis' information was, in general, very crude, and little or nothing of India or its inhabitants was known in his time, or rather, his statement, as it appears in the memorandum, may be misunderstood by the good folks of Bath. The nature of the slavery in this country I have explained above, but the main point is,— "Is it permitted?" Is it recognized by the British or no? The natural inference from the memorandum alone would be that it was; but, as I have already answered this in the negative, I have nothing more to say on the subject except that if the magistrate at Dacca suffered two boats, "laden with children of all ages" destined for slaves, and evidently kidnapped, to pass up the river without inquiry on his part, he deserved a proper jobation, and ought to be ashamed of himself for his negligence. You see what a long story I have made of this, so beware of putting similar questions about India for the future if you wish the contents of my letters to be entirely personal.

And now let mé turn to thee, O, Diana of Park Street, huntress of the 'oolves, dweller in the 'oods, called by the gods "Shap Habbey," and by mortals Hemma! Truly I have to return you my thanks for your share in the last letter received by me. I have in my last given you my thoughts on the subject of the vein of self-depreciation which pervades it, and I will not, therefore, repeat my lecture, but I must have nothing of the kind again, or if you feel disposed to describe self, drop the person, if you will not speak of it in favourable terms, and let the mind be the theme. I cannot say I approve much of your style of novel-reading. If you think a novel worth reading, peruse it with a decent degree of attention, but stuffing down volume after volume in pancake fashion at the rate of three a day is, in my humble opinion, a pure waste of time, and must ultimately produce a surfeit. If you read a novel which is not worth perusal, you are a goosecap for your pains. Do not think me censorious.

December 12th—

Since I wrote the last two pages I have been labouring under an attack of the small-pox. I have been unwell, very unwell, and, although I am now convalescent, I am still as weak as an infant. No one can tell the miseries of this loathsome disease before he has either experienced it himself or seen its effects on others. I was first seized with a fever, and after it had subsided the pustules broke out in every part of my body, even in my throat, and I lay for a fortnight on my back in a state of inconceivable wretchedness caused by the external inflammation. It is a most disgusting and a most trying complaint, and I trust that I may never hear of any member of my family at home having been attacked by it. A young newly-married couple were attacked by it at Delhi a short time ago. It first seized the wife, a young, pretty, and accomplished woman, and I shall never forget the anguish of the husband as he bent over his wife in the progress of the disease. Poor fellow! I used to see him wandering about like a ghost, restless and uneasy, for he thought that the light of his eyes was indeed to be taken from him, scarcely hoping that her good looks would escape the effects of the malady. I was almost as much pleased as himself to see her on her recovery perfectly free from any mark, for she was a great favourite of mine, and I had known them both intimately since their marriage two years ago. It will, I fear, leave its marks on me. I was never vain; indeed, I had never any reason to be so, but I could gladly have spared this ill-fortune, which is not likely to improve my looks. It certainly came on at a most unlucky time, for I had set my mind on seeing the Governor-General, and had determined to make the best of the opportunity afforded me by his arrival here in stating to him my wishes with regard to my future employment. I had good reason to believe, too, that my verbal representation would not be ineffectual, and I hoped, by bringing myself forward to his notice, to obtain a situation, or, at least, to secure a promise of one, as I know well that more can be effected by a personal interview than by fifty letters. Of this opportunity I have been deprived, unluckily enough. The Governor-General is here at present. He arrived four days ago, and halts a week; but whilst the other young men, my contemporaries, are dining with him daily, ingratiating themselves with those about his lordship, and enjoying a thousand opportunities of pressing their respective suits with him, I am confined to the solitude of my room and shunned as an infected person by all. This, as you may suppose, does not improve my spirits, which are at their lowest ebb, but I have, fortunately, something elastic in my composition, which, by leading me to look on the bright side of everything that may happen, blunts my feelings of disappointment and teaches me to search for the good out of the evil. I am not either, I would flatter myself, quite forgotten by these arbiters of our destinies. A friend who is living with me tells me that all in his lordship's camp, including Lord William himself, entertain a high opinion of me, and that several of the secretaries had expressed their intention of calling upon me, but that they were apprehensive of the small-pox contagion. He said, too, that Lady William Bentinck had expressed to him her regret at my illness and her disappointment at not having had the pleasure of seeing me at Delhi.

I received yesterday a volunteer visit from Lord William's private secretary, a gentleman high in his lordship's confidence, and, on my expressing to him my sense of his kindness in visiting a sick man, he said that he came as much by his lordship's desire as from his own wish to see me. He then added that he should be happy to communicate any wishes I had formed, with regard to my future employment, to his lordship, since my illness had deprived me of the opportunity of making them known to Lord William personally. I said that my wishes were directed to the possession of some more active employment than that afforded by my present duties; that my prospects had changed for the worse instead of the better during the last two years of my life; and that I saw little likelihood of my getting forward in the confined field of the Delhi territory, which, as a field for exertion, had deteriorated sadly since my first arrival here four years ago. With regard to the choice of a situation, I said that I would leave it entirely to his lordship, my only wish being that it would be somewhere in the Upper Provinces, to the climate of which I had now become accustomed; and I hoped that, whatever determination his lordship might come to regarding me, the result might be made known to me soon, as I was weary of my present situation, which held out to me little or no prospect of advancement. He said in reply to this that my name had already gone up to his lordship as one amongst others eligible for an appointment, and that he hoped to have the satisfaction of communicating to me before long the result. He then took his leave of me very kindly. All this may be flattering, but it is not so satisfactory as a personal interview. It shows, however, that I am not forgotten.

DELHI,

December 15th, 1831.

Dearest Mother,

Two days ago I despatched a letter to you, but as I am an invalid at present, and have little to occupy me, I commence another without delay to make up for my late deficiencies in my correspondence. I send you a few lines, which I must own are very indifferent, but I have not patience to revise, so you must take them as you find them.

1.

In the glow of life's summer on pleasure's gay brink,
  As thro' mirth's fairy mazes we roam,
Full lightly we value the flowery link
  Of the mem'ries that bind us to home;
But oft by the dark cloud of sorrow opprest,
  When the heart pines in anguish alone,
Oh! 'tis then that we flee to our haven of rest,
  And muse on the days that are gone.

2.

For the day-dreams of fancy in life's early bloom,
  In their hues so delusive and vain,
And the mild rays of friendship that beam'd thro' the gloom,
  To sink in the darkness again;
And Hope, golden Hope's ever-vanishing rack,
  All, all o'er his pathway have shone;
Yet sweeter's the thought of his home-beaten track,
  And dearer the days that are gone.

3.

Bright, bright is the vision of childhood's fair spring,
  With its rainbow of laughter and tears,
When the spirit soared high on a . . . wing,   *{ Hiatus valde deflendus!* Supply an epithet here yourself. I can't think of one, for the life of me.
  In the light of its own joyous years.
And still in the twilight of life fading fast,
  As the way-wearied pilgrim toils on,
He wistfully turns to the pleasures long past,
  And sighs for the days that are gone.

4.

Then let others—the gay and the thoughtless—unite
  In the gleam of the world's sunny smile;
Or weave the frail flowers of fancied delight,
  And bloom in its garlands awhile:
But mine be the draught from affection's pure springs
  Ere the heart's glowing colours have flown;
The visions of home that fond memory brings,
  And the dreams of the days that are gone.

Oh! Emma, Emma, I dread thy family scrap-book. It is a bugbear to my Grub Street wanderings; and the fear of having everything written by me, good or bad, chronicled in it, haunts me sadly. Let us suppose, now, Emma displaying her family literary treasures before some critic—say Mr. Hopkins, since you mention in your letter that parts of my epistles are occasionally submitted to his perusal. *Scene*—The drawing-room, Park Street. The curtain draws, showing Emma turning over the leaves of her family scrap-book; Mr. Hopkins standing near her. *Emma*. " Here is a small poem written by my elder brother, Samuel Sneade Brown, of the Bengal Civil Service, aged twenty-two years and nine months." *Mr. H.* (elevating his eyebrows). "In-deed! An ode to the Governor-General, I suppose, or a ditty on the Ganges?" *Emma*. "Oh, no, quite the contrary. Permit me to read them to you." [She reads in a pathetic tone of voice.] *Mr. H.* "Hum!" *Emma*. "Are they not pretty—quite affecting? Composed, too, on his recovery from an attack of the small-pox." *Mr. H.* "Ah! I thought so. Poor people! They are always talking about their hearts. Heart, with them, stands poetically for liver; the last line but two confirms this. Who ever heard of a 'heart's glowing colours'? Now the liver of an Indian, they say, has as many colours as a chamelion, and changes as often; so the allusion is obvious. The word 'draught,' too, evidently refers to the potions administered during his illness, or it may refer to your visit to Cheltenham. In the latter view of the case, the last lines may be supposed to express a wish to participate in the laxative effects of the Cheltenham waters; but as the meaning is not very clear, I would propose an amendment as follows :—

> ' But mine be a draught from the Cheltenham springs
> Ere my lights and my liver are flown;
> The laxative feel that a glass of 'em brings,
> And the ease of the days that are gone.'

Indians are often costive [*aside*]. Again, 'home-beaten' is a compound adjective, signifying 'beaten at home.' A tender *retrospect* that—he couldn't help looking *backward* to it. Excuse me, Miss, but he must have had Tom Jones' Squire Western in his eye, where that worthy says, 'Homer! why, I have the marks of Homer on my back yet.' " *Emma* (blushing). "Oh! Mr. Hopkins." *Mr. H.* "In the third stanza, instead of . . . , I would propose the substitution of 'dew-sprinkled,' or some such epithet, a much more apposite one if the state of childhood's under-garments are taken into consideration. Besides, it is mighty poetical!" *Emma*. "I'm sorry that you do not like this poem; but, if you will permit me, I will read you one or two more composed by my brother, which may please you better." *Mr. H.* (buttoning up his coat). "No, no, thank you; quite enough—quite enough! Good morning." *Emma*. "But, Mr.

Hopkins———." *Mr. H.* " Oh! to be sure—good morning." [Exit Mr. Hopkins.] Emma sola—she meditates for a time : " Well, after all there may be some truth in Mr. H.'s criticisms. The next time I write to Sam I'll beg him to make the alterations proposed." [Puts up the family scrap-book in a velvet cover, and exit.] So ends my drama. Do you remember Fred's blunder of " Excite Betty " ?

The weather now is almost as raw and cold as an English November day. I have a plate of rosy apples before me—turnipy enough in taste, but they answer my purpose. I am as fond of *garbage* (your favourite word) as ever. By-the-bye, I hope you have an apple tree or two in your slip of a garden behind your house, as you may expect to see me up in it half-an-hour after my arrival six years hence. Oh! Eve, Eve, thy trial was enough to shake thy constancy. The good Baxter, I was amused to find the other day, enumerates amongst the eight heinous vices of his youth, " a sinful excess in the eating of apples and pears." This is, indeed, going to the extreme of self-condemnation.

I have been reading much of late our old English dramatists, and the pleasure which I have experienced from the perusal of them has been unbounded. Beaumont and Fletcher's works in particular delighted me. The melody of the versification, the exquisite beauty of the sentiments, the lively touches of humour, and the true and vivid development of all the feelings and passions allied to human nature, combine to render their dramas a text-book for the lovers of nature and poetry. I am never wearied of reading them; and after laying them aside for a time, I take them up with redoubled pleasure. I got their works up from Calcutta a short time ago, in fourteen volumes, and they are a treasure to me. Shakespeare is so hackneyed in our youth, that the pleasure we feel in reading him at a time when we are able to appreciate his excellences is partly blunted; but the works of the contemporary dramatic authors (which are so strangely neglected by the generality of the reading public) burst fresh upon me with all their beauties, and dazzle me the more as they were before but slightly known to me. Massinger's works I have, too, and Ford's, and I intend to get Ben Jonson's. Massinger, in pomp of diction, surpasses the rest; but he falls far short of the honeyed flow of words which distinguishes Beaumont and Fletcher. Ford is more rugged, but more forcible, than any, with the exception of Shakespeare, in the delineation of the passions; but he frequently violates human nature, and the subjects of many of his dramas are monstrous and revolting. It is much to be regretted that a vein of licentiousness runs through most of these compositions, so as to render them unfit for the perusal of families; but I observe that an edition of our early English dramatists, commencing with Massinger, has already issued from the press as an appendage to the Family Library. It professes to leave out all objectionable passages, and to be purposely adapted for the use of families. I must beg, therefore, that you will procure them, volume by volume, as they come out, to complete my present of the books composing the Family Library. With Beaumont and Fletcher you will be delighted. Their works are like old gold compared with the tinsel of the poetry of the present day, or the stiff verse of the preceding age.

Delhi,

December 24th, 1831.

Dearest Mother,

'Tis Christmas eve—Christmas!—what a thousand associations are connected with that word! What numberless images of past days start up before me at the sound! 'Tis like an enchanter's wand, which summons up the shadows of the departed. Christmas! To me the word is almost synonymous with home, for it includes the happiest portion of my life. The Midsummer holidays, with their walks and rides, and excursions and tours,—and apples beside,—could never be compared with Christmas, ushered in by its goose and Christmas boxes,—its hollies and kissing-bushes,—its mince pies and cheerful greetings. Well do I remember the great earthen pan in the store-room, filled up to the brim with mince meat, and many a time have I wickedly dabbed my hand into it when your back was turned, and run out with my mouth filled with the crude mixture, doubtful whether I should lick my lips after it or vomit it up again. Many a time,—sinner that I was,—have my thoughts at church, in the morning, been taken up with the expected repast in the afternoon; nay, for days and days before, how have I gloated at the prospect of the feast which Christmas-day held out to me, whilst airy visions of goose and apple-sauce presented themselves, in my sleep, to my enraptured imagination! But oh! what a downfall to my hopes, when the cook covered the goose with pounded sugar, instead of salt; and, alas the day! when, after hacking away at its joints for half an hour, without making the least impression on its venerable bones, you laid down the knife in despair, exclaiming, in a calm, but resolved tone : " Children, I *cannot* cut it."

> Then rose the loud lament from earth to sky,
>   Then war'd the greedy, and grew pale the fair.
> But in her visage nought could they espy
>   Save anguish deep and motionless despair ;
> Fix'd was her look, and resolute her air ;
>   Then slow she said, " Alas ! it may not be,
> Nought may my wonted skill avail me there ;
>   Remove the goose !—this is my firm decree."—
> E'en Emma heav'd a groan, and Ellen sigh'd "Ah, me !"

'Twas, indeed, a picture which might well have rivalled that of Niobe and her children. Who can forget the stewed pears, and the toasted cheese, and the sally-lunn and the salted pigs' feet Peggy used to give me (under the rose), before I went to bed, and the roast pork and the big, baked potatoes with butter? Who, I say, can forget these? Tender, tender reminiscences! Don't you recollect when you shut me up in the dining-room, one day, for being naughty, with an injunction to learn, by heart, a certain number of verses out of Proverbs, to be selected by myself? The task was accomplished by me, but my choice, by a strange coincidence, happened to fall on unlucky verses, for there was something about eating in every one of them,—such as " Better is a dinner of herbs," &c. You must pardon me, therefore, for giving my guttling reminiscences the first place in my letter. What a source of pleasure were the Christmas boxes! Happy days! When Joe was made happy with " The Giant and the Dwarf," and when Noah's Ark raised Fred to elysium. Then, the purchasings beforehand, and the deep mystery observed by all; and the expectations, excited by the sight of the covered table, and the pleasure of giving, which equalled that of receiving. I love these old customs. They promote the interchange of kindly feelings. They furnish food for pleasure at the time, and for pleasing recollection afterwards. Occasions like these are remembered with delight in our after years, when other circumstances of our childhood are forgotten. Do you not remember the Christmas when you read the " Iliad " to Ellen and myself, and when we froze, with childish horror, over the ghost-tales in the " Old English Baron" ? Also, that woful Christmas, when William Wordsworth broke his leg, and we were forced to subsist, for weeks together, on Mr. Allen's lard ? And Mr. Ogilvy's recitations, when I was taken for a man servant, by Mrs. Strange's footman,—and the children's balls, which used to be my abomination,—and Manuel Johnson, dancing with his thumbs in his flap,—and my blubbering, at an earlier period, at Mrs. Crozier's, because they bothered me so to dance? If ever I feel lonely, or sigh over the recollections of past times, it is at Christmas. It is then that I find myself driving over the waters of life, without a home or resting-pl But it is of no avail to yield to thoughts like these.

January 8th—

I have just returned from the death-bed of a friend, who died under circumstances peculiarly painful to me. His complaint was the small-pox, and I cannot disguise from myself the distressing reflection that he received the infection from me. It is far from my intention to boast of the attentions which I had it in my power to show my poor friend. I did to him what I should wish others to do by me, and my anxieties were redoubled by the reflection that, had it not been for me, he would never have been reduced to that distressing condition. Whilst sitting by my poor patient I heard him frequently utter the names of his parents, and sisters, and relatives, and then pause, as if wondering why they did not reply to his call. I heard him allude, often, in a way which made my heart ache, to the scenes of his childhood and youth. From the last few words uttered by him, previously to his sinking into final insensibility, I found his mind to be still wandering amongst the scenes of home. Whilst he stood on the verge of a grave in a foreign land, he fondly fancied himself in the arms of his family, and amid the pleasures of his boyhood. And yet, 'tis a mercy that it should be so. He called to me on one occasion during these wanderings, by name, adding, in a slow and solemn tone, "Brown! have you not seen the City of the Dead?—'tis a wondrous place—its shadowy buildings—and cypress groves—and its pale, pale inhabitants!" I was affected to tears. He breathed his last without a sigh or a struggle. I selected the best spot I could find for his grave, in this dank and dismal burial-ground,—a rising mound, between two trees,—and we yesterday committed his body to the ground, with deep-felt sorrow. His father is a distinguished man in parliament. You may have seen him mentioned in the papers as Maurice Fitzgerald, commonly called "The Knight of Kerry," and the chief political opponent of O'Connell, and his family are highly connected, and of noble descent.

January 12th—

A fortnight ago I received an intimation from the Private Secretary to the Governor-General of my appointment to a station in the district of Mooradabad, on a salary of 700 rupees per mensem. This nearly doubles my present allowances, and will probably pave the way, in the course of two or three years, to some higher appointment. The station is situated near the Ganges, in a rich and fertile, and, I believe, a healthy, part of the country. It is not more than 100 miles or so distant from Delhi, and is nearly in the same line of latitude. The appointment, on this ground, is satisfactory to me, as I should not have liked to have descended amongst the damps and heats of the tropics, after enjoying, for the last four years of my life, the comparatively pure and refreshing climate of the Upper Provinces.

CAMP,

January 27th, 1832.

My heart is sad within me this evening. I have been thinking of all I have lost, all I have wished for in past days,—of scenes half obliterated by time, and of pleasures which exist no more. A passage in a book which I was reading awakened a thought, and with that thought came a tide of recollections which forced me to relinquish the volume and betake myself to my reflections. Many, many moments like these occur in the course of my solitary life, during which the past is my world, and the present is forgotten or remembered only with a pang. They are transient it is true, but not the less acute ; and they leave behind them on their departure a train of impressions which my heart yearns to communicate to another. But where is that other to be found ? I am essentially a solitary man— solitary not merely in my situation, but in my feelings. I have acquaintances, but no *friends*. I esteem them for their qualities of mind and heart, and I am bound to them by a long and familiar intercourse ; but I think not as they think, and my feelings are different from theirs. I am conscious that they could not participate in my thoughts ; and, consequently, I shrink from disclosing them. Many feel a relief during moments like these in committing the ebullitions of their hearts to paper. They fancy that their mind has in this way been eased of its burden and they are satisfied ; but what result could I expect in entrusting mine to the barren page of a journal, save the harassing probability of its meeting at some future period the eye of indifference or prying curiosity ? Man would never complain did he not look for sympathy. India affords none to me, and I am compelled to hush up my feelings in my own bosom; but the eagerness of my spirit to find it prompts me to take up my pen and pour forth my heart before those who, though they are separated from me by seas and continents, are the only persons in the wide world able to feel with and for me. I snatch up my létter, but the mere mechanical act of writing is sufficient to scatter and weaken the force of my thoughts, and in a moment they are gone, together with the feeling that gave to them life and vividness.

I am not a happy man, dearest mother, though I am far from being a melancholy one. Melancholy—habitual melancholy, at least —is as alien to my constitution as well as to the natural temperament of my mind; but I bear about with me an aching void, a dissatisfaction with self. I derive no pleasure from the present. Regret mars the past, and doubt dims the future. Alas! Regret with me is ever the handmaid of Memory. She is a sad instructress; her lessons are drawn from the past, and her monitory voice sounds in our ears when remedy is impossible and grief unavailing; yet Regret even is not without benefit if we choose to profit by her instructions. She teaches us to prize for the future what we before thought lightly of. She leads us to estimate as we ought the advantages which we enjoy during the period of their continuance; and, instead of trampling upon the flowers in our path from wilfulness or neglect, to collect them in our bosom whilst they yet bloom. But I must break short, for my fit of gloom is over, and I shall not resume my pen until I find myself in a more cheerful mood.

January 29th—

Light and shade—light and shade—such is life, and such must be my letters, which profess to be a kind of journal of my feelings and actions. I am on the road to my new appointment at Sahuswan, where I expect to arrive in the course of two or three days. I left Delhi ten days ago, and after spending six days at a friend's house on the road proceeded hither. I am now encamped on the banks of the Ganges. I have just had my dinner, consisting of a fowl made into cutlets by some inexplicable method unknown to me, a basin of fine fat soup, curry and rice, and a Hansi cheese, washed down with a bottle of beer and two glasses of sherry. The latter I have well earned by my day's exercise.

I set out with my guns about two o'clock to a large tank about two miles off in quest of wild fowl. I found lots of them there— teal, wild duck, wild geese, solan geese, *et hoc genus omne;* but they were difficult to get at, as the tank was wide, and they were sailing about in the middle of it. I took off my shoes and gaiters, tucked up my knee-breeches, and proceeded cautiously into the water " as far as I was forkit;" and after wasting a few minutes, standing in the interim perdu amongst the reeds, I observed a fleet of teal approaching me. I delayed until they were close by, took a murderous aim, and fired both barrels off into the midst of them. Whuzz-zz—up flew hosts of wild fowl with a noise like stage-thunder, and up flew the self-same teal, to my infinite mortification, quite uninjured ; and this, too, after I had calculated on bagging at least six of them. I loaded again without delay, and fired off both barrels again at a number of ducks careering above my head. This time I was more fortunate, as I slew three, a very paltry number, but better than nothing. By this time, however, all the birds were gone, as wild fowl are not in the habit of waiting for a third shot, so I let my spleen evaporate by shooting a cyrus—not Cyrus the Mede, but a huge bird bearing that cognomen, nearly as large as an ostrich, which frequents the marshy grounds in this country. It was a wilful act, for the creature was unfit to eat; and there was no glory to be acquired by the feat, as the cyruses are almost as stupid as penguins, and stand to be shot at with the utmost sangfroid ; but as I killed him with a ball from my rifle at a decent distance off, and as there was no one to witness the deed except my own servants, I felt little compunction and no shame.

February 6th—

Well, I have arrived at my new station, Sahuswan, and am considerably disappointed in the expectations which I had formed of it. The country in its vicinity is intersected by innumerable rivulets and streams, the soil is swampy, and the air loaded with moisture. There are two or three very large stagnant lakes near it, which cannot contribute to its healthiness. Indeed, during the rains it is spoken of as a notoriously unhealthy spot ; and the appearance which the face of the country presents leads me to place full credit in those assertions. In short, in point of climate it is the very antipodes of that of the Delhi territory to which I have hitherto been accustomed. There the air was dry but healthy ; here it is just the contrary. There the soil was sandy and the country unattractive ; here the vegetation is rich but rank, and the numerous trees give it a picturesque appearance in the eye of a casual observer ; but appearances are nothing if the reality of a good healthy climate be wanting. It is the peculiarity of all Oriental countries that beauty of landscape is seldom if ever found to be combined with a favourable climate. The more exposed, the more unpleasing the face of the country may be, the better for health ; for in India fevers lurk under the leaves of every tree and float upon the surface of every pool. Add to this disadvantage in the climate of my new station, it is 110 miles distant from the nearest stations. Bareilly and Allygurh are the two nearest places. There is not a soul here except my superior, and medical assistance if required could not be obtained until it might be no more needed, as there is no doctor here; and the two above-mentioned places are the nearest at which one could be procured. In addition to this second disadvantage, which is of no trifling importance in a place like this, there are no accommodations to be met with here, so I shall be under the necessity of building a bungalow for myself, and of living under canvass until it is completed.

Mr. Wyatt, my superior, plays upon the piano, indifferently enough I must own, yet the semblance even of music is pleasant in such a lonely place as this. He singeth also, but not in the very best style. He evidently, however, fancies himself a second Braham, and he gives me a specimen of his powers in both ways almost every evening after dinner. Whilst he is accompanying with his voice the jingling of his piano, I sit and think upon past times; for every air and melody is to me fraught with recollections which I love to dwell on. Solitude has led me insensibly to form a world of my own, stored with its peculiar images and feelings, in which my imagination delights to wander. A tune, a note, a word is sufficient to summon before me one of the scenes of this my mental Elysium. My lips may be with the passing scene, but my heart is "over the hills and far away." Oh, if we knew what India really was before we set foot upon it; if we knew the mental privations which it entails on us, the sullen monotony of its existence, the absence of the innocent gratifications which tend to enliven our earthly pilgrimage, its life of unsatisfied wishes and hopeless longings,—how many would there be who would prefer penury at home to its empty advantages!

CAMP,

February 20th, 1832.

Dearest Mother,

This month is our Indian May, when the country presents itself to us in its most attractive form. The air is mild, temperate and healthy, the sun very far from oppressive, and the landscape beautified with the waving corn-fields. Hills and dales, daisies and primroses, there are none; and the screeching of the paroquets, and the everlasting caws of the crows, excite sensations very different from the song of the birds in England, yet nature has arrayed herself in her best costume, and we should be thankful. I have met with many sequestered spots in the course of my evening walks, which have reminded me forcibly of home. I have seated myself occasionally on some mound, and, had it not been for the blending of the broad leaves of the plantain, or the stem of the cocoa, with the darker foliage, could have fancied myself once more on the banks of the Wye, or in the Weston valley; but the illusion is short-lived. The ever-bright sky becomes, after a time, tame and uninteresting, and the prospect, which looked so inviting from a distance, changes its features on a nearer approach; the lake turns into a weedy swamp, and that which before appeared a park, proves to be a thick-set jungle. The lover of nature in England derives as much delight from a confined as from an extensive prospect,—from the survey of the varied surface of a single field, as from a wide view over flood and fell; but nature in this country must not be examined in detail; even in her general aspect she is unvaried and inanimate, like the enchantresses of Gothic story: she seems seductive at a distance, but, on a closer inspection, she exhibits rottenness and deformity; or if she charms the eye for an instant, her powers of pleasing are not her own, for we admire her not for her own sake, but for the fancied resemblance which she bears to the scenes of home. But to drop my similes. The broad Ganges is, I confess, an exhilarating object, and the groves of trees, combined with the verdure of the country at this season of the year, form a very pleasing landscape. My thoughts, notwithstanding, are constantly reverting to our English May, and, with my recollection of that month, the banks of the Wye are inseparably united. I shall never forget the beauty of the country in the vicinity of Clifton during our fortnight's stay there; and the brightness of that morning, when we left Monmouth and proceeded along the banks of the Wye, is peculiarly stamped on my memory.   How simple, yet how touching, is Chaucer's apostrophe to May—

> " O Maye, with all thy flowrès and thy green,
>   Right welcome be thou—fair, fresh Maye."

I have been reading Chaucer's works lately; to me, they are particularly pleasing, from their simple, yet vivid, descriptions of natural scenery.   His diction is antiquated—many of his words are obsolete, and his lines are broken and rugged; yet there is a freshness of thought and feeling in many of his poems, which we may look for in vain amongst the jingling rhymes of the present day; nor is he deficient in harmony, for instance—

> " Hard is his heart that loveth nought
>   In May, when all this mirth is wrought,
>   When he may on the branches hear
>   The smallèr birdès singing clear,
>   Their blissful sweet song piteous."

Chaucer's sketch of the character of a good pastor ought to be made the text-book for all young clergymen.   I intend, when I have leisure, to present it to you in a modern dress, for it is too valuable to be neglected; but I do not mean to fill my letter with a dissertation on Chaucer's works.   I have noted down my thoughts upon them in my memorandum book, which I may send you at some future time.   Most of my pleasing reminiscences are drawn from the events of our tours and excursions; even the shades in the picture, caused by the inequalities of my temper, throw the lights into a stronger contrast, and the trifling mishaps which we met with enhance the interest of the retrospect.

By-the-bye, Mrs. Mary Brown, I have a bone to pick with you. Pray tell me what you mean by this paragraph in one of your last letters—" I hope that your brothers will be, like your own dear *elegant self*, persons of refinement," &c.   When the cockney, in a country inn, called the waiter Ganymede, the waiter swore " that he wouldn't be called such names—no, not by no man."   On the same grounds, Mrs. Brown, I have to inform you that I won't be called " Elegant Self," or, if you persist in using such a term, I must inform you that " Elegant Self " is a stout young man, aged twenty-three, with a good broad derrier, and a pair of legs to match.   As his morning dress in the jungles, " Elegant Self " weareth a pair of white corduroy breeches and leather gaiters, a shooting-jacket and a white hat.   At other times, and in other places, his dress resembleth that of other civilized beings, except that now and then a button gets loose without his perceiving it, and that, on one occasion in particular, he put a white nightcap into his coat pocket, strings and all, instead of a handkerchief, drew the aforesaid nightcap out of his pocket during dinner

time and wiped his nose therewith, to the amusement of the company.
It is currently reported that "Elegant Self's" eyes are not the best
in the world; but as he generally weareth spectacles, except in riding
or walking, or at meals, it is impossible to say what his eyes are like
—whether they resemble gooseberries in a glass bottle, or a pair of
pea-pods. We regret to state that "Elegant Self's" phiz is greatly
marked with the small-pox. The red spots occasioned by that dis-
figuring complaint, which are still visible, will, we hope, disappear in the
course of the next two or three months; but the marks of the pitting,
alas! will, we have much reason to fear, be permanent. It would
not be in the power of words to record the distress which the news
of "Elegant Self's" altered charms occasioned amongst the fair sex.
Two spinsters cried themselves blind, and four married ladies miscarried. The fate of a seventh was still more melancholy. Like the
nymphs of old, she dissolved away in tears, until she vanished in a
puddle!!! Her disconsolate husband is at present engaged in the
heartrending task of pumping up her liquefied remains for the purpose
of interment. "Elegant Self" goeth out shooting sometimes, but we
cannot confidently assert that he is much of a shot; he killed, it is
true, two wild geese the other day with a ball from his rifle, but we
incline to attribute his success, on this occasion, to chance. It is
credibly affirmed that "Elegant Self" ate the said geese afterwards
with infinite satisfaction.

A RIGHT GOOD BALLAD ON ELEGANT SELF.

Oh! Elegant Self's an astonishing creature,
His proportions so queer, such a Phœnix in feature;
Ye Muses and Graces, preserve me from blunders
Whilst I pen a brief ode to this wonder of wonders!

First his head—'tis a sight that would stun all beholders,
For 'tis stuck on a neck, and that neck on his shoulders;
Nay, more—'on my conscience, on searching you'll find
That his face is before, and his bottom behind.

*   *   *   *   *   *   *

So much for his person—his wit is immense,
For he writes in fair grammar, and sometimes talks sense;
And when asked how he is ('tis annoying, yet true),
He replies, "Pretty well, sir, and pray how are you?"

And his manners!—oh, dear! 'tis delightful to see
How he munches plum-pudding and swallows hot tea;
Nay, 'tis thought that he'll beat my Lord Chesterfield soon,
For he eats with a napkin and handles a spoon!!

Oh! Nash and Beau Brummel are nothing to him
In his elegant gaiters and small-clothes as trim;
He's the Jacky of fashion—the prince of all beaux
From the crown of his head to the tips of his toes.

To conclude—he composes such exquisite doggrel,
So movingly fine that 'twould make e'en a hog rail;
So he begs to take leave in a bow most profound,
With his stern in the skies and his nose on the ground.

Self-depreciation, my dear mother, is worse than vanity. Vanity is being over-pleased with what God has given us; self-depreciation is being over-discontented with the same—so, of the two failings, the latter is by far the worst. I gave Emma a good scolding, some time ago, for her habit of self-depreciation, and in disclaiming the propriety of the term "elegant," as applied to myself, I do not wish to be thought a self-depreciator—my sole object is to recall to your mind that I am not an Adonis in person, or a Lord Chesterfield in manners, or a Lord Bacon in abilities. I always hated puffing, even though prompted by affection; and if you hold me up to your friends as something extraordinary, you will disappoint yourself and them, and make me ridiculous. But enough of this. Pray let me know how Emma's very interesting affair with the Bristol silk mercer gets on— yes, I fear that in that arbour scene Emma *harboured* an 'opeless affection. You must pardon these jeux d'esprit, if they deserve that name. I have no family news to fill my letters with, and I cannot always be writing in a grave strain. Besides, I love a joke from my heart—merriment is one of the ingredients of my composition, and as I find no one to laugh with at this place, I must laugh with you by letter. Emma was always the legitimate object of my funning, and she must still consent to be the butt. There is nothing in the world like a little harmless fun—now and then.

Dear "Shap Habbey,"—I have just read over your long letter a fourth time with increased pleasure. One sentence only requires explanation—"I was never drawn forth in my childhood, and, consequently, I have rolled myself up in a *great reserve*." What on earth can that be! A *great reserve!* I have consulted Johnson's Dictionary, and half-a-dozen French ones, in vain for the purpose of discovering its meaning. Perhaps an initial *p* has been omitted; but why you should roll yourself up in a great *p*reserve, even admitting this reading to be correct, passes my comprehension. We roll paste up in a great *p*reserve when we make roley-poley pudding or three-cornered tarts. Perhaps it may be a Park Street phrase for a shimmy or petticoat, or some other article of dress. Do, pray, explain this phrase, for you have no idea how the ambiguity of the meaning weighs upon my mind. The words "*drawn forth*," too, puzzle me not a little. How, or when, or where were you *drawn forth?* Was it out of a well or a river? In that case, *reserve* may be an abbreviation for reservoir. Still the meaning is not clear, particularly as I have no recollection of the occurrence referred to.

SAHUSWAN,

May 6th, 1832.

Dearest Mother,

We had a most fearful storm here yesterday—none which I have yet witnessed in the country could equal its fury. You can have no conception of the violence of an Indian north-wester, and it would be vain for me to attempt to describe it. I can only mention briefly its effects. About three o'clock yesterday afternoon I became aware of a sudden lull, the invariable herald of one of these tremendous hurricanes. A deep darkness suddenly fell on the face of the earth, and to this shortly afterwards succeeded the distant growl of the approaching tempest. On it came, roaring and bellowing, bearing with it such dense clouds of dust and sand that objects were invisible at a distance of two yards. My tent happened, fortunately, to be pitched on low ground and in the midst of a magnificent cluster of trees, but their protection availed it nothing. The tent-poles waved to and fro like twigs, the ropes creaked and groaned; and as I had reason to expect every moment that the whole tent would give way, I fled hastily outside, preferring the brunt of the storm without to the chance of being smothered under the folds of the tent or crushed by the fall of the poles. A smaller tent, in which I used to sleep, was pitched in an open space at a short distance from the trees. Scarcely had I emerged from the larger one when I witnessed its fall. It was blown flat to the ground, the bed inside was crushed to atoms, and bed, bed-clothes, and tent were all whirled across the plain at an incredible rate; the pillows and mattresses seemed to have wings. "After the feather pillow," shouted I to one of my servants who was standing close by; "Never mind the rest." No one heard me in the roar of the storm. The tent and its contents were speedily hidden from our sight by the driving sand-sleet, and I was making the best of my way to a tree for shelter, when I received such a thump on my head that I was almost knocked down. It was from a solid mass of ice *considerably bigger* than a hen's egg, which was followed by a shower of lumps of a most prodigious size. I ran with a basket on my head, which I had snatched up in my hurry, to the spot where my horses were picqueted, as I foresaw that unless they were held fast by the grooms they would break loose half-maddened by the pain occasioned by the blows of the hailstones. On reaching the spot I found that they had already escaped, and were kicking and plunging in the plain, none of my Syces venturing to go after them in the midst of this pitiless pelting. I hastened back, accordingly, as fast as I could, and took my station behind a clump of young trees, which were less likely to be rooted up by the wind than the older ones, several of which had already been blown down with a loud crash not far distant. Here, then, I stood wet to the skin, bruised, and shivering, holding the basket on my head with both hands, and twisting with pain from the thumps of the hailstones which forced their way through the branches. With the hail were mixed branches of the surrounding trees, some of them of the thickness of my finger, which had been shorn off as if with a razor by the pieces of ice in their descent. My tent was close by, but I was afraid to enter it from fear of its being blown down like the other. My servants had all fled hither and thither for shelter; several of them had ensconced themselves behind a thatch which I had put up to preserve my traps from wet, but the thatch was turned over upon them by the wind, and they lay hollowing and bawling underneath, unable to extricate themselves. To add to this confusion, a herd of about fifty oxen, maddened by the blows of the hail, came rushing at full speed, tail on end, to the grove for shelter, overturning and trampling on everything that came in their way. I narrowly escaped being run over by them; two seemed disposed to dispute with me my right to the trees under which I stood, and six or seven forced their way sans cérémonie into my tent, where I found them after the storm was over manuring my tables and chairs by way of expressing their gratitude. In short, such a scene I never witnessed. The hailstorm lasted ten minutes, and the mischief it did is incalculable. My own individual loss has not been trifling. The outer covering of my large tent was rent to atoms as if it had been cut into fifty strips by a pair of scissors; this was owing to the hailstones. My small tent, bedstead, &c., have been demolished; an outhouse adjoining my bungalow, which I had just tiled, was laid bare, the tiles being smashed to pieces by the hail, and, as for my own person, I have half-a-dozen severe bruises on different parts of my body—one of them the effect of a single hailstone, which struck the calf of my leg, being as large as the palm of my hand, and quite black. The swelling was so large and gave me so much pain yesterday, that I experienced considerable difficulty in walking to my bungalow after the storm was over. The luxuriant mango-grove has been stripped of its mangoes, boughs and leaves, which lie on the ground one or two feet thick throughout the clump. Sad havoc was made amongst the poultry, the hailstones having demolished several of my chickens, and my unfortunate horses were bruised to a mummy.

Such is an Indian hailstorm. You may smile, if you please, at my account of the size of the hailstones; but I here declare again that many of them—and particularly the one which struck my leg and which I picked up immediately afterwards—were *considerably* larger than a hen's egg. They were, in short, solid, shapeless masses of ice—some round, some oval, and others square and jagged. You may conceive how severe the blows must have been from these, and with what force they must have fallen from the height of half-a-mile, their violence being greatly increased by the fury of the wind, which dashed them fiercely against us. After the sky had cleared, I saw sheep and cattle lying sprawling in every direction over the plain, unable to rise from the effects of the hail; and whilst I was standing near my bungalow, I observed a huge wolf creep out of some low jungle and commence gnawing the side of a bullock which was too weakened from the storm to defend itself against its attacks. We hastened to the poor animal's rescue, but the wolf had contrived to lay its ribs bare before we arrived, the bullock being unable to rise owing to its bruises. "Sam has put this in at the end by way of a finale, I suppose," I hear you say. "Yes," says Emma, "Sam is wont to sacrifice veracity to romance now and then, as my beloved Charles observed one day." *Fred:* "Oh, a slight lapsus, which may be justified by a reference to the ancients." *Joe:* "Yes, that last is certainly a crammer."

May 11th—

What a beautiful object is a herd of antelopes! I met a large herd of these beautiful animals in the course of my ride this morning. I have seen hundreds of them since my arrival in India. About Sahuswan they are very numerous, yet the sight of them always arrests my attention wherever I meet them. They are smaller than the English deer; but in elegance, fleetness, and beauty, they far exceed any animals in the creation. It is most enlivening to see them bounding along in line, headed by the stag-antelope, springing fifteen or twenty feet at every bound.

Reports from the interior of the district to-day mention the death of no less than eighteen individuals—chiefly children, women, and old men—owing to the hailstorm. They were literally battered and bruised to death by the hail whilst they were on the open fields without any means of shelter. What say you to this? One of them, an old woman, was torn to pieces by a wolf whilst she was lying on the ground enfeebled by the effects of the hail, in the sight of two or three others close by, who were in the same situation, though too weak to assist the poor old creature. When they went from the neighbouring village the next morning, to search for those who were missing, of the poor women who had been overtaken by the hailstorm in the same spot, they found only one alive. Two had been torn to pieces by the wolves and jackals during the night, both of them having probably been attacked before they were dead. The third had died of exhaustion; the feet, the palms of the hands, and the skull of one, were all that remained, except a few scattered bones. In several instances of deaths from wild beasts which have come under my notice, I have generally found that they do not devour the hands and feet of human beings. Some time ago a native in a village not far distant was reported missing. Search was made for him, but in vain, until two decayed hands were discovered by a dog belonging to a herdsman who was grazing his cattle in a jungle. A few bones near them proved the fate the poor wretch had met with. With regard to this exemption of the hands and feet, you may remember Jezebel's fate, these being the only remains of her which could be found after she had been torn to pieces by the dogs.

May 23rd—

I send you a few lines addressed to yourself, which I wrote a few days ago with watery eyes. Surely, my mother ought not to be excluded from the subjects chosen by me for poetizing upon. They are not poetry; yet they may please you, despite of their length and the large space which they occupy in my letter, as conveying the expression of my feelings towards you, my ever dear parent.

> Let others sport on fancy's wing,
> Or wake to loftier themes the string,
> Mine be the grateful task to sing
>   My mother !
>
> My muse no poet's flight essays,
> Yet green her wreath and sweet the praise
> If thou command her homely lays,
>   My mother !
>
> And be her meed one accent mild,
> One tear-drop for thine exil'd child,
> Or smile but once as erst you smil'd,
>   My mother !
>
> Well may that theme a tribute claim
> Richer than waits on wealth or fame ;
> There's music sweet in that blest name,
>   My mother !
>
> 'Twas she who watch'd my infant years,
> With smiles approved, rebuked with tears,
> My wanderings chid, and sooth'd my fears,
>   My mother.

'Twas she who taught me first to pray
For grace to guide and strength to stay,
" Allur'd to heaven, and led the way,"
                    My mother.

That smile of love, that fond regret,
Those looks—they live in memory yet;
Hush'd be life's pulse ere I forget
                    My mother.

Her voice to all my cares allied,
Her form for ever at my side,
My friend, my guardian, and my guide,
                    My mother.

Time's wing has swept those features now,
And snows have blanch'd that honour'd brow,
The clear, bright eye burns faint and low,
                    My mother.

Yet to my heart thou'rt dearer still,
And tenderer thoughts my bosom fill
To see thee tread life's downward hill,
                    My mother.

Oh! be it mine in that lov'd land
To hear once more those accents bland,
To kiss thy cheek, and press thy hand,
                    My mother.

Oh! be it mine, beyond that sea,
To pay by love and piety
Some part of all I owe to thee,
                    My mother.

Long may'st thou live, ador'd, possest
Of every wish that warms thy breast;
Long happy, blessing still and blest,
                    My mother.

Till when beneath the verdant sod
Thou tread'st the path that all have trod
To meet thy Father and thy God,
                    My mother.

SAHUSWAN,

May 30th, 1832.

Dearest Mother,

Administration of justice in this country is simple in itself; the forms are few, and the method, without being despotically summary, is adapted to the habits of the people; but it is too often clogged and impeded by the carelessness of those who have to administer it. It is my constant object to simplify my proceedings to the utmost of my power. The business of each day is despatched by me as it comes on: I suffer no delays, and keep no business in arrears. I am easy of access, and ready to listen to the pettiest, as well as to weightier grievances, with impartial attention. It is by giving a willing ear to the complaints and representations of this poor people that we are able to make them sensible of the benefit of our rule, compared with the injustice and oppression which marked all the measures of the native governments in former times. It is by this that we secure their good opinion—I do not say their gratitude, for that is an exotic which rarely blooms on these shores, and naturally enough, for surely it would be vain to expect any feeling of that kind from the conquered towards their conquerors.

Here is egotism and philosophy for you; but I must stay my pen and get to my business.

June 2nd—

I have had to dig two wells on my grounds—one for my garden, and one for the use of my house. The expense of two wells of masonry in the Delhi territory would have been enormous, owing to the distance of the water from the surface in these sandy regions; but here, where water is to be found at the average depth of seven or eight feet, the cost is comparatively trifling. The method of well-making in universal practice in the Upper Provinces is peculiar. The sides are built first, with brick and mortar, on the surface of the spot fixed upon; the height of their structure corresponding to the requisite depth of the intended well. They are then left to dry, and when well cemented into one compact mass, the soil is removed gradually from beneath the foundations, and the whole fabric sinks. They go on in this way, scraping the earth from beneath, and baling up that which accumulates in the centre during the progress of the descent of the masonry, until they reach the water. Here, again, they follow the same method by the aid of divers, until the foundations have sunk several feet below the point to which the water rises. When, owing to the distance of the water from the surface, it is found to be impossible to raise the masonry to the height required previously to the digging operations, several feet of masonry are completed first, and when this has been sunk they add several feet more, taking care, however, to keep all the building work above ground until they have reached the water. Both of my wells were thus completed in a single day; the masonry having, of course, been prepared beforehand. This simple and ingenious method is rendered necessary from the looseness of the soil in this country, which, if unsupported, falls in after a hole has been dug to the depth of a few feet. The expense of a timber frame-work in the first instance, such as is raised in England preparatory to the commencement of the masonry, is thus rendered unnecessary; whilst the diggers, being protected by the sunk walls, can continue their work with the most perfect security. It would not, however, be possible to follow this plan in England, as the hardness and stony nature of the ground would present a sufficient obstacle to its removal from beneath the foundations of the superincumbent walls. I remember meeting with an account of this method of well-making in India some years ago, in an old book of travels, and scouting it at the time as a traveller's fiction. Large wells are in this way built towards the westward to the depth of 150 feet, which could not be effected in the midst of that loose sand by any skill or contrivance in the world except in this mode.

The method of shaft-sinking in England is different from this, in as far as the timber frame-work to support the sides of the pit is erected as they dig downwards, instead of the sides being built first, and the digging taking place last of all. Here is a dissertation on well-making for you!

June 22nd—

I received this evening your letter of January, written from Ayott.

Well, and so Joe's complaint is pronounced to be a goitre. You really must not think me unfeeling when I mention that I could not help smiling on reading your lamentable narrative of the supposed disease, which—judging it at least from your description of it—appears to be no other than the very formidable one of a double chin. As you have given me no diagram of the complaint, I confess I feel under no apprehensions for Joe's general health. Why, I have a goitre myself, if an incipient double-chin can be termed such, which promises in time to become a dew-lap worthy of a parish bull. Poor Joe, he is only to drink twice a day. He is never to move out of a certain staid pace. He is to be bled and blistered, and, of course, take oceans of physic of Mr. Ridout's providing, &c., &c.,—and all this for a trifling glandular affection, which Mr. Ridout has so finely magnified into a goitre, frightening you to death, and making poor Joe's hair stand at end "like the bristles of the fretful porcupine." But then (as Mr. Ridout says), the most remarkable circumstance of all is the palpitation of his heart after violent exercise. Oh, sage Mr. Ridout! Why, if there was really anything the matter with Joe, did you send him to Ridout, who is merely a London apothecary in a wholesale way? I feel for your anxiety on the subject, which I cannot but think has been causelessly excited, for I have that confidence in the soundness of all our constitutions that I am not apt to be alarmed by the faculty's prediction of complaints which arise, in general, from feeble frames or corrupted blood. I augur, therefore, nothing more serious in this case than the abduction of a few golden guineas from your purse, and the administering of sundry doses of physic to poor Joe, which will be of infinite use to him in the end, in serving to keep down the heyday of blood peculiar to the critical age of fourteen,—goitre, indeed! Fiddlestick! Now don't call me cruel and hard-hearted. It is my nature to start off at a tangent when any sudden opinion is pronounced on apparently insufficient grounds; and my incredulity, I confess, too often leads me into the opposite extreme of paying too little attention to the probabilities and possibilities of a case, thus started; but many things, with me, go by the rule of contraries.

I am happy to learn, from one of your former letters, that Emma is so agreeable in conversation, but, "Shap Habbey," remember one thing, and do not be angry with me for mentioning it particularly, as I quote myself on the occasion. Be careful, lest, in your wish to render yourself agreeable, you overstep the line of those retiring habits which become all young ladies in a mixed company. Young ladies should always keep themselves in the background in society. I do not mean that they should be shy, or reserved. They should talk *to* others, but not *for* others. Gaps in conversation ought not to be filled up by a young lady's voice; nor should she impel forward the current of such talk amongst strangers, whenever it flags. The line between the two extremes, of being vastly agreeable and vastly disagreeable, is so small as almost to be imperceptible, and many young aspirants after the one over-reach their mark and fall, unwittingly, into the other. I do not think this caution unnecessary, since I was myself an example of it at your age. I thought myself monstrous agreeable in company, and this impression was kept up by the remarks of you all. The consequence was that I talked and chattered as much in mixed society as I should have done on the occasion of a morning visit. This was not observed by you, nor even by myself, until Mortlock mentioned it to me one day, in his friendly manner, and I then saw what a fool I had been making of myself, and how completely my efforts had failed, inasmuch as they had created an impression directly contrary to that which I flattered myself I had excited. Remember, I merely speak of mixed society. A young lady or a young gentleman cannot talk too much in a family circle, provided he or she talks sensibly. I have not a doubt on the latter point with regard to Emma; but, whether a young lady's conversation be sensible or not, it should be restrained within certain bounds amongst strangers. Yes, I see that you are greatly indignant that I should have the barbarity to suppose that you could ever speak or talk in an unfeminine manner; and there stands my mother, all agape with astonishment at my presumption in venturing to lecture on a subject of which I know nothing. I can't help it, however. What is writ is writ, and I am too far off to be scolded. So, if you feel yourselves outrageously angry, beat Fred for me. He will make an excellent substitute. There! at him, Emma, with the duster. Hoho! Mrs. Brown! Charge him on the left flank with the parasol, like you did me in days of old, when you made that murderous attempt on your sweet son's life, near the garden gate of old Winifred, endeavouring, with bloody intent, to precipitate him, headlong, into the fosse of the field, in the sight of the servant of the bearded Gorges. But enough of this.

June 24th—

Nothing can be more dull and uninteresting than the tenor of my present life. Day passes after day, and leaves no trace to distinguish it from those which preceded and followed it. My life is a confused medley of sleeping, reading, and business. You who live in happy England, and meet white faces wherever you go, cannot well imagine an existence like mine, unbroken by the voice of cheerfulness, or the murmur of sympathy. My sole recreation, if such it can be termed, is to play, for five minutes in the evening, with Jack, my monkey, and a most scientific and accomplished monkey he has become, under my tuition. He eats mangoes like a Christian, drinks milk out of a mug, and, when disposed for a "lark," sparrs with my dog Bob, alias Robert, Duke of Normandy, in a most gallant style. This, or a battle between the said Bob and one of my Turkey cocks, in which Bob is sure to be worsted, or a a little rifle practice, with balls, at a bottle placed at the distance of 100 paces, or a walk to my garden, to see how my cabbages grow, or a short ride, constitute the chief amusements of the "elegant-minded" Sam.

One of my servants died to-day of the dysentery,—one of the most lingering and hopeless modes in which death can attack the human frame. I had his body carried to the Ganges, where it was burnt, and the ashes thrown into the stream, this being the mode of burial in use here. A handful of the ashes was preserved by those present, in a bag,—which will be sent to his father,—for the purpose of being thrown into the Ganges at one of the most sacred places, Hurdwar, where the river first issues from the Himalaya Mountains. The cremation of corpses is, in my opinion, a much better and cleanlier mode of disposing of them than the consignment of them to dust and the worms; but our prejudices are in favour of the latter custom, and prejudice is not to be disputed in such matters. When I was at Hurdwar I saw some thousand little bags of ashes thrown in the stream in one day, by the relatives and friends of the deceased, who had come from afar to discharge the duty of scattering them on the bosom of the holy Ganges. There is much that is pleasing, mixed with a mass of grossness and superstition, in the Hindoo religion. The latter certainly predominates; but it is not so bad as Mr. Ward has represented it in his book. The symbols they adore are horrid, and not to be mentioned, far less described. The sight of them, in every temple, impresses on the mind a painful feeling of the utter degradation into which superstition resolves itself. It may appear a paradox to assert that any written creed of superstition should be worse than the tenets and actions of those subjected to it, but I believe this to be the case, notwithstanding, with the Hindoos. Their minds and superstitious observances are infinitely purer than the doctrines of their Vedas.

Sahuswan,

July 31st, 1832.

Dearest Mother,

My last was despatched a day or two ago. Sahuswan is at present the most cheerless place imaginable. The rain is pouring down in torrents, and the view from my bungalow overlooks a waste of water which has been accumulating for the last month in the lowlands and hollows at the foot of the rising ground on which my house is situated. As for Wyatt's bungalow, it is altogether insulated—I envy not its occupant his proximity to these pools and swamps, or its thousand miseries from the animal world generated amongst them. On visiting him the other day I found him sighing and groaning over the torments of flying ants and cockroaches. I am a little better off in this respect, my bungalow being well elevated above the marshes; but I, too, have had my plagues. First, there was the plague of mosquitoes. These I had endured with all the patience and fortitude I could muster, until my powers of endurance began to give way before their unremitting attacks. I was forced to case my legs in the evening in stout leather gaiters and thick shoes, wearing an ample dressing-gown to protect the rest of my body. These elegant habiliments did not tend to lessen the heat, as you may suppose, but I preferred an increase of heat to the misery of mosquito bites. You have no idea of the state of nervous fidgetiness to which I was reduced despite of these precautions. The very sight of a mosquito, or its shrill hum, was sufficient to throw me into a fever. Persons can form no conception of the miseries of such a mosquito-plague until they experience it in their own person. They were, however, at last in part dispelled by the rains in the end of June, and since that time I have been comparatively free from them. But this plague was succeeded by another, namely, the plague of frogs. Frogs croaked in hundreds in every corner of my bungalow. If I went to the book-case, half-a-dozen leapt down from the shelves where they had been spawning; if I opened a portfolio, I was sure to find a frog inside. They were never silent. Croak, croak, croak in dozens under the mattings of the rooms and behind my boxes. Every fall of rain drew their voices out into full song, so that my house presented all the accompaniments of an English horse-pond. Pharaoh was surely never so tormented. The picture in the old Bible book frequently recurred to my mind; but the plague of frogs in my case was not quite so bad as that of mosquitoes. They dirtied everything in my room, and kept up a terrible clatter, but they had not, fortunately, stinging powers. Well, this plague at last passed away also, and was followed by a third, namely, the plague of rats—not the puny rats of England, but good, big, bouncing fellows, nearly as large as tom-cats. The first evidence I had of their nightly visitations was in a book which had accidentally fallen on the floor shortly before I went to bed, and which I found half eaten up in the morning. Happening to awake in the middle of the next night, I had a full opportunity of witnessing their gambols. At first I thought that a host of village dogs had got into my room, for I could scarcely believe that the pattering of their feet on the matting could have proceeded from the paw of any animal of less size. I sat up in my bed, and looked around me. Half-a-dozen were busily employed in demolishing the leather on one of my trunks; one was mounted on the table, licking up the oil which had oozed from the lamp; one was dragging off, close to my bed, a Bath newspaper. Some sweet-scented shaving soap, for which I had paid five rupees, had become the prey of another; and how many were digesting the contents of my books I knew not, only the noises and scratchings I heard near the book-shelf convinced me that there was a goodly assemblage of them there. The latter evil was quite unendurable, so I got softly out of bed, with my cutlass, and selecting one of my tormentors, chased him into a corner and chopped him in two. The only result of this gallant exploit was that my mat was piteously dirtied with the rat's blood, and the corner stunk famously for the next week to come. Ten minutes afterwards I heard the rats as hard at work as ever, tearing and scratching and galloping backwards and forwards in fine style. The next night I kept my little dog in the room, but the remedy was worse than the disease. The barkings and chivyings and contests between the dog and the rats, who were no wise intimidated by the presence of my ally, kept me broad awake the whole of the night. The next day I borrowed a rat-trap from Wyatt, and set myself to work in making figures of four, as we used to call them at school. A few were caught in this way, but their number was so inconsiderable that I was in no way relieved of my guests by this contrivance. I then got some *nux vomica* from the Bazaar, and mixed it up in balls of flour. The poison is a deadly one, but how many were thus killed I know not. The plate was cleared every night, but still there was no apparent diminution in their number. When I shall get rid of this plague, and what my next is to be, I cannot tell. I have, however, taken precautions to place my books on shelves out of their reach, so they may gnaw away at the outside of the boxes at their will. It is no small nuisance to have one's house infested with them, and to hear their work of destruction going on in half-a-dozen places, but there are no means of stopping their inroads. They burrow in the ground like rabbits, and as I am obliged to keep my doors and windows open at night, on account of the heat, they go out and come in at pleasure.

So much for my domestic miseries. Outside, the snakes are so numerous that I never venture to walk to any distance from my bungalow. I shot one the other day behind my poultry yard, which measured five feet in length, one of those beautiful but deadly cobra capellas. Add to these, the wolves and foxes and jackals, although the three latter are only to be dreaded on account of the sheep and poultry. The quantity of water in the vicinity has attracted thousands of birds here of every description and from every quarter. The huge pelican, the stork, the adjutant, the cyrus, the crane and the bittern, and every species of water-fowl, from the solan goose to the diminutive teal, are all to be found in hundreds on the large marsh in front of my bungalow. Nothing could well be more cheerless and melancholy than the face of Nature as she has presented herself to me for the last month at this place—the dank and dismal sky, the moisture-loaded trees, the plain covered with high rank grass, and the dull, reedy, waveless swamps. But if the sights are sombre, no less so are the sounds. The clanging cry of the cyrus, the wail of the bittern, and the howl of the jackal, are the only sounds which break the stillness of the evening. Often have I exclaimed, whilst gazing on this dreary prospect from the verandah of my bungalow, "This is indeed solitude." I certainly never knew before what real solitude was. Change of scene and place kept up a certain degree of interest in the deserts of Hissar, but the dull monotony of this place, where I have been rooted for the last six months, becomes every day more insupportable. The cold weather is fortunately approaching, and were it not for the prospect of emancipation from my head-quarters which it holds out to me my spirits would be sensibly affected. I feel not my isolated situation during the day, for business turns my thoughts into other channels; but it is the dulness and cheerlessness of the evening which weighs on my mind. It is distressing to have nothing to look forward to after one's daily toils are over—no recreation, no friendly intercourse, no meetings round the hearth or board. Fortunately for me the love of reading, which I have had from my childhood, supplies a source of occupation to my thoughts at these times and prevents them stagnating in dull inactivity; yet even reading becomes irksome when our situation precludes us from communication with others. "Why," I asked myself the other day on taking up Gibbon, "should I read this book? Few persons, if any, study for the sake of study. Men read to acquire information, and to exhibit their attainments to others. Of what use, then, will the perusal of this book be to me ? " I found however that unless I set to to it I must sit all the evening with my legs on the table twirling my thumbs, so I commenced upon it perforce, despite of my soliloquy.

You may perhaps ask me, why, if I find myself lonely and melancholy in my present situation, I do not get changed to another, where I might be likely to find a pleasant society ? A pleasant society, unfortunately, is a *rara avis* in the Upper Provinces, and my habitual shyness and dislike of the common routine of what is called society in this country is such that I would prefer spending six months amongst deserts and jungles to being thrown for a week into the empty nothingnesses and irksome amusements of an up-country station. I cannot force myself to sneak up to the Judge by abusing the Collector, or attempt to gain the good graces of the Collector by crying down the Judge. I cannot propitiate their vices by talking scandal of their neighbours, nor could I derive any amusement from making love to their chitty-faced daughters; neither could I hope to acquire that unenviable title of "a good fellow" amongst those of my own age, since no one can lay legitimate claim to it who does not share in their debauches, lose his money at billiards, or subscribe to the Sporting Magazine. I am, therefore, better where I am; but at the same time that I admit this, I must be allowed now and then to lament that my lot in life has been thrown beyond the reach both of rational pleasure and kindly sympathy.

You may tell me to look forward to my return to England, and so I do; but am I to be blamed for regretting that the simple pleasures permitted me in my career of life arising from the free exercise of the feelings and affections are to be summed up so briefly and in a period of such brief duration? The prospect, besides, is a distant one. We cannot live on hope alone, and this hope is to me like the mirage of the desert, for it recedes the nearer I approach it.

September 2nd—

I send you a few lines written yesterday evening. I would I could respond to the feelings expressed in them from my inmost soul; but, alas! the pen too often traces thoughts to which the heart is a stranger.

> In youth's fair morn Thy Grace my bosom warming,
> Ere my bark launch'd on life's eventful sea,
> Heedless of pleasure's shoals, of sin's fierce storming,
> Full many a vow my feeble heart was forming,
> To flee to Thee, my God! to flee to Thee!

But, oh ! too early from its onward track
   That fragile vessel wander'd madly free;
Folly obscured its skies with vapours black,
And passions whirl'd it on their boisterous wrack,
   Away from Thee, my God ! away from Thee !

Yet still, oh! still, Thy sun of love o'erpowering,
   Gave it the long lost goal once more to see;
On its dim course a stream of radiance show'ring;
While mercy steer'd it through the tempests low'ring
   Again to Thee, my God ! again to Thee !

'Scap'd from the wind's deep voice, the billow's chiding,
   Say, would that restless heart again be free ?
Oh! may it yet, Thy arm of pity guiding,
Anchor at last in joy's still haven riding,
   At peace with Thee, my God ! at peace with Thee !

And in that hour, when flesh and heart are failing,
   And the awed spirit waits Thy dread decree,
Oh! may it then glide on, in triumph sailing,
Beyond the clouds, beyond the storm's loud wailing,
   To be with Thee, my God! to be with Thee!

Camp, Budaoon,
September 8th.

Dearest Mother,

   Once more I am under canvass, and the change is a really refreshing one. After having been confined for the last seven months to the marshy, melancholy Sahuswan, it is with no little delight that I find myself enjoying the temperate breezes of this month in a spot which is, without exception, the most beautiful and picturesque of any I have yet met with in this country. Budaoon is about twenty miles from Sahuswan. I came here partly for business, and partly for a change of air, and the aspect of the place has pleased me so much that I intend to prolong my stay here to a week or fortnight. The ruinous old town puts me in mind of the vast silent piles of ruins which are scattered over the face of the country in the direction of Delhi. These tenantless and mouldering edifices form a striking object—they appeal to the feelings as well as to the eye; the decaying shrines of the bigoted Mussulmans of past centuries, the shattered mausoleums of the former princes of the land, and the scanty relics of the Hindoo structures of a date prior to the Mahomedan conquest 800 years ago, each tell their own tale of human mutability. To an Englishman, it is true, the charm of association is wanting in these scenes, and we all know the power of association over the imagination,—

how interesting it renders the broken tumuli on Lansdown, and the otherwise shapeless ruins of Crucis and Furness Abbey. Still the sight of human grandeur vanished, and human pride laid low, must influence the feelings more or less in every age and country; and such were the scenes which were presented to me at every step in my afternoon ramble to-day. The very names of the builders of many of the magnificent edifices which I stopped to admire were unknown; the rank grass was growing in the once splendid mosques; the mausoleums were unapproachable from the thickness of the surrounding jungle and underwood; and a few solitary beings creeping here and there amongst the sea of ruins were the only ones left of the thousands and tens of thousands who formerly gladdened this once famous city. The widespread desolation recalled to my mind the beautiful Persian distich, "The owl hoots from the hall of Afrasiab, and the spider spreads his tapestry in the palace of the Cæsars." Again, "I passed by the abode of the mighty, where the son of Selim was awing nations with his frown; I passed again the next day, and, behold! the dove had built its nest on his judgment-seat." You may remember the beautiful passage in the Psalms, where the wicked is likened to a green bay tree; and the powerful images, in Isaiah, descriptive of the annihilation of Babylon. The images are eastern, and it is only in the east that the poetry admits of exemplification. Yet vast as is the desolation here, it did not strike me so forcibly as many of the scenes of the same kind which I happened to visit in my wanderings in the territory westward of Delhi. The ruins of Budaoon are enlivened by a fertile and beautiful country in its vicinity, by a meandering river quite English, and by groves of mango trees. In the Delhi territory, on the contrary, the aspect of the surrounding country suited well with the internal desolation of these cities of the dead. I still retain a vivid impression of the feelings experienced by me at the sight of the vacant, noiseless city of Indore, situated in the midst of a circle of bleak, rocky cliffs; nor shall I soon forget the view from the summit of one of the old bastions of the fort of Sirsa, on the borders of the Bikaneer desert, where the town lay in ruins at my feet, and a howling wilderness extended as far as my eye could reach to all points of the horizon. Did you ever read Southey's Curse of Kehama? If not, pray do. It is a wild and fantastic, but an interesting, tale, and so faithful are the sketches of Indian scenery, and so truly Oriental the whole tissue of the poem, that it is difficult to believe that the writer of it never visited the country. You will find there a most beautiful and poetical description of the submarine city of Bali. You have only to fancy it above ground, and to put me, Suet Dumpling, alias the Buttermere Jug, with spectacles on nose, a stout stick in one hand, and a silk handkerchief in the other mopping the moisture from my brow, and toiling and puffing up hill and down dale for all the world like Sisyphus, with this single exception, that he shoved up the unruly stone before him, whereas I drew along a stone's weight of bottom behind me—you have only, I say, to substitute this most unromantic figure in the place of the disconsolate father in the poem, the Ladurlad to whom the portentous curse became a blessing, the undaunted explorer of the hidden mysteries of the ocean. You have only, by a slight stretch of the imagination, to effect this change in the scene and character, and you will have a far better description than any that I can give you of my wanderings to-day amongst the ruins of Budaoon. I took up the Curse of Kehama the other day for the first time since I left the Charterhouse, where I originally met with it, and I read it over with great delight. It is one of those fanciful fictions which we feel at the time of perusal to be directly opposed both to reason and probability; yet we read it, notwithstanding, with interest, and we close the book with a smile of pleasure. Thalaba, though equally Oriental in its cast, is infinitely more extravagant in its fictions; besides, there is no moral, as in the Curse of Kehama, to render its wildness excusable; yet many of the descriptions of natural scenery in it are admirably correct, as well as poetically beautiful. The opening stanzas, " How beautiful is night," have often recurred to my mind on nights of moonshine, when I was encamped on the sandy wastes in the Hissar district during the cold weather two years ago, the scene around me not being dissimilar to the one described in the commencement of the poem.

The aspect of the country here is so different from that presented by the sandy wastes of Hissar, that one's pleasure in moving about from place to place is enhanced by the richness of the scenery. Wherever I halt, I always find my tent pitched under a cluster of shady mango trees, tenanted by hosts of paroquets, doves, and a thousand other birds, who give a life to the scene which was wanting on the treeless sands of the western desert. Every little village here has its grove and garden; and every mile, almost, I cross one of the streams which find their way down here from the Himalayas, a good, clear, fresh running stream, the very sight of which is delightful. The change is certainly a pleasant one; to me it is everything; for one of the few gratifications left me in this ungenial clime is the susceptibility of enjoyment from natural scenes. I know not how I could reconcile myself to a second residence in the Delhi territory, after what I have seen of this part of the country. Besides, I am quite smart and spruce with my new tent, which I have lately purchased, my former one having been destroyed by the hail-storm in April last.

CAMP,

October 9th, 1832.

Dearest Mother,

What a pity it is that the climate during the after months in the year in this country does not resemble the equable temperature of October; then, indeed, would India be the most delightful country on the globe, and we should have little cause to regret our sojourn here if we could but forget that we were exiles. Here am I encamped in a beautiful glade in the centre of clusters of mango trees, grouped together in English park fashion; the doves are cooing round me, and the sun is shining mildly through the branches on the close-cropt grass. At a little distance is the village well, where the women are drawing water, and a little further off is the hut of the village priest, before which a group of villagers are seated, singing in chorus, in a not unpleasing manner, some of their hymns to the goddess Ravuti, on the occasion of the festival of the Dussera. Some pilgrims, who are on the return from Hurdwar, with their carefully-covered pots full of the holy water of the Ganges, have alighted, and are cooking their victuals under some trees in front of my tent; and not far from them, under a separate cluster, a band of strolling jugglers have taken up their quarters with their dancing bear, which they are exhibiting to the naked little urchins of the village. My servants and camp-followers are lying here and there in the shade, some asleep and others cooking their meals; and a little beyond the circle occupied by my tents some twenty or thirty Zemindars are squatted on their hams round a native, who is writing out petitions for them at their dictation, to be presented to me when I commence the business of the day. So now you have a strictly Indian scene, and you may judge for yourself how preferable this part of the country must prove to the cheerless sandy wastes of Hissar.

I am happy to find, my dear mother, that my letters give you pleasure; but that I work them up for effect I strenuously deny. The mere act of writing in this cramped hand and small-sized letters occupies me treble the time, and my thoughts and phrases have therefore more time to form themselves into order and suitable expression than in my ordinary letters. I certainly have no intention of writing to *you* for effect, and as I hate a laboured letter myself above all things, I should be the last to think of substituting artificial diction in the place of the free and open style of natural expression which alone renders letters interesting as transcripts of our natural thoughts and feelings.

I frequently see accounts of missionary meetings in the Bath papers. India, of course, forms a prominent topic of discussion in all of them; the progress of conversion in this country is dwelt on in glowing terms by the zealous and pious, but certainly self-deluded, speakers; and hopes are held out which the results of the missionary labours in Hindostan up to the present time can by no means justify. I will therefore give you my own settled opinion on this important subject. There is no denying, in the first place, that the exertions of the missionaries have totally failed. We have been in possession of a large portion of India for seventy-five years, and yet, during this period, the number of professed converts has been so small as hardly to deserve notice, and of that number hardly one-tenth have proved sincere believers. If you inquire the cause of this failure, before answering your question I must give you a sketch of what British India really is. Our government in this country is, as far as the natives are concerned, a pure despotism—one of the most cheerless and uninviting kind. All offices of trust and power are held by Europeans. The natives are protected from oppression, it is true; and they enjoy, under our laws, many advantages which they never even dreamt of under their own tyrannical rulers; but if they have nothing to dread, they have at the same time nothing to look forward to. They feel themselves to be a conquered people, and a conquered nation is always the last to adopt the religion of its conquerors; separated from them as we are by a total dissimilarity of language, feelings and pursuits. But this sullen resistance is not the only obstacle we have to contend against in our disinterested efforts. We have to attack a superstition, the growth of ages. The savages of New Zealand have proved far readier converts to the Gospel than the civilized inhabitants of Hindostan—and why? Simply because they were ruder and more ignorant. Their minds were found to be blank, unoccupied by any preconceived prejudices or impressions. They listened with wonder, and received the Gospel with eagerness; but here the case is very different. The Mahometan faith, though of a thousand years' growth, is, comparatively speaking, of a recent date. Its adherents are, in consequence, more bigoted, more self-opinionated, more fiercely intolerant. The Hindoo superstition has become a habit. It is to be traced in every action of their lives, in almost every word they utter; its very rites are festivals. Can then the chains which prejudice on the one hand and habit on the other have riveted on the minds of the native population, be loosened by exhortation or argument? Can the iron grasp which idolatry, in the twilight of knowledge,

W.   I has fixed on their reason be shaken off by the exertions of a few obscure individuals, many of whom are ignorant of the prejudices peculiar to those whom they address? I say *No;* and far, far be it from me, in saying so, to disparage the efficacy of that Spirit of grace and power without which the toils of these zealous and pious missionaries would be nothing, and worse than nothing. But you mistake the nature of the means to be used in the furtherance of this great work. Was not our Saviour even preceded by John the Baptist, to prepare the way before Him; and should not we prepare the minds of the bigoted and prejudiced to receive the faith of the Gospel by enlightening their intellect and enabling their understanding to perceive the excellence and superiority of that religion, before we attempt to impress it on their hearts? Miracles were found necessary, in the infancy of the Gospel, to shake the prejudices of the multitude, by affording them palpable evidence of the divinity of the despised Nazarene; but miracles ceased with the occasion that dictated their necessity. When, by the exertions of the first missionaries—the apostles—the doctrines of the Gospel had been diffused over the countries of the ancient world, mankind were left to complete the work by the lights held out to them by reason and experience. The prayers of the pious may avail much, but we are not justified in supposing that prayers alone, without means, will prosper. We must first raise the altar, and dig the trench, and lay the sacrifice upon it, and then, but not till then, should we invoke the purifying fire from heaven. If then we had, in the first instance, applied ourselves to the education of the native classes in this country; if we had opened their *minds* to a sense of the gross idolatry and absurd superstition of their forefathers, the result would have been far different. Yes, if one-third of the vast sums yearly contributed by the pious community at home had been devoted to the establishment of schools for *general* knowledge in this country, and if these schools had been thrown open to all, of every class and denomination, who chose to frequent them, Hindooism could not have maintained its ground, as it now does, in Calcutta and elsewhere. It is not yet too late to effect a radical change in the present mistaken system, if system it can be called; but so little is known of India at home, and of those who are qualified to guide the others in undertaking this task, so few, unfortunately, take any interest in the question, that my hopes of a change are far from sanguine. I could write volumes on this subject, but enough for the present.

October 24th—

I am encamped once more on the borders of a clear, flowing stream, which glimmers brightly in the sunshine, imparting a feeling of life and freshness truly delightful to my English tastes. I have been wandering hither and thither for the last month, partly on business and partly for pleasure, shaping my course as the whim seized me. This is the kind of life I love in the cold weather.

CAMP NEAR THE GANGES,
October 30th, 1832.

Dearest Mother and Emma,

Thousands and tens of thousands have assembled here for the annual festival, and the hum of the multitude is like the surge on the seashore. The scene is a gay and striking one. The booths form a street three miles in length. Just behind the booths the officiating Brahmins and priests have taken up their quarters on the banks of the stream to assist the devout in their ablutions, each Brahmin having a separate ghaut for his disciples. These ghauts are situated about twelve feet from each other; they have no steps, but the sand is cleared away by the Brahmins, and a pathway formed to the edge of the stream to facilitate the approach of the bathers. The Brahmins give me more trouble than all the rest put together. The owners of these ghauts are constantly squabbling with their neighbours; and their eagerness to entice the bathers to their respective ghauts, for the sake of the douceurs given to the Brahmins on these occasions, produces a spirit of rivalry which is sometimes sufficiently amusing. I saw a poor man this morning pulled almost piecemeal by the contending Brahmins, each endeavouring to drag him to his own ghaut. One had hold of one arm, and a second was pulling him by the other in a directly opposite direction; whilst half-a-dozen in front were bawling out at the top of their lungs the superior virtues of their ghauts and themselves. I didn't wait to see the issue of the struggle, but on my return I observed him standing up to his middle in the water puffing violently and surrounded by the different Brahmins, who were squabbling as lustily as before. It appears that, not being able to establish a separate title to him, they had dragged him down to the water jointly, and given him about twenty more duckings in the holy Ganges than was either necessary or usual. The scene put me in mind of the descriptions of London in the "Fortunes of Nigel," where the 'prentices are represented standing each before his own shop puffing off his wares, and calling out to the passengers "What d'ye lack? What d'ye lack?" "This way, this way," cries one of the Brahmins to a fat little merchant who had come to wash away his sins, "don't go to that fellow's ghaut; his grandmother was a low-caste woman, and he can't read the Vedas or repeat the Slokas." To this the other retorts with a shower of abuse which I should be sorry to be forced to translate, so that all peace and quietness in the bathing ceremonies is entirely out of the question.

November 10th—

Well, the fair is over, and very glad I am that it is so. It has been a busy and an anxious time with me. It is no trifle to be made responsible for the preservation of peace amongst two hundred thousand people, with a police not exceeding forty in number. The people conducted themselves, however, in a very orderly manner, so that my attention was chiefly directed to the prevention of robberies and thieving, which used to be very common under the former magistrates. In this I was singularly successful, and the shopkeepers and visitors have in consequence returned to their homes pleased and satisfied. Many gangs of thieves had assembled, as they are always in the habit of doing at these fairs; but I so frightened them by the arrangements made by me beforehand, and by the information I had gained with regard to their haunts and practices, that they all left my part of the country and went off to another festival of a similar kind, about a hundred miles distant, to try their luck there. I was forced to make my rounds two or three times each night as well as by daytime, a duty which, I confess, I performed very unwillingly, but this vigilance had the desired effect in keeping the police on the alert; so that, with the exception of one or two very trifling cases of theft at either extremity of the fair, no individual amongst the thousands assembled there lost a fraction of his property during the week of its continuance.

November 17th—

Five years of my dreary sojourn in this country have nearly passed, and five long years have yet to come ere I can form a hope of revisiting England. I look back upon them as from an eminence, and they present the same cheerless aspect as the expanse of the Western Desert viewed from the ruined bastions of the fort of Sirsa. If there have been no deep sorrows, no agitating anxieties, there have been, at the same time, no pleasurable excitements, nothing that could deserve the name of rational enjoyment. They form a dull flat, unstudded by trees, unenlivened by streams; one that presents no spot on which the eye can fix. Few can tell what a life in India really is without experiencing it themselves. Yet others make the most of it, and contrive to eke out their days with one pursuit or another. There must be, therefore, a twist in my disposition, which incapacitates me from bearing it with the same sang-froid. A touch of the hermit drives me out into these jungles; yet man is a social being, and solitude sometimes hangs with a dead weight on my spirits, and makes me wish for some kind of companionship. I get a companion, and again I become tired of him, and betake myself as before to my daily haunts. Thus it has always been and thus it will ever be with me. On looking over some of my papers the other day I found a few disjointed lines which I remember writing in a fit of deep gloom on a dismal, cloudy day at Sahuswan a few days after my arrival here from Delhi in January last. I send them you not for their sentiments, which are rather unchristian, and not for their poetry, to which they can lay no claim; but merely to convey to you an idea of the feelings which this solitary life sometimes gives birth to.

To die—'tis but to lay
  Life's joyless burden down,
To rest in peace beneath the sod,
To tread the path that all have trod
  When hope's bright dreams are flown;
To fold the weary hands to sleep
Where tearful eyes our vigils keep,
Where bloom the flowers and willows wave
Their verdant ringlets o'er our grave,
And rippling streamlets murmuring nigh,
Whisper a ceaseless lullaby;
Or meekly to prepare our bed
In silence 'mid the silent dead,
Where soft the distant anthem swells
And sweetly chime the sabbath bells.
  And is this Death?—oh, no;
'Tis like the scent of autumn's rose
In the still hours at evening's close;
  Or like the summer's breath,
That gently sighs itself away
On some green bank with flow'rets gay,—
  'Tis anything but Death.

Yes; but to die—
*   *   *   *   *
To rot beside some nameless lake,
Where fowl their thirsty pinions slake,—
Where hiss the snakes and bitterns scream
In wailing notes the requiem;
Or near a reedy stream to lie,
Whose sluggish waves creep silent by,
Sullenly stealing on their way,
Unlighted by the sun's blest ray;
Or in the last dark hour to press
The howling, arid wilderness;
To fall unlov'd, unwept, alone,
The very name and grave unknown;
No stone to mark the lonely spot,
No sigh to mourn the sufferer's lot.
*   *   *   *   *   *   *
Oh! 'tis a thought that inly burns
  A grief too deep for tears;
'Tis more than language can express—
'Tis agony—'tis bitterness.

CAMP ON THE GANGES,

Dearest Mother, *January 10th*, 1833.

Once more on the banks of the Ganges. I really wonder not that the natives should have exalted into a divinity this noble river. The sight of so vast a moving volume of water cannot fail to be delightful to the eye wearied with a dreary succession of jungles and deserts. This feeling—common to all—which we regard as a natural one, becomes superstition with them, by their ascribing it, in their ignorance, to an unearthly influence. Sweet streams abound in this part of the country, and numerous lakes are formed at the foot of the rising grounds by the accumulation of rain water, and by natural springs, which afford excellent sport to every one who can handle a gun. I went yesterday to one which had not been visited before by any European. It lay in a semicircular hollow of low hills, sprinkled with jungle, and put me more in mind of one of the Cumberland lakes, or rather, I should say, one of the Welsh lakes—the Ogwen, for instance—than any I have yet met with in this country. Nothing can be more disagreeable, in general, than an Indian swamp—for they hardly deserve the romantic name of lakes—filled as they always are with rank grass and reeds, and encircled by a moist, plashy shore; but this one happened to be free from these unpleasant accompaniments; and, although the water was far from transparent, it looked pretty from a distance, even under the rays of an eastern sun. Thousands and thousands of wild fowl—from the small teal to the stately wild goose—were sailing about on its surface; and gigantic cranes, from three to four feet in height, were standing on the edges, with their long bills fixed intently on the water, ready to pounce on the minnows.

You ask me, dear Emma, to write some more poetry. Here is my reply:—

No laurels grace my muse's wreath—her strains are faint and low—
She haunts in dreams the green hill side, the silvery streamlet's flow.
When sorrow clouds the brow, she flits across the ocean's foam
To drink the notes of other days and sing the songs of home.
Then would'st thou that thy brother wake his homely lyre once more;
Oh! say, can rapture's accents breathe from India's sterile shore?
Or canst thou bid me change its tone, and stem the rising sigh,
When cold the glance of friendship's grown, and dim the once bright eye?
Yes, oft I've tried in fitful mirth to chase that gloom away,
And struck the chords at fancy's call, and basked in pleasure's ray;
But thoughts will rise of home and friends, and childhood's joyous years,
And sad and sadder grows the strain, and, melting, ends in tears.
Vain falls that mirth on exiled hearts—those transient flashes vain:
Oh, give me then my hawthorn glades, my blue, blue hills again.
Oh! bear me back to days of old, to England's sun-bright powers,
'Mid hallowed visions of the past, and dreams of happier hours.
Yet be it mine to breathe a wish—a brief, but heartfelt prayer—
Be happy, long as life may last, and innocent as fair;
Thine be the light of inward bliss, the sunshine of the breast,
The heart that, dovelike, roams the world, but seeks a holier rest.
May Love, and Joy, and meek-eyed Peace, and Grace to thee be giv'n;
Hope, that aspires to brighter skies, and Faith, the Christian's heav'n.

Mr. Hopkins (after Emma has finished reading). "Pray, Miss, did your brother ever attempt the harp?" *Miss E.* "Oh! no. He tried once on Ellen's harp, but mamma boxed his ears for meddling with it." *Mr. H.* "Ah! your mamma, at all events, must have benefited from the instructions of *Boxer* (Bochsa). I suppose, then, your brother, in his allusion to the harp in the piece of poetry you have just been reading, must have meant the *Jew's harp?* Well, really, it's as doleful a ditty as I ever heard sung in the streets to the tune of a hurdy-gurdy; and then your brother is so constantly talking of 'visions' and 'dreams,' that he seems, when he writes, to be under the influence of a kind of poetical nightmare." *Miss E.* "Well! but, Mr. Hopkins, don't you admire the sentiments? Listen to some more."

ENGLAND.

Know ye the land where the fountain is springing
　　In music and mirth through the long summer day;
Where the thrush and the skylark their anthems are singing—
　　Now thrilling in rapture, now melting away?
Know ye the land where the earth ever vies
With the gleam of its waters the hues of its skies;
Where the dew-stars shine bright on the sun-wakened flowers,
And the emerald mantle that hangs o'er its bowers
Sheds a soft ray of beauty—oh! lovelier far
Than the warm glowing tints of the easterly star;
Where the hearth blazes bright when the autumn is o'er,
And peace sits in smiles at the cottager's door;
Where the husbandman's carol, the reaper's glad call,
And the songs of the harvest-home, clearer than all,
Ring in echoes of mirth o'er the mountain and dell,
And sweet is the chime of the church-going bell;
Where grief is forgotten, and exile unknown;
Where the music of gladness is heard in each tone,
And the spirit is borne of the free and the brave
In the voice of each breeze, and the gush of each wave—
And know ye this land? 'Tis the isle of the west—
Far—cradled afar on the blue ocean's breast—
Where the hearts of its exiles in dreams ever roam,
'Tis the clime of my fathers—'tis England—'tis home.

Mr. Hopkins. "I've seen some lines very like those in Lord Byron's works." *Miss E.* "Oh! yes. I suppose my brother meant them to be an imitation." *Mr. H.* "If not, Miss, you may adopt, in your brother's defence, the excuse of Puff in the 'Critic,' who, when taxed with cribbing a passage out of Shakespeare, replied 'that it wasn't surprising that two men should happen to hit upon the same idea, and that the only advantage Shakespeare had over him was that he had happened to hit upon it first.'" *Miss E.* "Well; but, Mr. Hopkins, you must listen to another piece of poetry by my brother, entitled 'India.'" *Mr. H.* "High diddle diddle, the cat and the fiddle! I wish you good morning, Miss."

SAHUSWAN,
March 10*th*, 1833.

Dearest Mother,

Happening to meet with an edition of Miss Edgeworth's works the other day I commenced upon them with all the assiduity of a novel-reading Miss, and scarcely suffered myself to take my proper quantum of food or exercise until I had reached the end of the fifteenth volume. They are very admirable tales in every way, and I certainly do not look upon the time occupied by their perusal as misspent. They are as different as possible from the novels of the present day, in avoiding the sins of diffuse and wordy descriptions, and in pourtraying characters by a few characteristic touches rather than by a dry preliminary catalogue of their vices and virtues. What can be a more admirable tale than "The Absentee" or "Ennui," or a dozen others. By-the-bye, I am at present deep in the study of Mrs. Dalgairns' "New and Approved Practice of Cookery," which I took into my head to order up from Calcutta a short time ago, hoping to be able to find some means of ringing a new change on my belfry of dishes. Now it would be easy enough for a man with my relish for good things to cook up some most delicious bonnes bouches from Mrs. Dalgairns' receipts, but the materials are unfortunately wanting at Sahuswan—I have the cart but no horse to draw it. You cannot imagine how melancholy the reflection made me, or the despairing look with which I turned over page after page, miserable as a half-starved chimney-sweeper at the door of a confectioner's shop. At last I lighted on a few receipts, the ingredients for which were procurable here. No time was lost in making the trial, and such messes as we had for the next week or fortnight at table you never saw. In vain did I hold long conferences with my khansaman,—in vain were the receipts translated word for word into Hindostanee, to assist his memory; my looks of eager expectation when dinner was announced quickly changed into sighs of disappointment as soon as the covers had been removed—the puddings were squash and the dishes of meat indescribable and untasteable. My companion for the time being, wearied at last with these successive failures in my culinary experiments, voted them a bore, and wished Mrs. Dalgairns at Jericho. "Before the arrival of that ill-fated volume," he exclaimed, "we had now and then something eatable, but now we are favoured with dog's meat one day and pig's wash another." Only conceive how mortifying to my feelings as a gourmand and a tyro-cook! However, faint heart never won fair lady, and I wooed Mrs. Dalgairns accordingly most assiduously. My companion actually went so far yesterday as to pronounce my white soup "tolerable;" so I meditate a fricassee to-day which I hope will astonish his weak imagination. The best of it was that he undertook the other day himself to show me how to make melted butter, and turned the tables upon himself most completely by this ill-advised offer, for such woful stuff I never saw. I had a good laugh against him in my turn, so that he was forced to conform his taste to mine for the future. I have got once more into my bungalow, and find the change pleasant enough just at present. I have my books about me, and small as my bungalow is it is more commodious than my tents in this weather.

Have you ever happened to meet with the "Passages from the Diary of a late Physician," in Blackwood's Magazine? If not, get the late volumes and read them. They are most powerful sketches of scenes of human frailty, passion and suffering, painted with a master's hand, and with so close an attention to verisimilitude that it is difficult to believe them fictions.

I hope you let Fred subscribe to a library during his vacations. On arriving in this country I was surprised to find myself deficient in the commonest general information. Beyond the Oriental tongues, and the classics, and the little of history and law which I had picked up at Hayleybury, I knew nothing. This I ascribe, in a great measure, to the want of a father in my youth, as well to the want of a stimulus to induce me to turn my attention to those points of information which not to know in the present day is disgraceful. This stimulus can be supplied by the interest which every young man of sense ought to take in passing events, and which can only be excited by his admittance to reading-rooms and sensible society. It is only in the society of men that a young man feels his deficiency in manly information, or is actuated by a desire to overcome it. The nature of the studies at Oxford is too confined, and your life at home is too retired, to admit of the chance of that deficiency being impressed on Fred's mind so forcibly as it was upon mine on my entering into life; but he must recollect that for a gentleman something more is required than a mere knowledge of Latin or Greek, or an acquaintance with Euclid. Nothing, in my opinion, can be more absurd than the system of education at the universities. What oceans of valuable time are sacrificed to the study of the dead languages, whilst all useful information is carefully excluded from their antiquated precincts! It is all well and good to stuff the classics down lads' throats at school, because their minds at that age are not sufficiently formed to enable them to appreciate the value of the more useful studies; but it appears to me something worse than ridiculous to force young men to devote the most precious part of their lives to the acquisition of that which is, after all, a mere accomplishment. However, as things are conducted on this absolute plan at the universities, Fred cannot help himself. It is his interest, unfortunately, to devote himself to the classics, but it should be his aim, at the same time, to blend with them the studies which will be useful to him in after life, when he will be apt to look upon all the paraphernalia of classical knowledge, which he has spent so much time in tricking himself with, as useless lumber. You may prick up your orthodox ears, perhaps, at these opinions, but you will find them confirmed by experience.

March 27th—

The wolves are really becoming very troublesome here. Whilst at dinner yesterday evening, we were alarmed by shrieks and squalls in the direction of the out-houses. Running out, helter-skelter, we found that a wolf had made a pounce on one of my washerman's children, about twenty paces from the bungalow. The child thought it was a dog, and took no notice of it, but her father happening to come by just at the time, caught her by the arm and pulled her into the house. Had he been a moment later, the child would have fallen a prey to the ravenous beast. They tell me that two or three prowl about the bungalow every night. They never attack grown-up persons, whether sleeping or waking, but they make no bones of children. About six weeks ago I happened to be riding near a village one evening, and hearing a hue and cry, galloped to the spot, where I found a little girl about ten years old lying on the ground in the agonies of death. A wolf had pounced upon her close by the village, seized her by the throat, pulled her down, and tore open her entrails. I have sent some men to-day to search for the holes of my nightly visitors, and if they are successful, I shall have them dug out and shot or speared.

SAHUSWAN,
April 10th, 1833.

Dearest Mother,

Information reached me the day before yesterday of a suttee being about to take place at a village ten miles distant from Sahuswan. I mounted my horse immediately, attended by four armed horsemen, and hastened to the spot without delay. Night overtook us on the road, and we lost the way. A precious half-hour was spent by us in finding it again. We pushed on with all possible speed, and arrived at the village two hours after sunset. On approaching it, the frantic cries of " Jy, Jy !" and the blaze flashing amongst the trees told us too truly that the deed was done. The crowd dispersed instantaneously in all directions as soon as they heard of my approach, and all that we found was a smouldering fire and the half-consumed corpse of the unhappy victim of their superstition. The pile had been fired by the eldest son of the deceased, a mere lad, who exulted in the thought of the honour acquired by his family from his mother's self-cremation. I was successful in apprehending the persons who had taken an active part in the tragedy, and I trust they will meet with the punishment their barbarity so richly deserves. Suttees are much less common in this part of the country than in Bengal. This is only the second that has come under my notice, whereas hundreds and thousands were sacrificed annually in the Lower Provinces until a stop was put to them by Lord W. Bentinck's humane prohibition. Strange that such an inhuman rite should have been permitted to disgrace our management of India for so many years.

A case came before me the other day of so peculiar a nature that I cannot avoid mentioning it. Indeed, it deserves to be recorded. A native of this part of India, on his return to his home, stayed several days at the house of his sister, who had been married during his absence. He had served for many years in one of the native states in Central India, and had contrived to amass about a thousand rupees, which he was carrying to his friends in his native village. Finding his sister in indigent circumstances, he generously gave her two or three hundred rupees out of his scanty savings, and, after remaining with her two or three days, prepared to take his departure on the morrow. The woman in the meantime, in the hope of securing the remainder of the sum, was planning his destruction. She mentioned her intentions to her husband, but, on his rejecting the proposal with horror, she resolved to undertake it herself unknown to him, in the belief that a sense of his own interests would lead him to hush the matter up after the crime had been perpetrated. Her intended victim rose very early on the morning of his departure, and, accompanied by his brother-in-law, proceeded to the Ganges to bathe, intending to return to the house and take his meal before he set out. Whilst they were absent the son of his sister, an only child, about twenty-one years of age, came in from the fields where he had been tending the cattle since sunrise, and, feeling wearied, flung himself on the bed on which his uncle had slept, and pulling the sheet over his face, as the natives are in the habit of doing to protect themselves from the insects, fell fast asleep. His mother, I should have mentioned, was not aware of her brother having gone to the Ganges that morning. Thinking the time ripe for the performance of her diabolical resolution, she quietly approached the bed on which her son was sleeping with a drawn sword, and, without removing the sheet, struck him on the neck with such force and with so true an aim that she almost severed his head from his body. Her unfortunate son died without a groan or a struggle. The face continued covered with the sheet as before, and the woman, panic-struck for the time, quitted the room without removing the corpse or making any attempt to conceal it. Her husband shortly after returned. Meeting him with a triumphant air, she exclaimed, " It's done!" "What's done?" asked her husband. "The money is ours, and my brother's never likely to demand it of us again." "Impossible!" replied her husband. " Tell me at once what you have been doing." She made no reply, but, leading him to the room, showed him the corpse covered as before, with the blood streaming in torrents from the gash in the sheet. Her miserable husband, seizing her by the arm, led her close to the corpse, and, pulling back the sheet, exposed to her view the features of her only son! She neither wept nor trembled, but considering it a visible interposition of Providence, and a just retribution for her intended crime, proceeded without delay to the nearest police-station, and, delivering herself up, made a full confession of her guilt. She will shortly be sent to take her trial, and will most probably meet with the punishment her crime deserves. When I first heard this tale of blood, Rich's play of the "Fatal Curiosity" recurred to my mind. I certainly never thought that it would have been my lot to witness on the stage of life an event which I looked upon as an overwrought fiction of a tragic dramatist.

April 30th—

Thus far had I written when I was called off on some business. I was prevented from resuming my pen again, and the day after I went for a change of air and scene to pass a couple of days at an acquaintance's house about fifteen miles from Sahuswan. I returned again last night in order to avoid the heat of the sun, and reached home about half-past two this morning. I had just flung myself on my bed, heartily tired, when your letters of October and November, which had arrived during my absence, were put into my hands. I instantly called for a light, and continued reading them until seven o'clock, when up I got, blinking terribly, ordered breakfast, ate it, and seated myself at my half-finished letter with a pen in my hand eager to notice and pass my comments on the news contained in them.

My dear Emma, if you find occasion to allude to serious subjects, do not spin out your exhortations to too great a length. Do not think you heighten the effect of your remarks on these points by repeating them half-a-dozen times in the course of one letter, or imagine that the heart can be softened, like the metals, by reiterated strokes without a pause between. Alas! you are but inexperienced if you think this plan will succeed with a man of my impatient temper. An appeal which might otherwise sink into the heart becomes tame when repeated and irksome when reiterated. Let me give you a fable to the point, from which I leave my mother and you to draw the application;

A young tree grew once upon a time in a sheltered spot near the banks of a pleasant stream, drawing life and freshness from its waters. And when the springtime was nigh past, and the young tree had put forth its leaves and blossoms, behold a flood came down from the hills and formed another bed for the stream at a distance from its former channel, and the tree began to wither and dry up from lack of moisture. And the heart of the fairy of the stream yearned for that young tree when she saw it despoiled of its freshness, and she said within herself "I cannot change again the course of my stream, yet will I bring moisture to my young tree so that it perish not." Then the fairy flew to the sources of her stream among the distant hills, and turned one of the springs into a higher channel, and it flowed like unto a thread of silver on the high lands and poured itself over a rock on the roots of the tree, and the roots were evermore moistened with its incessant trickling; yet the young tree revived not. Then the kind fairy was sorely grieved in her heart, and she said to the tree, "When the stream left thee I watered thee with a spring from the distant hills, and yet thou revivest not." And the young tree replied, "O benevolent fairy! whilst thy stream was yet with me I stretched out my roots to its waters and my young branches overshadowed it, but now it is afar off. Yet how can I forget its benefits since I still discern in the distance its gliding current and hear the faint music of its murmurings? Suffer me, then, to remain awhile; or, if thou wilt, pour on me the gentle dews and the soft rain, and it may be that in the coming flood-season thy stream may yet regain its former channel; then will the honey-bee again sing to my blossoms, and the voice of the turtle be heard amongst my branches. Recall, then, this trickling streamlet to its source. Thou has led it here to soften my roots with its moisture, but thou little thinkest, kind fairy, that by its constant dropping thou art changing them to marble."

I bow with the utmost deference to your correction of my genders in *cher ami*. My knuckles are still tingling with the rap given them. It is but fair that you should retaliate now and then to my quizzings and criticisms. Tit-for-tat for ever! Pray what is the meaning of the term "*wonder*struck?" I have been reading the "History of the Jews," which is a very sensible and instructive book. You found fault with it, as far as I can recollect, for the views which Milman takes of the origin and objects of the Mosaic code, but without sufficient reason, I think. The box of books despatched last year by you has arrived, and is on its way up here. I am looking forward to its arrival anxiously. Your last letters convey the most delightful accounts of Ayott.

Sahuswan,
July 10*th*, 1833.

Dearest Mother,

Since I last wrote, I have received one—two—yes, three—letters of various dates; letters did I call them—folios rather, brimful of love and affection and interest. How to repay the debt I know not, for mine are Gullivers compared with your Brobdignags. You must not scold me for having passed over a month in my correspondence once in the way. I have but lately returned to Dumpling Castle; last month, the hottest of the year, having been spent by me partly in tents, and partly in the bungalow of my acquaintance, the Indigo Planter. The weather, too, has been more oppressively hot than I have ever yet felt it in this country, owing to a suspension of the rains, which ought to have set in about the middle of last month, but which have only just commenced. Oh, the utter misery of waiting all agape for the first refreshing showers, after three months of burning winds and torrid sky,—of speculating on every petty cloud that may happen to make its appearance on the horizon,—of sighing and perspiring, and perspiring and sighing by turns from heat and vexation. You, who cannot put on a new bonnet or petticoat without being harassed with fears of showers and thunderstorms, can scarcely form an idea of the delight with which they inspire us. I would have given my best coat—and I have no great assortment of them—to have got a good ducking last week. The excessive heat, added to the dire consequences which always follow a suspension of the rains in eastern countries, began, in fact, to be fatal to man and beast; and had we not been visited by a few partial showers yesterday, we should, probably, have had cholera, fever, and a thousand other epidemics raging, independently of drought, famine and starvation. Even yet we have not had rain enough to revive the parched and burnt-up country, and, unless it descends to our heart's content in the course of the next ten days, the doom of this district, at least, is sealed. Heaven avert so grievous a calamity!

July 25th—

I have had much to occupy me since I last took up my pen. One of my principal revenue officers, a native of some rank and consequence, having been guilty of every kind of villany and oppression under the imbecile management of my predecessor, I dismissed him from his situation, and summoned him to answer the charges preferred against him. Having ample reason to dread an inquiry into his conduct, he fled the district, and concealed himself in the territory of an independent chief, about 150 or 200 miles distant. The instant I heard of his having absconded, I mounted an active fellow on a mule belonging to me, which I had purchased a few months before, and started him off in pursuit. The fugitive had got the start of me by two or three days, but I found I had not over-calculated the powers of my mule. The hardy little animal, and his no less hardy rider, completed the first 100 miles in twelve hours. He then rested, and started off again in the evening on a fresh horse furnished him by an acquaintance of mine, and riding all that night and part of the next day came up with the culprit and apprehended him. He was seized and lodged in a place of safety, but in the course of the next night he poisoned himself in a fit of despair, by swallowing an immoderate quantity of opium. His putrefying remains, which were sent to me immediately afterwards, conveyed to me the first intelligence I had received of the success of the pursuit, and produced an impression amongst the native community here which will, I hope, have a good effect in deterring others from similar practices. The affair has made some noise in this part of the world, for it is not often that our native officers venture on such a rash step.

We have had abundance of rain, I am happy to say, since I last took up my pen. For four days and nights the rain came down incessantly,—a steady, soaking, deluging rain, which has put the whole country about Sahuswan under water. We have a small boat on the lake now, and have actually hoisted a sail—a sort of make-believe; however, we manage with it tolerably enough, and feel the same degree of pleasure in the novelty that a child does in his pieces of wood and handkerchief launched on a trough of water. We sailed along merrily this evening, and I could almost have fancied myself on one of the rivers at home—the country around looked so fresh from the recent rain, and the western skies so beautiful. It is only in the rains that we are ever treated with anything resembling an English sunset, yet still how different are the leaden clouds and the dull aspect of the horizon from the bright, balmy, joyous spring and autumn evenings in dear old England!

Camp,
September 28th, 1833.

Dearest Mother,

They say you may judge of a man by his books. If that be true, I give you an opportunity of forming an opinion with regard to my character and habits by furnishing you with a list of the volumes out of my small library which I have selected for my study during my excursion in the jungles. They have been my companions on many a weary travel and many a dull day, with some slight variations; but I tire not of them, and never shall so long as I preserve the tastes of my boyhood. Gibbon's Decline and Fall; Clarke's Homer; Corpus Poetarum Latinorum; Herodotus; Shakespeare; Beaumont and Fletcher's Works; Ford's Dramatic Works; seven volumes of the Edinburgh Review; Don Quixote; Mrs. Dalgairns' Cookery; The Cook's Dictionary; Biddulp on the Liturgy, a copy of which 1 had before you sent me the last; and some other books of a serious kind. These are my standard volumes. My delight in the works of the old dramatists is exhaustless; their study has spoiled my boyish predilection for the mawkish poetry of the present day. You sent me some time ago a pretty poem by Mrs. Hemans, the point in which hinged upon the natural affinity observable in the effects of pleasure or sorrow, each exhibiting itself in a tear. With how much force and beauty is this idea expressed in a few words taken from one of Middleton's plays—

"*Juliana.* My joys start at my eyes. Our sweet'st delights
Are evermore born weeping."

CAMP,
November 6th, 1833.

Dearest Mother,

I have been reading "Corinne," or rather a translation of it. My chief inducement to take it up was the mere recollection of its having formed one of the few novels which you permitted Ellen to read. She read it, I recollect, years and years ago, at Cheltenham, in the original, of course. For my part I could not get through it. "Corinne," as far as I remember, was the first novel Ellen was permitted to read, the object being to improve her in French. "The Scottish Chief" was the first novel I was "authorized" to read, the permission being fettered by the condition that I should first read the preface attentively,—a task which I believe I undertook with more willingness, and got through more quickly, than any that was ever imposed upon me. This was at Weymouth. I except the "Old English Baron" and "The Mysteries of Udolpho," the first of which you read to us yourself one Christmas night—I recollect the occasion as if it had been yesterday. Freezing with interest and excitement we sat up until eleven o'clock at night (a rare occurrence), cowering over the dying embers in the grate of the parlour at Winifred, and following up every pause with, "Oh! dear mamma, pray go on, now do go on a little further." How I bolted up the stairs afterwards, six steps at a bound! How I screamed all the time, "Hold the candle a little longer!" How I ducked my head under the clothes, when I was safely in bed, bunging up my ears with my fingers to exclude all ghostly noises! One other novel you permitted me to read in my boyhood, namely, "Frankenstein;" and it I read under the shade of one of those beautiful lilac trees near the new bower on Winifred House lawn, the very day before we left it for ever. Dear Winifred! If ever I see thee again it will not be with dry eyes, for if things remain as they were, every stick and stone to me will have its history. And here am I, whilst I am recalling recollections of past days and Christmas pleasures, encamped on the skirts of a vast jungle, fifty miles distant from any European, overlooking an Indian lake as large as Grasmere, the wild geese screaming in their flight over my tent, and the wolves and jackals howling and yelling in the distance. True, I am seated by my stove, and my tent looks as warm and comfortable as it well can, but where is the family hearth? Where "the fond, familiar faces"? Even echo cannot here answer "Where?" for echo dwells not in the dank jungles or muddy marshes of India; but despite of jungles I have got a "fatted calf," or rather a good fat bullock, ready for Christmas, to which I hope to be able to do justice.

I have not written to my uncle for an age. The fact is, I cannot write from the jungles. The uniform tenor of one's life here, and the absence of all excitement from without, renders one, against one's will, torpid and listless. We cannot amuse others when unamused ourselves; and I have no events to chronicle like my uncle Charles, no births or marriages, no lyings-in or happy deliveries. Strange that one who is so fond of mirth and merriment as myself should be imprisoned year after year in the centre of deserts and jungles! Yet my mirth bubbles as before, although it overflows not its cistern.

I have just returned from an excursion into the heart of the jungle, partly for the sake of sport and partly for change, in which I was accompanied by Bentall and another junior. We spent three very pleasant days together, and parted each to his own camp miles and miles asunder. Such is society in the out-stations. Meetings like these are pleasant for the time, but after they are broken up the sense of loneliness falls with a double chill. I returned to my camp to-day through a wild tract of country, quite melancholy and gloomy, and I experience now a dead weight on my spirits. I like these meetings in the jungle. People meet at large stations, and the meeting is only acknowledged afterwards with a distant bow; but a social party in the jungle, be the persons who compose it who they may, is always remembered and reverted to with pleasure. Certainly if there is any portion of my life in India to which I shall be able to look back with pleasure, it will consist of the odds and ends of my leisure time which have been devoted to these social meetings. The interest, too, attending a day's sport in the jungles here, which have never been visited yet by any European, is not of a nature to be easily effaced, any more than the chances of the sport. I am very far from a professed sportsman, and am equally far from being an expert one, but the exercise and the excitement make me not only relish a little relaxation of this kind at the time, but mark it out as not ill-spent. Really to enjoy it I ought to keep an elephant, but this is a luxury which I do not, or rather must not, think of, from economical motives.

CAMP,

April 6th, 1834.

Dearest Mother,

I have received your last box of books. Many thanks for its contents, which have amused and interested me for the last three weeks. My time is not my own now, otherwise I should have acknowledged its receipt earlier; in fact, I am sensible of having been rather lax in my correspondence of late, but I have had so much to occupy my mind and divert my attention that I have scarcely been able to give my thoughts, far less my pen, to you; yet my heart and my affections are unchanged, and, I hope, unchangeable. If they had been disposed to stray, your annual budget would have been of itself a magnet of virtue sufficient to recall them. I am in debt to you all; to Fred deeply, I fear irretrievably and unpardonably; to Joe, to Emma, to Ellen; even Miss Pilot and Mrs. Oates call upon me for some token of recollection. I must not fail to them though I do to you. You must not be jealous of this show of preferences on my part, but I cannot, in common gratitude, suffer their kind and valued notes, received with the box of books, to pass over unacknowledged. Mrs. Oates' kindness in remembering me I feel deeply, for it is not often that the same attention is paid by age to youth. To Miss Oates, too, something more is due than a common expression of gratitude. Miss Pilot I look upon as one of you, but she begs to be excluded for a time from your circle for the sake of receiving a separate letter, and she must not be disappointed. Fred's essays and Joe's verses I promised some time ago to answer in kind, but it is easier in this case to say than to do. The hot weather is coming on with rapid strides, and the tagging of rhymes and metres in English or Latin is not a task to be undertaken when the thermometer is at 90°.

The letters and books in your last box are amusing enough, but nothing comes up to the items in Fred and Joe's account-books. You mentioned, I think, in one of your letters some time ago your having cried over an account-book of mine kept whilst I was at Mildenhall. I don't know whether you intended me to pay a similar tribute of tears to Joe's memorandums; if so, your expectations were answered, but they were tears of merriment. For instance: "House of Lords and Commons, 1s. 6d.,"—a contribution, I presume, towards the liquidation of the national debt. "Item, Woman and Fat Pig, 1s." This is to be ranked, I suppose, as a charitable donation. "Item, Humbugs, 2d." Horribly extravagant this! "Item, Inquisition, 1s." This is very obviously another act of public munificence for which the Spaniards will undoubtedly canonize him. From the other pages I gather that Joe had contrived to effect a very amicable and advantageous composition between his conscience and his stomach, for items of ginger beer, buns and tarts, liquorice and Shrewsbury cakes alternate with donations of pence and halfpence to little boys and girls, women with ten children, and bull-beggars. But I forgot—you deprecate jocularity in my letters, so let me compose my features and proceed.

We have had an extraordinary mild season for this period of the year hitherto, which is fortunate for me, as I shall have to remain under canvass until the end of May. My health continues good, and I have lost, happily, the tendency to fever which harassed me during four months of the cold weather, to my great discomfort. You are now revelling amongst the buds and blossoms, the green fields and genial breezes of the opening spring. I envy you. Four years hence, but not before, for I date my ten years from the period of my actual service, I may be embarking on the steamer to join you all; but I must not anticipate. How, indeed, is it possible for the most buoyant hope to overleap the dreary interval of four hot seasons? I have read the books received with your box with much interest. Mr. Baxter's account of himself I cannot admire. The subject is a disagreeable one, and there is nothing to interest or even to pity in the author. Such gross fanaticism is far worse than open profanity. "Rome in the Nineteenth Century" is written in a spirited manner, and by a lady, too! She must be a blue-stocking, but she is certainly the most agreeable one I have ever met with, either in books or society. It has set me longing after Italy again,—not, perhaps, with the fervour of my early days, but with a deeper interest. The author of "Spain" is no great shakes. "Thomason's Life" is not only well worth reading but worth remembering. I should not forget the pretty little bijou, "The Parting Gift." It had well-nigh made me poetical again, but I have had quite enough of the muses, and so, I think, have you. Sentiment in me is horribly misplaced, whatever you may say to the contrary. "Miss Graham's Memoirs," Emma's gift, put me in mind of Lyme and Morcott. It touched a string that still vibrates, though it has long been hushed; yet the sound that it once gave is not one to be forgotten. The budget of letters of all shapes, sizes and subjects, not omitting notes from Emma to this and that Miss Thingumbob, written on rose-coloured paper about the size of my thumb, were, as I said before, only outdone by Fred and Joe's dot-and-carry-one memorandums, which, if they were sent me for an example, it would be vain for me to attempt to rival. I anxiously expect your next letter. May Emma's lot in life, whatever it be, turn out as fortunately as Ellen's! I dreamt a few nights ago, —dreamt, mother!—that your silver cord had been loosed, and your pitcher broken at the fountain, and I awoke in a flood of tears,—the bitterest, as they were the first, I had shed for many a long year. May that event only be delayed until after my second departure from England, if I am permitted to see its shores again. But why mourn in anticipation? Why forestall the future? I do not commend the two volumes of "Keith's Commentary on the Revelations," received with your last supply of books. Human reason always has erred, and always will err as often as it attempts to particularize prophetical events, those alone excepted which have influenced the world at large in past ages. It is worse than useless to aim at applying the grand events shadowed forth in prophecy to our own times, or even to those of the past generation. Mr. Keith's book—at least, the latter portion of it—is made up, half of fanciful speculation, and half of idle dreaming.

SAHUSWAN,

September 15th, 1834.

Dearest Mother,

I sent off a letter to you yesterday, but I commence another without delay to make up for lost time. I expect shortly to receive some further accounts of you all, and of Emma, the destined bride, in particular, whose prospects in life have occupied more of my thoughts than you might be, perhaps, willing to believe,—judging, at least, from my dilatory correspondence of late. It is the certainty that I have always felt of preserving my original interest in all of you, happen what may—I mean the interest that naturally attended me during the first one or two years after my arrival in this country— that has contributed to bind my heart so closely to you. You must give me credit, then, for a similar feeling.

I do not think that any of your letters has miscarried since my arrival in this country; and such letters—so full, so satisfactory, so tenderly affectionate—it has fallen to the lot of few to receive. Oh! that unlucky fable! I will discard Æsop for ever afterwards, and content myself with the Polite Letter-Writer. Mole-hills become mountains in your teeming fancy.

You tell me to reflect before I set down my thoughts on paper in writing to you. Why, at that rate, letter-writing would be as bad as theme-writing, and quite as uninteresting. You are accustomed to the vivid expression of feeling poured forth by my brothers and sisters in their letters to you, and you probably think me tame and cold in comparison, and not without reason. They meet you over the Christmas hearth; they walk with you over the spring meadows; their feelings and thoughts are yours, and yours are theirs. They have not yet learnt by experience that exile and absence subdue, whilst they strengthen the force of the heart's best affections. The current of theirs runs through a pleasant country, kissed—if I may be poetical—by the overhanging trees and flowers; mine is in a desert —its sources still shine to the eye of the traveller, but its future course is a mist. Yet there may be "a meeting of the waters." But I will not pursue the simile further. You must not doubt my affection until you have reason to do so. The warm feelings expressed by all of you towards me are very dear to me, and I frequently regret that I cannot respond to them in the same glowing terms. Remember the captives at Babylon : "How shall we sing the songs of Zion in a strange country?" So it is with the heart; its lyre hangs on the willows in exile, but its feelings are unchanged. Oh! for the time when it may be once more restrung!

You make frequent mention in your letters of Sir A. Agnew's bill for the better observance of the Sabbath. I am glad to see that it has been thrown out by a large majority in the House of Commons. The Sabbath will never be better observed by tacking a penalty to the neglect of it. Legislation has nothing to do with the matter, and its interference has always been productive of double mischief. Many persons would abstain from worldly pursuits and amusements on the first day of the week from proper feeling or example, who, if forbidden or prohibited from doing so, would run into the opposite extreme. Any attempts of this nature appear to me exceedingly injudicious. Under the bigot Laud, in Charles the First's reign, sports of all kinds were in a manner enjoined on the people of England on the Sabbath, and thousands, who frequented and encouraged them before, ranked themselves immediately amongst the Puritans, simply because they would not be compelled to indulge even in recreations. Mr. Percival's motions in the House of Commons are—or, rather, were—of the same caste. Such ill-judged people, however sincere they may be, do infinite injury to the cause they advocate.

SAHUSWAN,

April 15th, 1835.

Dearest Mother,

I have just despatched a letter to you, and lose no time in commencing another. I have just been reading over again your transcripts of Emma's letters. What a bustling little mother she has become! How deep she is already in the mysteries of housekeeping! I wonder if she is allowed to keep a cookery-book? She could hardly be so venturous, considering the jobation I got once for a similar offence, beginning, as usual, with the evil effects of indigestion, and ending with the "gallows," or "gallis," as Peggy used to call it, in the wind-up of her lectures to me. Poor Emma! having to sit up, dressed pretty, to receive the congratulatory calls of the Frome folks! What a penance! And then her first arrival with her husband at her new home in the still of the summer's evening; her cottage ornée, which, whether large or small, must be lovely; and the quiet tea-drinking of the young couple, both of them looking as domestic as possible, and as pleased as Punch. *That* is an evening which Emma, I will be bound to say, will long remember! Her feelings must have been like mine when, after knocking about Calcutta for a few days, weary and unsettled, a stranger in a strange city, I found myself at last in rooms I could call my own.

Your description of your journey to Lyme, over the moonlit hills, of your quiet drive by Charmouth and Up Lyme, and of your stroll in the Cobb under the same moon, which, to my memory, appears to have been always shining there, make my heart ache with longing. It was a happy luck that fixed us at Lyme ten years ago. No other spot I have yet seen would have retained the same hold on my affections. Odd enough, the very day I received your last letter, I was reading one of Miss Austin's admirable novels, "Persuasion," in which Lyme and its beauties are mentioned in glowing terms, not excepting the Pinney cliffs and the identical brook—for I am sure it must be the same—welling from them in its brief course to the sea.

One of the few times I ever moralized in those days was when I was standing on a bright January morning near the second brook, a few hundred yards beyond Titania's Green, which is crossed by a stepping-stone. The stream was beautiful in its brightness and mirth, singing amongst the rocks and stunted shrubs, but its life was so brief in its passage from its source to the ocean, and apparently so uncared for and uncaring, and, moreover, so useless to the purposes of man, that I felt as if I would not have been that brook for worlds. But a truce to sentimentalizing.

By-the-bye, my birthday is in a day or two. I have been trying to make out whether I am twenty-five or twenty-six, and can't discover, for the life of me; the former, I believe. If so, I have reached the top of the hill of life; that of such of the Brown family who have come out to this country appears limited to fifty years in the course of nature. My walk for the future will be downwards. *My* climacteric has been attained already. With the exception of my first two birth-days at Delhi, the rest have been passed either amongst the deserts at Hissar, or the Sahuswan swamps. Where did I get my hermit dispo-sition from? Dull as the days pass at Sahuswan, and cheerless as are the evenings, I prefer it vastly to the larger stations, and I shall leave it, whenever I do leave it, with regret. Yet, what a life is mine here! how entirely blank! how pointless, and apparently how aimless! It seems as if my thirst for reading was given me expressly in anticipation of my lot in life—to prepare me for the jungles of India, and make them endurable. Not that I'm at my books all day long, but I turn to them with a pleasure which I do not see in others.

I often picture to myself the idea which each of you will have formed of me, when the time comes for my return to England. You will be looking for a very *elegant* young man; Emma for a very romantic one, a spouter of sonnets, and a writer in ladies' albums; Ellen for the same as she knew me, with the leading traits of my character brought out into strong relief by ten years' working; Fred for a bit of a parson, and bit of a humorist; Joe for a big-wig, armed with wise saws and modern instances; and my two brothers-in-law for a piece of mosaic-work, composed of all the above except the first, of which I shall assuredly never be found guilty. Am I correct or not in my ideas on the subject? I much fear the reality will disappoint you all, as it always does dreamers, and where is there such a dreamer as Affection? Now, my ideas with regard to you all are much more sober, yet why they should be so I know not. I can picture Ellen by that time a quiet, peaceful, loving matron; Emma a bustling, joyous, happy one; what Fred and Joe will be I can judge by myself, with the additional advantages,—mind, of better dispositions, called forth by happier circumstances and higher privileges.

By-the-bye, now that you have left Bath, you need not send me any more Bath papers. The chain which bound me to it is broken, and I should not care if the pump-room were to fall into Bladud's bath, or the two cliffs meet, as Joanna Southcott prophesied, provided Sion Hill and Charlcombe, and the Weston fields and vales, are left to welcome me back again with their cowslips and chervil, as of yore.

Dear Bath! I was not there at the time of life likely to make me tired of it. I left in my hobbledehoyism, and all my recollections of it are, in consequence, tinged with a *couleur de rose*, instead of being counteracted by dull Park Street realities. Yet why should I call Park Street dull, since Ellen was married and Emma wooed there?

I wonder what kind of a house you will take at Hampstead? One, I suppose, about five yards from the road, with a gravelled walk up to it, a patch of sickly grass on each side, and an iron stand in front of the window, to hang out mignonette-pots upon; for this is the fac-simile of all houses at Hampstead or elsewhere in the environs of London. Well, never mind; if you become disreputable, I shall *cut* you, and live in lodgings in town—ahem!

———————————

SAHUSWAN,

May 10th, 1835.

Dearest Mother,

I have just been looking over Ackermann's Picturesque Tour to the Lakes, containing about fifty admirably coloured sketches of the scenery, beginning with Coniston Water and ending with Penrith. It almost appears as if the artist had accompanied us step by step in our tour, for there are only two or three out of the whole number which I do not recognize. They have set me a-dreaming the whole day. One would have been sufficient for that purpose, but the whole form a kind of magic mirror, not merely of the scenes themselves, but of the recollections connected with them. I have Somer-dale, and Buttermere, and Crummock, and the verdant valley of the Calder, on the table before me, and Wast Water, and Kirkstone, and Patterdale, and the still vale of Furness,—a ruin which, from its wild situation and utter loneliness, made a deeper impression on me than any I have yet met with. And here, too, are Seathwaite and the Langdale Pikes, and Rydal Water, and here—let me see—yes, here I have it—here is the identical mountain stream on the bank of which I lunched in my pedestrian excursion from Wast Water to Buttermere the day previous to the episode of the jug; and here is the spot where we had a squabbling match, or, rather, where I took to one of my "vagaries" one peaceful summer evening in our walk to Rydal; and here is Scale Force, attained by us after so many frights in crossing the Crummock Water, when we were supplicated not to laugh lest the reverberation might upset the boat; and here we have the Old Man and the Yewdale Crags. I shall never forget the first view we had of Coniston Water on our road from Ulverstone on that balmy May evening at Calder, or our rambles together over the hills above Ambleside. These sketches make me melancholy. They make me feel quite an old man, not so much in years as in the vividness of my feelings. I could not muster up now one-tenth part of the excitement and enjoyment which the simplest of these scenes afforded me then,— and where can you find a truer landmark of the passage of Time than this? Time may do many things in our favour, but it cannot restore even a shadow of the pleasurable sensations peculiar to our earlier years. No wonder, then, that I should draw so largely, or so frequently, on these two scenes of my recollections, Lyme and the Lakes; or that I should be led to sentimentalize occasionally, almost against my will, over the days passed amongst their beauties. Dear mother! it is not one of the least of the thanks we owe you, that you should have laid your-self out to gratify to the utmost our youthful tastes; you have had your reward for once to-day in *my* thoughts, and it is not one likely to perish. Three years and a half hence I shall start for England, if my life be spared. I shall by that time have been nearly eleven years in this country, and by the time I arrive in England I shall have been absent from you twelve. What an age! Twelve long, long years, spent by me for the greater part of the time in comparative solitude,—in an utter dearth, at least, of the heart's best affections. Surely, surely, those who picture to themselves, in glowing colours, the advantages of India, can have little idea of its melancholy realities. If the fruit has a golden hue, like the fabled apples on the borders of the Dead Sea, it is bitter to the taste—they look alluring at a distance, but when we grasp them we find them ashes. I shall be an old man of thirty when we meet again, a frowzy old bachelor; and you will be a comfortable old lady, and Ellen will be a matron of a respectable age, and Emma will have lost her youthfulness, and my brothers will be as I am now. O Time—Time, I wish thy current swifter now, but I shall have to look back many a time with a longing eye to thy sources in the distance.

May 18*th*—

An event has occurred here since I last took up my pen which had well-nigh ended in a deep and bloody tragedy to all of us. I was sitting yesterday in my public room transacting business, with a number of natives about me, when I heard, of a sudden, shouts and screams proceeding from the room in which Louis was sitting, and which was separated from mine by a small corner room. A number of the native officers and others who were in attendance in Louis's court precipitated themselves at the same moment through the corner room into mine, and made for the doors, which were wide open. A sudden panic seized the men who were with me, who ran out after the others, leaving me nearly alone. Suspecting the real state of the case, namely, that some attack had been made on Louis, and fully expecting every moment a similar attack on myself from the headlong haste with which the people fled from his room through mine, and thence to the outside of the house, I looked round me for something to grasp at, but seeing nothing, and not feeling disposed to run away, like the rest, from an unknown danger, for they were all too frightened to tell me what had happened, I ran out into the verandah and seized a thick stick from a man who was making off after the rest as hard as he could manage, at the bottom of the steps. I had hardly got it into my hands, when a man turned round the corner of the house, on the outside, and confronted me, at the distance of a few paces, with a bloody sword in his hand. I guessed immediately what had happened, but recollected myself sufficiently to stand my ground, or rather to retreat slowly up the steps, holding the stick as a guard, for I fully expected him to run at me, in which case, had I taken to my heels, I should infallibly have been murdered. This show of resolution,—for I confess it was only a show,—seemed to daunt him, for he turned round and took to his heels. Mrs. Louis, at the same moment, ran into the verandah, in search of her husband, half frantic. I supported her into a small room next mine, keeping a watchful eye round me, for all the doors in the house were open, as they always are in this country, and I thought it not unlikely that the man would make his way back again into the house by another door, after he had disappeared round the corner. On entering it, and slamming-to the doors, we saw Louis come in, covered with blood, from the opposite verandah; and had scarcely time to exchange words, or make any more preparations for defence, when the shouts from outside told us of the capture of the rascal who had wounded him. The circumstances were as follows:—One of the native guards had been summoned by him to answer for some misconduct, and, on its being proved, he had just issued the order for his dismissal, when the man pulled out his sword and made a desperate cut at his head; the blow, fortunately for him, missed his skull, but shaved off a piece of the scalp at the back of his head, and cut deep into his shoulder. The man then attacked the native officer who was standing by Louis, gashed him terribly down the arm, cutting off one of his fingers with the same blow, and aimed a second at his head, which cut through the thick folds of his turban, but did not penetrate further. This was the work of a moment, but it saved Louis. Louis, on finding himself wounded, fled through the two centre rooms of the bungalow to the corner room, which opened in the side room where I was sitting, and was half through the door when the fellow, who had pursued him after wounding the native, came up with him and aimed another desperate blow at his back. Had he been half a foot behind-hand, he would have been cut nearly in half, but the blow fell short, the point of it inflicting a trifling wound in the small of his back. Louis then slammed-to the door, and escaped through the room into the verandah. At this moment, I was sitting with my back to the door through which Louis escaped, and within a few feet of it, but the uproar and confusion was such that I neither saw nor heard Louis, although he passed close behind me in his flight to the verandah. The fellow, baulked by the door, ran back through the centre rooms to the outside of the house, and made round to the side room where I was, with the determination, as he has since declared, to do for me too. On reaching the steps, within a yard or two of the place where I was standing, almost alone and quite unarmed, he was met by my people rushing tumultuously out, and attacked them right and left, with a view to clear a way for himself to my room. He cut down three men on the steps within a few feet of the door, and a fourth at the foot of them; one man lost his hand at the wrist, which was cut clean off, and the others were wounded one after the other with three or four sword-cuts. By this time all had fled, and there was nothing to prevent him making his way into my room; but thinking that I had fled with the rest, he ran to a small bungalow occupied by the public officers, a few yards from the public one, with the intention of doing some more mischief. Here, again, he was baulked by the men shutting the doors in his face. He then returned again towards my room, and it was at that moment that I met him at the foot of the steps. My escape was, therefore, three-fold, for had he only opened the door through which Louis escaped, in the first instance, which there was nothing to prevent him doing, I must have been killed, as he would have come upon me from behind, and would have found me quite unprepared. All this, which has taken a long time to tell, passed in less than two minutes. Mrs. Louis and the children's escape was no less providential than Louis's, who got off with a deep but not either a severe or a dangerous wound, for Mrs. Louis had only left the room, into which the rascal pursued her husband, a minute before, and the children, who usually remained in the centre room during the day, had just been put to bed. Had any of them been there at the time, they would certainly have been mur-dered. "Ah," said the fellow, when he was caught, " I've done for one Sahib, at all events; and the only thing I regret is that I didn't do for the other, too (meaning me), and all of them." I sent for a native barber-surgeon immediately, and got him to put a stitch through the lips of Louis's wound to keep them together, after which I physicked him to keep down fever until the arrival of the doctor, whom I instantly sent for from Moradabad, sixty miles distant. He arrived late last night (the 18th), and found Louis doing well; in fact, I hope to see him convalescent in a fortnight.

May 29th—

I have investigated the case as magistrate, and have committed the rascal to take his trial to-day. Louis is on his legs again, and the other wounded men were able to come into court and give their depositions, six in all, besides Louis, with the exception of the poor fellow whose hand had been cut off. One of them had lost three of the fingers of his left hand. He met me a few minutes after the assault, the blood spouting from the stumps, and the forefinger, the only one left, projecting from his mutilated hand in sign-post fashion. He had had the coolness to pick up his three fingers, which he brought in his other hand to show me. Their half-black, half-blue colour was quite sickening. He asked me to-day whether he should burn them, for it appears he had kept them by way of evidence. It is quite surprising how soon the natives of this country recover from wounds which would keep Europeans on their backs for months. This is no doubt owing to their vegetable diet. The ruffian has been three times before me. I did not feel at all satisfied with his restless looks whilst I was engaged in the case to-day, and I accordingly armed myself with his own sword, which had been produced in the course of the examination, for he was standing only a few paces off; and past scenes had convinced me that I could not rely on natives for any effectual assistance in the first moment of surprise, although, in general, I do not consider them cowardly. The sword was covered with blood from the point to the hilt, so I must have cut rather an imposing figure. In fact, for the future, I shall take care to have a sword at hand during public hours. The sudden gusts of fury to which natives are subject cannot be forestalled, so that it is better to be always prepared, and with a good sword in my hand I should not be disposed to shrink from an encounter with a half-madman, although I should be very unwilling to court it. I observed in the paper a day or two ago a similar circumstance which had occurred in another part of the country, where a man, or rather a fiend, had killed fourteen people in a fit of momentary fury. In fact, in this very district, only a short time ago, a man killed his wife and four children without any assignable cause. He thrust their corpses into a heap of dried cow-dung, in front of his house, which he set fire to, and afterwards betook himself to his ordinary business, as if nothing had happened. But I will not attempt to entertain you with our Indian Newgate Calendar, except in as far as it concerns ourselves personally. To give you an interlude in our affairs, the old lady—Mrs. Louis's mother—on hearing the shouts and screams, fled for refuge to the bathing-room, which she had just reached, when one of the servants, frightened out of his life, overtook her, pushed her down, stepped over her and passed himself into the room, closing and bolting the door in her face, where he remained as snug and comfortable as possible, until all was over, the poor old lady hammering away, out of her wits to get in, the whole time. I could not help laughing when she told it me, afterwards, with a very dolorous and indignant expression of countenance. *You* will no doubt sympathise with her. I still wonder at Louis's escape, which, all things considered, was quite wonderful, or rather, I should say, providential. It appears the rascal had been summoned by me, on one or two occasions before, to answer for his misconduct,—whereon, I presume, his spite against me. But I have given you enough of this, for once. I hope I shall not have occasion again to detail any similar event, as far as I am concerned. You, who live in happy and peaceful England, see little of the "red knife," but this, as I said before, is not the first scene of the kind I have witnessed. Let me only live to see you once more, and then——; but I will not anticipate either good or evil. The events of the last fortnight prove the folly of both.

SAHÚSWAN,

June 3rd, 1835.

Dearest Mother,

Yesterday and to-day have been holidays, and I have enjoyed the respite by reading over again " Rob Roy " for the sixth or seventh time. In fact I have been romancing, and my return to my usual duties to-morrow is looked forward to by me with something of the same kind of feeling which I experienced as a Charterhouse lad towards the close of the Sunday evenings, when the time came for my return to my prison, for I never could look on Charterhouse in any other light. Even in this country and at this season, when the hot wind is sweeping along with its furnace blasts from daybreak to sunset, I find it possible to enjoy myself, after a fashion, on a holiday, seated behind a lattice with a novel in my hand, without my jacket and waistcoat, and fortified on one side with some hock and soda-water, and on the other with a huge water-melon, not forgetting a case of cigars. " Very luxurious indeed," you will say. I am glad you think so. For my own part, a stroll by one of the summer-brooks of old England for a single hour would amply make up to me for all, and more than all, that could be adduced in favour of this country and its appliances, for I cannot call them comforts,—for all, that is to say, except the novel. I read " Rob Roy " for the first time when a snivelling little school boy, during the two months' probation I under-went at Charterhouse, in the early part of 1821 ; I have taken it up again since many a time, under very different circumstances, in England and in this country ; and like every other often-perused book, it has a charm, independently of its own attractions, in the instructions connected with its readings. Books of this kind become dial-plates, as it were, of our tastes each time we resume them. The interest I gave to the story years ago is now lost in the amusement derivable from the dialogue and the delineation of character, and passages which I invariably skipped formerly are those to which I first turn to now. But I will not fill my letter with my dissertation on Scott's novels.

June 8th—

To-day's dawk brought me tidings of the assassination of one of my old Delhi friends, a young Irishman of the name of Blake, who arrived at Delhi in 1829. I knew him intimately. We have lived together for months at a time, and the pleasantest days passed by me there were spent in his and Trevelyan's society. All my excursions to the Cootub were made with him, and our trio, when Trevelyan was with us, used to be a happy and social one. He had been deputed on some political business to one of the native states, and was murdered there in open day with two other gentlemen; the particulars I have not yet heard. He was a fine, high-spirited, talented fellow, and I mourn his melancholy fate most sincerely. My May letter, which communicates the particulars of my own narrow escape from a similar fate, you will probably have received before this reaches you. My former Commissioner at Delhi was assassinated three months ago. He too was a man of a noble character, and his mild and unoffending disposition made his fate the more tragical. The laws in this country are far too mild; they are written in milk and water, and present little or no check to the furious outbreak of the passions in which the natives frequently indulge, and which lead invariably to crimes of the deepest dye. The tiger of a man who put all our lives in jeopardy here last month is not likely to be sentenced to any severer punishment than seven years' imprisonment—and imprisonment in this country is far from oppressive. I really believe myself that the only effectual mode to check the recurrence of an attack like that made on us last month would be to take the law into one's own hands on the spot, and make short work with the assailant. There can be little doubt that the man would have been cut to pieces here on the spot, as soon as the people had summoned courage to seize him, had it not been for our interposition, which I am half sorry for now. For my own part, I should feel no more compunction in taking summary vengeance that in stamping on a noxious reptile. Attempts of this kind would not be so frequent if they were attended with personal danger to the assailant. I have had an old cavalry broad sword, which I bought at an auction three or four years ago, well sharpened; and, if I have it at hand on any future occasion of the kind, I shall not let it remain idle. As for Louis, he walks about now with a pistol in his breeches pocket, which is more likely to prove dangerous to the wearer than to any one else.

SAHUSWAN,

July 29th, 1835

Dearest Mother,

      I have just received your letters of December and January. Many thanks for them. Your gentle reproach about my dilatoriness in corresponding during the past year will not be lost on me for the future. I cannot but plead guilty to it; but my mind was occupied by sundry matters of pressing importance at the time. My public business, moreover, was heavy, and engaged me unceasingly, from morning till late in the evening. I had no time even to read, except in snatches during meals,—or rather, during breakfast, for, whilst we were living together, books of course were prohibited at dinner time. Under these circumstances, I could only think of you, instead of writing to you. I am sorry that only "bits" of my letters are interesting; my only subject is self, and that, as long as I remain at Sahuswan, must be a barren one. Yet, dilatory as I may be occasionally, I believe that there are few correspondents like myself in the country, as I am sure there are none like you at home. I had half a mind to marry a black woman, and send you two or three whitey-brown children home; this would give you something to talk about, and me something to write about,—and this would be your proper punishment.

      The man who made the attack on us here has been sentenced to perpetual imprisonment, with labour, in a jail in Calcutta. He poisoned himself the other day, in the jail at Moradabad, where he was waiting to be conveyed to his destination,—a fit end for such a villain.

      I am glad you are pleased with my savings. I have now an inducement, beyond mere self, to continue my remittances. I ought to have commenced earlier, but the failure of Alexander's house, which first put into my head the idea of remitting direct home, would have absorbed all, besides giving me cause for regret for the future. So all is as it should be. I was never expensive, but I am habitually careless of my expenses. This, I am now gradually getting the better of, the nearer the time for my return approaches. I cannot play the miser, but I can curtail unnecessary expenditure. Servants' wages, in this country, are a heavy drag on one's pocket. The salaries of the individual servants are low enough, but there is no breaking through the trammels of caste and habit. There is no blending together different offices in this country, as in England, where the same wench who removes the slop-pails washes her hands and cooks the dinner, and where one man acts as gardener, groom and house servant. I find it impossible to reduce my household establishment below thirteen servants, who cost me 10*l.* a month, which I pay as unwillingly as a farmer his tithes. This number may appear immense to you, but there is no alternative. These include a washerman and a tailor. By-the-bye, I found the latter busily engaged, the other day, in *patching* the heels of my stockings with pieces cut from some old stockings. He had no idea of the mysteries of the back-stitch,—not he! He evidently thought he had hit upon an admirable plan to mend Master's stockings, particularly as I had rated him soundly a short time before for sewing up the holes in the heels, so as to leave a kind of bag, which used to set me a limping like a pig in a string, whenever I had occasion to shoulder my gun.

If I can contrive to save 3,000*l.* before my return I shall consider myself lucky, but this I doubt. I do not intend to return before the cold weather of 1838. You need not fear my walking in some day before my time has expired. I should not be able to enjoy myself at home unless I had fairly gone through my probation in the first instance. I should feel as if I had run away from school a few days before the holidays, and so have incurred a whipping for nothing. Three years is a fearful long time to wait before I can even make any preparations for my departure; but there is no use in grumbling. It is, I think, eight years to-day (August 3rd), since I set foot on board the " Palmyra," and four more years will have nearly elapsed before I can hope to embrace all of you again.

SAHUSWAN,

September 23rd, 1835.

Dearest Mother,

I am behindhand this month in my correspondence, but I cannot help myself. My public labour is incessant : Louis is gone, and I have no one here to assist me.

I have been busily engaged of late in physicking my servants, who have all been more or less attacked with fevers. In fact, this has been a most trying season to all, both Europeans and natives. The latter have died in thousands and tens of thousands, like sheep with the rot. The absurdity of their system of medicine passes belief, and they have not come to me in general until it was almost too late. Whole villages have been depopulated by epidemic fevers, which have swept over them like a pestilence. The cold weather is, fortunately, fast approaching. Two months more of the balefully unwholesome weather we have lately had would be too much for me. Oh! for a mouthful of the genial breezes of good old England!

To give you an idea of my present labours. I rise at seven, swallow a cup of tea, smoke a cigar, and am in my office by eight or a little after, where I have to sit for eight, nine, and sometimes ten hours, not like a clerk in a counting-house at home, with my pen behind my ear, but occupied in a round of business of every description, calling for an unflagging attention and prompt decision. I return to my bungalow afterwards, with little or no appetite for my dinner, and, after a short ride, have to set to again until nine or ten o'clock with public correspondence, &c., &c. The day's work is not unfrequently followed by a restless night; for mental fatigue is felt in the stomach, and not, as some wiseacres pretend, in the head; and I never was a good sleeper, in this country at least. I certainly can say for myself that no man was ever more worthy of his hire than I am. It remains to be seen whether my labours will ever be acknowledged. They would have been, and, in fact, were, and handsomely, too, by Stockwell publicly ; but my present Commissioner is a man of a different stamp, and I look for nothing from him by way of commendation. So little, in general, serves to conciliate those under one, that I am surprised any public officer should miss the path. But there is no use in grumbling.

September 26th—

Your April letter has just reached me. It is delightful, as all your letters are. It breathes of home, and Chalcombe, and brothers, and sisters, and friends, and enjoyments, which have been long strangers to me. I feel, whilst reading them, as if I were personally in the midst of you. The conclusion, it is true, brings me back to the hard, dry world again; but your letters will not only bear reading twice, but many times, and each perusal renews the feelings of the first one. I always keep your letters on hand for a full year before I deposit them along with the rest in my sanctum. I open the latter occasionally, and dream away over its treasures of affection like a miser over his gold. It is, indeed, a rich mine; and although you frequently asked me formerly to destroy our family correspondence, I cannot bring myself to do it, nor could I ever even think of doing so. I would as soon commit a sacrilege. No; let them be preserved, from the first letter of dear Ellen, dated from Martigny, and written on French paper, to the very last. They comprise the history of a loving family for eight long years, at the most eventful period of their lives, and they *must* not perish. How tame must mine appear when contrasted with the full details, the *earnest* affection, and the fond appeals of yours! I have a woman's heart in many things, but a man's pen; and in this, and the absence of any other object but self to interest you, lies, I would hope, this main difference. I have now nearly ninety letters of yours, independently of those from my brothers and sisters, and they are so many leaves in the book of existence.

Dear Mother, I observe a slight, a very slight, and, to any other eye but mine, an almost imperceptible tremulousness in your hand of late, which tells of increasing years more plainly and affectingly than any picture could. They were merely a few strokes, the formation of a letter or so; but they caught my eye, and my heart, and my memory at once, and my eyes swelled with tears, and I felt my heart each time draw, as it were, into itself. My heart, dearest parent, is like a sealed fountain in the wilderness. Neither presence nor life itself will remove that seal. It will be removed only by your death, and then the waters will flow forth freely. Oh! India, India! what have I gained, and what have I not lost, by visiting thee?

Dearest Mother,

I have just been reading Munro's Life, which I had dipped into but not gone through before. His character is an interesting one,—a stern and frigid one apparently to the world, but with veins of deep feeling running through it, which are brought more vividly into notice by the contrast. In his correspondence there is a constant reference in his letters to his sisters to a particular spot in the grounds of his father's small property, which as a boy he was fondly attached to, where a small stream runs over a dam. This spot seems to have "haunted him like a passion" during his first residence in India. He was no romantic lover of scenery, and that amongst the Ghauts in the south of India, which, next to the Himalayas, has not its parallel in this country, is noticed by him only cursorily, but he never meets with a mountain stream without recurring, in a touching manner, to the single favourite spot of his childhood. Well, after nearly thirty years' uninterrupted residence here, he returns home, and proceeds without delay to his old home, then in the hands of strangers. The following extract of a letter to the same sister will tell his feelings:—

"I have been twice at Northside, and though it rained without ceasing on both days it did not prevent me from rambling up and down the river from Clayshoup to the aqueduct bridge. I stood above an hour at Jackson's dam, looking at the water rushing over, while the rain and withered leaves were descending thick about me, and while I recalled the days that are past. The wind whistling through the trees, and the water tumbling over the dam, had still the same sound as before; but the darkness of the day, and the little smart box perched upon the opposite bank, destroyed much of the illusion, and made me feel that former times were gone. I don't know how it is, but when I look back to early years I always associate sunshine with them. When I think of Northwood-side I always think of a fine day, with the sunbeams streaming down upon Kelwin and its woody banks. I do not enter completely into early scenes of life in gloomy, drizzling weather."

What a touching picture! It has gone home to my heart with the melancholy force of reality; and what beautiful, simple nature in the expressions!

March 15*th*—

I have just received your very interesting letter of September containing the termination of Ellen's tour in Wales. You say well that she writes delightfully, and so too does Emma, each in her own character. Their tour has interested me much. I have followed them in their wanderings, for every rock and stream is deeply imprinted on my memory. No wonder—it was my first tour, and I expended so much of my youthful enthusiasm on it and my subsequent ones that I shall feel at a loss where to draw from for a fresh supply on my return, unless I go over the same scenes again, "chewing the cud of sweet and bitter fancies." But then it must not be alone,—and where and how can we ever expect to go over them again together?

The hot weather has commenced already. I may, perhaps, be able to get under some sort of shelter next month, but I shall be exposed to great inconvenience, and my thoughts will be my only companions. One's life in this country is truly one of expectancy, an expectancy so strong that in our eagerness to reach the goal we tread down the few flowers scattered in our path. Well, there is no use in repining.

And so you were taken ill at Ayott? I cannot pity you very much, for I have had similar seizures arising from accidental colds in this country. And you felt melancholy, too, at Ayott. Alas, my dear mother, you would never do for India. I cannot sympathize with you, for you have no claim to sympathy. You have never experienced the feeling of utter loneliness which haunts us on our sick beds in the jungles of India. You know not what it is to look round and meet no eye, no "fond familiar face" to comfort you. You never can feel the utter prostration of spirit incidental to such a situation, and, therefore, I cannot pity you. Do not think me hard-hearted. Our pains and pleasures are all comparative, and we cannot be expected to follow the golden rule in all matters.

Fred, I see by your letters, is in great request, visiting here and dining there, and doing the polite to all. I am glad to see this. It shows that he has not his elder brother's awkward disinclination to the company of strangers, which I have never been able to shake off, and never shall, I fear. In fact, it matters not what I am; I shall return to England like a bird let loose from its cage to drink its pure air and revisit old haunts and scenes for awhile, and then, returning again to my bondage, I shall run away and hide myself, as I used formerly to do when I heard a rap at the door, and shall not dream of making new acquaintances. I shall seek to enjoy myself, and not to play the agreeable to strangers. I never could reconcile the two, though most people can; yet, to please you, I will do my best to behave myself. I will bow pretty when I am told, and brush up my hair, and smile to show my teeth (that is to say, if I have any to show by that time), and make morning calls twice or thrice a year, and open the door to the ladies, and carry the umbrellas, and go down to town to pay the bills. I am heartily glad that Fred has nothing of this. It may make no vast difference, perhaps, in the sum of a man's happiness as far as self is concerned, but it tells in the end, particularly to those who are entering upon life at home.

CAMP,

June 4th, 1836.

Dearest Mother,

The post this evening brought me at last one of the well-known letters with the copper-plate direction. I wish I could write copper-plate. A hand like this would make my fortune in a writing academy. The letter proved most welcome, for I had long been looking forward to its arrival. It is dated November. I read it as I read all your letters, and as I shall never read another after you are gone. Little bits of description, and beautiful they are, too, and little bits of extracts from letters, and then little exhortations, and then a little bit of poetry. My dear mother, I shall never have a correspondent like you. Several of these little poetical pieces I had seen before, but it seemed as if I had never entered into one-half of their beauties until I read them in your handwriting. They are indeed "beautiful exceedingly," and beautiful is the task of the selector, and beautiful is everything in your letters, from the aforesaid copper-plate direction down to the postscript. I have hoarded all your letters carefully, and some time or other I intend to make a selection,—when I know not, but such letters must not be lost entirely. And now for the contents of your last, for every letter of your's makes me put pen to paper without delay.

I see by an extract from one of Fred's letters in your last that you have been urging him to study composition. How? by reading Addison, or Swift, or Cowper? no, but by writing frequent letters! Mercy upon us, my dear mother, who ever heard of anything like *composition* in a readable letter? You had much better recommend him to get by heart the "Polite Letter Writer," which may be purchased in any huckster's shop, price one shilling. The very idea of a letter written as one would write an essay is enough to sicken one. Every young man is more or less disposed to verbiage and composition in his correspondence, until his better taste shakes it off; it is certainly the last thing in the world to be encouraged. I have been guilty of it in my time, and even now I am sensible occasionally of a little inflation, but then this is the inflation of my feelings and not of composition, and I cannot help it, so pray don't talk of "style" in a familiar letter; or, if you must have style, let Fred compare the letters of Cowper with those of Pope, and he will soon see the difference. Again, I see that Fred has chosen his tutor at Oxford as being a dab at essay-writing, in which he finds, or fancies, himself deficient. Now, I take it to be an axiom that a man who has any ideas to express will find no difficulty in expressing them, and the less effort or study spent in spinning phrases the better. If there be a deficit of ideas, the essay writer may pump all the big-wigs and tutors in both universities without being a step nearer his object, but this I certainly do not take to be Fred's case. In compositions in the learned languages the case is exactly the contrary; style in these being much more looked to than their matter. When as a lad I had to write themes at Dr. Knight's on subjects regarding which I had not one idea to rub against another, I used to employ a set of phrases which, in my opinion, did equally well for every subject, so that all I had to do was to substitute one word for another, such as "avarice" for "ambition," and so on, and my theme was completed. Some parts of the system of education in force in the colleges and large schools, even at the present day, are so grossly absurd that I really should feel considerable hesitation in subjecting a son of mine to its yoke. But enough of this. I hope you are both of you quite well after your scolding.

Your letter is full of tenderness and affection, so full that I grieve over the deficiencies of my own,—but you know my heart. Most truly can I apply to you the beautiful lines addressed by Lord Byron to his much-loved sister, the only being on whom throughout the fitful fever of his life his heart fondly and constantly rested—

> Thou dids't remind me of our own dear lake
>   By the old hall that may be mine no more;
> Leman is fair, but think not I forsake
>   The sweet remembrance of a dearer shore.
> Sad havoc Time must with my memory make
>   Ere that or this can fade these eyes before:
> Tho', like all things that I have loved, they are
>   Resigned for ever or divided far.
>
> I feel almost at times as I have felt
>   In happy childhood: trees, and flowers, and brooks,
> Which do remember me of where I dwelt,
>   Ere my young mind was sacrificed to books,
> Come as of yore upon me, and can melt
>   My heart with recognition of their looks;
> And even at moments I could think I see
>   Some living thing to love—but none like *thee*.

And so do your letters, dearest mother, breathe a freshness and beauty, and depth of affection, which one must have been, like myself, a sojourner in a strange land for many long, weary years to feel as I do.

SAHUSWAN,
August 23rd, 1836.

Dearest Mother,

  It never rains but it pours. Yesterday I received your letters of March and April, and a letter from Emma. What delightful volumes! There is much in your letters to call for remark, but what surprised me most of all was a notice in one of Ellen's letters to you of her having taken up Shakespeare again. What! I exclaimed, Ellen, the Ayott Lady Bountiful, whom I had imagined absorbed in her girls' schools and boys' schools, and shoes, and petticoats, and shifts, read Shakespeare!! And then I chuckled inwardly at having found an *ally* where I least expected one, for, to tell you the truth, I was afraid that Shakespeare had been banished from her library as an improper book. Read Mrs. Jameson's "Characteristics," and see what an exquisite use of it an elegant and accomplished female mind can make. It is the most beautifully written book I think I ever met with, and brings to light a thousand beauties which the coarser minds of Shakespeare's men-critics and commentators for the last 200 years have passed over. As for any occasional coarsenesses that may be found in the plays, I can only repeat to the purer reader an anecdote of Dr. Johnson's. A lady, a wit and a blue-stocking, had been paying her court to the Doctor the whole evening most assiduously, and at last said, "My dear Doctor Johnson, I am so happy to find that there are no improper words in your Dictionary." "And I, Madam," said the Doctor, with a look of thunder, "am sorry to find that you have been looking for them!" I hope with all my heart that Ellen will continue her readings, as I shall then have someone to talk to about my favourite book on my return.

September 18th—

  Since I last took up my pen I have been to Budaoon, a large ruinous old town in my dominions, which I believe I have described in some former letter. The occasion of my going there was a serious one, being no less than a religious dispute between the Hindoos and Mussulmans of the town, which had well-nigh ended in a popular tumult. If an outbreak once takes place, consequences the most serious, independently of mere loss of life, are sure to follow. A dispute of this nature which occurred at Bareilly some seventeen or eighteen years ago, reached so alarming a height that a mere chance prevented our being swept off the face of Upper India like chaff before the hosts of infuriated Mussulmans. Many European officers have lost their lives in attempting to interpose in these religious quarrels, and it was only in the past year that a civilian in the Madras Presidency, who had endeavoured to quell a disturbance of this nature, was cut to pieces along with his guard, which consisted of eight or ten Sepoys. In short, a Mussulman, when his bigotry is once inflamed, is more like a wild beast than a man, and on the slightest indignity offered to his religion, or, in other words, to his place of worship or stated ceremonies, his sword is unsheathed, the green standard of the Prophet is hoisted, death is proclaimed to all *kafirs* (infidels), including, of course, Christians, and then woe betide the public officer, who is bound by his duty and the honourable spirit of his profession to act as mediator. Daniel in the lion's den is nothing to his situation. Fortunately, although matters had proceeded to a great length before I could arrive, the event in my case has been more fortunate, otherwise the above fragment of a letter would have been the last you would have received from me. The Mussulmans, it appears, had taken offence at some Hindoo procession, which they pelted with brickbats. An altercation ensued, crowds collected, and swords were drawn, but fortunately the police arrived at the spot in time and quelled the tumult. A day or two afterwards, a Hindoo drawing water early in the morning from a well in the middle of the town, fished up a piece of fresh beef (beef, as the flesh of the sacred animal of the Hindoo, is as great an abomination to them as pork is to Mussulmans or Jews), which had been thrown in by some Mussulman, and the same was found in several other wells in different parts of the Hindoo portion of the town. Pieces of beef were also found in several of their temples, which were defiled of course in consequence. They retaliated by throwing some filth into one or two mosques, which were defiled in their turn. The Mussulmans, although the first aggressors, were instantly in a flame. The town is about twenty miles from Sahuswan, and intelligence of the affair up to the last crisis reached me in the night, five days ago. I immediately started off, and a wretched ride I had of it. The night was as dark as pitch, the road deluged with rain and running through several deep swamps, and my mind wrought up to a pitch of anxiety which was fully justified by the occasion. I felt quite sick at the stomach from apprehension and anxiety, not personal, but general, although it would be absurd to affirm that there was not some slight sprinkling of personal anxiety into the bargain. On my arrival at Budaoon early in the morning, I found the conchs and gongs blowing and beating on the part of the Hindoos; and the Mussulmans, on the other hand, quite furious, and only waiting for the flash of the train to commence, but most luckily it had not yet been lighted. I immediately sent for the chief inhabitants of the towns, several of whom were personally known to me before. They attended in numbers, Hindoos and Mussulmans. I was apprehensive of their angry passions, which had now been thoroughly excited, finding vent on the spot, for a few words of abuse on both sides would have been sufficient to produce an instant collision, which would have spread like wild-fire, and God only knows what might then have happened; so I went out and harangued them, telling them I would have no tumultuous assemblage, and that it would be impossible for me to reconcile their differences or do justice to either party unless they separated, leaving with me whichever of their headmen they chose to depute. I had pushed into the middle of the crowd, and stood perfectly alone; they cleared a space for me, a sign which I hailed as a good omen, and which gave me undoubted confidence,—and confidence was needed, for most of them were armed, and they stood with their hands on their swords scowling at one another. A look of alarm or indecision, a twinkling of the eye-lid even, would have finished me. But separate they did, at least a few yards, and I then selected a dozen deputies from each party to confer with, telling the mob that they could not expect me to do anything either one way or the other unless they moved off. This, too, they did after a little persuasion, in which I was aided by their self-elected deputies, and I posted immediately afterwards two or three horsemen whom I had brought with me, the whole of my force, in the vicinity of my quarters. But the story is getting a long one. Suffice to say that by conciliation, cajolery, promises, kindness and threats applied to both parties, but more particularly to the Hindoos, who are less bigoted and consequently more easily worked upon than the Mussulmans, to whom my conciliation was chiefly directed, I succeeded in appeasing them, and left Budaoon, after three days' stay, —during which time I had prevailed upon both parties to re-consecrate, or rather purify, their temples and mosques, as well as their wells,— quite tranquil, no personal violence having been committed on either side. I trust that the dispute will not be revived, but there is no knowing, for mischievous persons are always at hand to fan the flame in all popular disturbances. At all events I have done all I could in the business, and longer I could not stay there, my duties calling me to Sahuswan. A magistrate's office in this country is no sinecure, and he is frequently thrown into difficult and harassing situations like the above, which try him to the core.

CAMP,

October 8th, 1836.

Dearest Mother,

I have just heard of the death of my poor friend Louis. He had gone to the hills, where his wife was, intending to bring her down, with the children, next month, and exposed himself incautiously in a shooting excursion at a season of the year which is universally unhealthy in the hills as well as the plains. This brought on a fever, which carried him off after a few days' illness. He is the first of our Sahuswan party—who will leave next?

If anything were to happen to Bentall now, I should feel as if the last five years had been spent by me in some cave or desert, apart from all communion with man, for there would be no one left with whom I could recall old days.

This day, twenty years ago, I was launched from the nursery into Dr. Knight's school at Bradford. Well I remember the day. What an age to look back to. Oh! Time, Time, Time! These deaths are saddening, and make one revert to the past instead of looking forward to the future.

I have just been reading the "Memoirs of Mirabeau." It is not the kind of work to please or interest you, but I have been wrapt up in it during the perusal. Eloise and Abelard, Mirabeau and his Sophie, Lord Byron and the Countess Guiccioli are merely counterparts of each other—the same burning, deep, and tender language of passion on the woman's side, with a similar return for a time on the man's, ending eventually in coldness, and silence, and estrangement. I like these commentaries on the human heart, afforded by the private biographies of eminent men. What a state of things in France prior to the Revolution does the life of Mirabeau present! Surely the Revolution, notwithstanding all its horrors, was a blessing in sweeping them at once off the face of the earth. Our Revolution— and depend upon it we shall have one before long, that is to say, a radical change in the Constitution suited to the temper of the times— will be a moral one, and we shall have to set the world an example in this, as we did, a century and a half ago, in a constitutional one. The times are critical, and, penned up as I am here, I pine to be in England, were it merely to be a close observer of events and changes, which will, probably, be perfected before my return. When that return may be, remains to be seen. If it were a year nearer, despite of the strong distaste I feel to go home before my ten years of actual service are well expired, still, with my present feelings, I should find it difficult to look forwards to another fifteen months of exile in the Sahuswan jungles.

October 15th—

I received to-day your letter of May. It is redolent of spring—the beautiful spring of old England, with its flowers, and buds, and blossoms, whereas mine is like a scroll from a churchyard. You talk of the lark and the songs of birds; I, of India and the grave. Shall I ever see again one of those hedgerows you speak of, or an autumn sunset, or a spring violet? Oh! this is a wearisome life, a life of dulness and deprivation, a scene of intimacies quenched by death or separation as soon as they begin to ripen. I groan in spirit over the past and future. I lament my youth, wasted in this melancholy country, and I look forward to my future years of service with a sickening feeling which I certainly never expected to experience in the outset of my career nine years ago. This is not grumbling or discontent, and must not be understood by you as such. My lot, as I have frequently said before, is fixed, and I shall abide by it to the end. Your description of the lark, tired with its soaring and song, and sinking exhausted amongst the grass and flowers, is quite beautiful, and made my heart ache; and so are your stories of bye-gone days about the birds. The bird you mention, which builds a nest like a reticule, and suspends it to a branch, is a very common one in this country, and I have seen half-a-dozen hanging to a bush, and waving backwards and forwards with every motion of the supporting twig. They are beautifully and, at the same time, strongly built, and I have pulled at an old one that I found on the ground with all my force without being able to tear it asunder. It is nearly a foot in length, with a little hole on one side for the bird to creep into, and yet this little bird is one of the smallest, if not the very smallest, of the feathered tribe in this part of India.

Dearest Mother,

Once more in my favourite encampment near the broad Ganges. It is an old mud fort, of which the mud walls alone are extant. Large mango trees have grown up in the area, which time has levelled and covered with a fragrant grass, cropt short by the cattle, like the grass-plots in England. From the mud bastions I overlook the Ganges, its banks, and the grassy islands in the centre, to the extent of four or five miles. At my feet lies a lake, studded with wild fowl, wild ducks, widgeon and teal, of every genus imaginable, and a plain abounding with hares and partridges. I came here first by chance, in the commencement of 1832, very shortly after my arrival in the district; again in 1833, twice, when I stayed nearly a month here; again in 1834, twice; again in 1835, three times. Every tree and bush has its separate memories, for this was our favourite meeting-ground, and much harmless fun and many a hearty laugh have passed on the spot where I am now writing to you. Of the four who used to meet here, three are scattered—one, my poor friend Louis, in his grave in the Himalayas; the second to Hurriana, the Hissar district; the third, Bentall, to Bengal. I have been out all day to-day, from eight o'clock to sunset, wandering through my old haunts, picking up such game as I could find, and sitting, or rather lying, amongst the long grass, enjoying the sight of the cheerful stream of the Ganges, and inhaling the fine fresh breeze which is always to be found on its banks. Still there has been a weight on my mind. Bentall may join me again elsewhere, if not here; and so may Wright,—but the grave cannot give back its dead. *They* sleep the sleep that knows no wakening, or, as my favourite Greek lines say, of which I gave Fred a very tolerable paraphrase some years ago—

$$\text{ἀνάκοοι ἐν χθονὶ κοιλᾷ}$$
$$\text{Ἔυδομεν εὖ μαλὰ μακρὰν ἀτερμονα ἀρρετον ὕπνον.}$$

Blake, my classical friend, who asked me to translate this quotation, which had struck us when we were reading old Homer together, at the Cootub, five years ago —where is he? And Elliot, an exclusive and fastidious man, who sought my society whilst he shunned the common-place, give-and-take sort of life at Delhi,—where is he? And Louis, my constant companion at this place, with whom I have passed many a pleasant evening after the day's exercise,—

where is he? These are melancholy thoughts. They oppress me occasionally; and as I am a man of habit, even in trifles, and make a point of visiting, if I can, my old haunts in the district every year, they are not likely to be soon blunted,—not, at least, as long as I remain here. I was encamped here in March last, for a week, with Bentall. After dinner we used to adjourn to the bastion fronting the Ganges, and carry on our conversation in the brilliant moonlight. This kind of life cements in one hour acquaintanceships and friendships which it would have required years in England to form; and so far, this is one of the advantages which I am willing to concede to India,—but then of what use are they but as food for regret? A day scatters and separates us for ever, and death only reduces the separation to a certainty.

November 12th—

I received yesterday the following letter from the private secretary to our Governor :—

"My dear Sir,—I am desired to ascertain whether you would like to be appointed Magistrate and Collector of the Hurrianeh division of the Delhi territory, in the event of that situation becoming vacant by Mr. Neave's transfer to another office."

Hurrianeh is the name of the tract of country of which Hissar is the station. How singular that I should keep knocking about between two such stations as Sahuswan and Hissar! Of course I replied that my object was promotion, and that I would willingly avail myself of any opening afforded me, either at Hissar or elsewhere; so it remains to be seen when I shall receive my appointment. My tactics are as follows. To Hissar again I am determined not to go, although I do not of course tell them so. I was sick, uncomfortable, and unhappy all the time I was there, and I feel a thorough disgust for the place and country. In the interim I hope to get appointed to Hissar, and to draw the allowances of the situation in the same way that the nominal Collector and Magistrate of this district is doing; and ten to one but that the appointment of Collector and Magistrate here, in which I am at present officiating, becomes vacant intermediately, in which case I shall apply to be appointed here instead of at Hissar; in other words, to have my appointment transferred from Hissar to Sahuswan. I do not anticipate much difficulty in effecting this, and then I shall have all I want. At all events, happen what may, as soon as I am myself gazetted for a permanent Collectorship, all that I have been striving for, for the last year, will have been gained. It is an important step in the service, and raises me at once to the highest rank and salary I could desire. I shall be fortunate in obtaining my promotion sooner than nine-tenths of the service.

November 14th—

I often blame myself for indulging in any feeling in my letters to you. You do not, and you will not, understand me,—or rather, the situation in which I am placed. Any occasional burst is looked upon as an ebullition of *sentiment*,—something, I suppose, in the style of the Sorrows of Werter; so, at least, says Ellen, who is the spokeswoman of the family in such matters, and justly too, for she is the cleverest and the most clear-headed of us. I, a man, to indulge in vapid sentiment! I detest the word, which is only suited to boarding-school misses, who half expire over the fashionable novels of the present day. If I live to return to England, you will see the superficies of my character—the character in which I have appeared in this country—a tolerably good-natured, good-humoured man, quick in his feelings, fond of a little quiet satire, and devoted to fun wherever it can be found. By placing all the other more hidden traits down to *sentiment*, you reduce me at once to the very common-place character which I have described, and which is shared with me by tens of thousands. My letters to you for the last nine years, if I ever happen to see them again, will contain, for me at least, a record not of facts but of feelings. They were clear and vivid at the time I wrote them down; they amounted almost to a passion, and they took its language. I never strained after *sentiment*, and all expression of sentiment implies an effort, for which I never had need. It seems as if you required to be, like myself, nine years in the jungles of India, to understand the difference. People look upon Indians as callous and hard-hearted men in general,—and is it to be wondered at? We come out to this country in the hey-day of our existence, with all the warm feelings of our youth about us; we meet, in our own countrymen, with a care-devil sort of demeanour and a thorough selfishness; in the natives, with plausibility and a show of everything that is amiable, and estimable, and attractive, which we find, after a short experience, to be but paint on a sepulchre; we are thrust into duties occupying the whole of our thoughts and time, which bring us in contact daily with crime and fraud of every shape and hue—the worst and vilest features of human nature. I never shall forget the constant shocks which I was receiving at that warm and trusting period of my life, on my first entrance on active public duties. And yet with all this, which one would think would be sufficient to fossilize any heart,—and which, as far as this world is concerned, has undoubtedly hardened my ears,—I have preserved an under-current of affections towards persons and things, which have grown with my growth and strengthened with my strength, until they have become as part and parcel of my being. Do not set down my occasional expression of these hidden feelings to *sentiment*. You should have known that sentiment is too luxurious a plant to live in this chilling country.

November 18th—

I have just returned from Sahuswan, where I was summoned by express by Alexander, to bury his eldest girl, who died suddenly after a lingering illness. Poor little child! I forgive her all her squallings and cryings. I saw her in her coffin, and she looked beautiful, almost angelic, with the tiny shroud wrapped around her, and her pale, cold face, so sad and peaceful, as if her long illness had worked traces on her childish countenance which Death even could not smooth. I felt quite melancholy in having to commit so young and fair a flower to the weeds and rank grass of the Sahuswan compound; but it was a happy release for her, for she was invariably ill.

Lay her i' the earth;
And from her fair and unpolluted flesh
May violets spring!

There are no accompaniments of this kind, I fear, in this country to make Death picturesque. Death here is bare, and divested of the sentiment of a churchyard and flowers. All is cold, icy reality. The first idea of death I ever had was on the death of little Monier. I remember, as if it were yesterday, standing near the coffin, which was placed in the room between your bedroom and the nursery, and looking at the little lump of clay within, covered with blossoms and early flowers, and wondering what death was, and whether this, which looked so beautiful, was death. And when was this? I quite forget the year, but the occurrence is clearly imprinted on my memory. It must be a long, long time ago, for everything around it is a blank and a shadow.

November 20th—

What I last wrote *is* sentiment, I suppose, if you must have the word in your vocabulary, as it refers to others, so I am sorry I wrote it.

The annual fair is at its height to-day, and I have the sound of 150,000 people—for I really do not think there can be fewer—buzzing, or rather roaring, in my ears. The multitude would astonish you. Their encampments extend a good five miles along the banks of the river, and the temporary shops or booths, of every article eatable and vendible, form a street two miles long. But I have described it to you before. To-morrow is the grand bathing day.

W.   M

HISSAR CAMP,
January 14th, 1837.

Dearest Mother,

Here I am, once more encamped on the very spot where
I first pitched my tents in this district seven weary years ago.
I would not live them over again for worlds. How different have
they been to all of you—I question whether you will not look back
upon them as the happiest of your lives. My return to this part of
the world makes me feel as if all the intervening period has been a
dream. Poor, dear, old Sahuswan! The people there regretted my
departure much, and it was painful to me to have to leave it without
bidding them farewell. I have had many kind messages and many
regretful letters from my native friends there, as well as from the
Alexanders and others, and I think I have reason to say that I have
left behind me there a name which will not soon be forgotten. Circumstances had thrown me much with the natives there, and we knew
each other mutually. There are many excellent traits in the native
character, so many, indeed, that it has often struck me as surprising
that they should have been found to exist at all, despite of the long
ages of their misrule and the baneful effects of their early education.
All they require is kindness and firmness, and with a little management you can make anything of them, from attached friends to
obedient subjects. I shall long remember with gratified feelings the
five years spent by me at Sahuswan, though, as I have said above, I
would not willingly live them over again.

January 20th—

Well, my diploma has at last arrived, and I am now Magistrate
and Collector of Hissar, on a salary of 2,000 rupees per mensem, or
2,400*l.* a year; and whatever I may think of my appointment in
other respects, I am singularly lucky in attaining so high a rank and
allowances within nine years of actual residence in the country, and
in so satisfactory a manner. I am no longer liable now to have my
salary retrenched a half or two-thirds on the occasion of unavoidable
absence, from ill-health or any other cause. The utmost I can lose
by absence is a seventh of my allowances; but what is much more
satisfactory to me, I have obtained a permanent rank in the service,
which has raised me by a single step over many of my seniors. I
cannot now fall lower, and if I live to return to this country I shall

have a good claim to higher promotion. Certainly nothing since I have been in India has given me more pleasure than the receipt of the letter announcing my appointment two days ago,—so wish me joy, and do not, for God's sake, revert ever again to private interest, which I despise, more particularly from the false impression entertained of its efficacy by one's friends at home.

I am pitched now at a spot which I visited first six and a half years ago, at the base of a ridge of volcanic rocks, which rise out of the plain perpendicularly almost, not far from the desert. If a man is at all disposed to the blue devils, never let him come to Hissar, for they abound here, and become, even to me, really oppressive. They have given me as Assistant here a great he-fellow, as big as myself, but with little in him to make a companion of; at all events, he will relieve me of a good deal of troublesome duties, and an official help-mate is needed at a place like Hissar.

January 30th—

Once more on the verge of the desert! Again amongst the sand-hills! I recollect encamping here six weary years ago. The face of this part of the country I need scarcely say changes not from century to century. It is ever the same. For changes we must look to ourselves, and changed I am in many respects since I was last here; but who notes the changes, or who cares for them? I have not one-fourth of the exuberance of feeling now-a-days that I had then. India has had the same effects on me that it has had on all, and were I to remain in the country without a break a few years longer, I should forget, or think but little, of anything at home but your affection.

CAMP, HANSI,
February 9th, 1837.

Dearest Mother,

I have just received your August letter. It contains my brothers' letters from the Continent, and highly interesting they have proved. I regret that they were prevented going to Venice, but, after all, at their age the Tyrol, I doubt not, has afforded them livelier pleasure. At least, I can say for myself, that I had a craving then which nothing but scenery satisfied, and Rome and Venice would have weighed nothing in the balance against Switzerland. *Now* I should give the preference to the former. The Himalayas have spoiled me for any mountainous scenery, and I would rather look on a green meadow with its daisies, and a little rivulet running through it, than upon Mont Blanc or the Jungfrau. Besides, Venice would have an interest now to me which I had no conception of in my nonage,—the interest of recollections and romance, history and fiction.

If life and health last I hope to return to England with 5,000*l.* in all, a larger sum certainly than I ever expected to realize by the time of my furlough. My savings were first in a manner unintentional, and even now they scarcely merit the name, which, by-the-bye, I am not partial to; they are bonâ fide the surplus of my expenditure, and it is to the out-of-the-way places in which I have been thrown that they have been owing, and not to any forced or self-imposed system of my own. I shall feel something like independent with 10,000*l.* in the Funds, and, much as the sum is, I am thankful that I have been able to raise myself and been raised above the passing hour. It will have been dearly purchased. Like Cleopatra, I shall have dissolved in the cup many a pearl of great price, many a listless and misspent hour, many a warm feeling, many an aching and unsatisfied longing, and the best and freshest part of existence already past and gone—gone, gone for ever, without a track or a flower, or so much even as could form itself into a dream of past enjoyment. I would to God, I sometimes inwardly exclaim, that I had never come to this deadening country, and then the thought of independence checks the feeling, but not always, for independence looks to the future, whereas I live in the past. My furlough at present terminates my horizon. All beyond that is like the sea in Mirza's vision, indistinct and colourless. You may think this rhapsody or affectation, and you will say so when you see me; but they are the true expression of feelings wrung out of my heart by silence and solitude. I would keep them to myself, but I cannot. It is a feeling, I am confident, that all men in this country more or less entertain, but they obliterate or drown it in the early part of their career, and take kindly to a life which, when examined, will be found the dreariest and dullest of all,—a bedizened corpse, a painted sepulchre.

Two or three civilians from this part of the world embarked at Bombay in the steamer last month, and must have arrived at Suez. The overland route by Egypt is getting in vogue, and I have no doubt that two years hence it will be adopted by many on the Bombay side and by not a few here in preference to the tedious sea voyage, which I will never encounter again if I can help it. By the end of next year the means of conveyance will also be greatly improved; the only difficulty to us will be the overland journey to Bombay from the Upper Provinces; but what is a trip of 700 or 800 miles to a man, who has once set his face homewards?

February 16th—

What a glorious day this has been, "the bridal of the earth and sky,"—a mild, genial, Italian spring day, beautiful, beautiful exceedingly. I gave myself a holiday, and have been rambling for many a long hour over sand-hill and plain, with my gun in my hand and my dogs at my heels, and never did I enjoy myself in this country more. I started at eight o'clock in the morning with my men and a basket of prog, which, by-the-bye, I never neglect in my shooting excursions, and, after killing five brace of hares and as many partridges, I lay down in the shade during the heat of the day, looking up to the brilliant blue sky, and actually fancied myself happy. Certainly if I can remember anything in this country with pleasure, it will be the days stolen from business and spent in rambling over the country; but then the day was an exquisite one, owing to the rain we had had before. In the hollows between the sand-hills game of every sort abounds—hares, partridges, quail, deer, pea-chicks, &c., &c.; not that I care much for them, for all that I kill I give to my men, who tuck into them furiously. What I like and what I feel is the healthful exercise and the feeling of independence, like that of a boy let loose from school.

Dearest Mother,

CAMP,

April 19th, 1837.

My birthday, and I forgot all about it until just this minute, when writing the date to the letter, and I am eight and twenty! How Time slips away! It is nearly ten years now since I left England. What a little eternity ten years appeared to me at that time, and lo! it is gone already on its way to the shadowless past. I was scarcely sensible of its lapse until I had reached the wrong side of five and twenty, and then the thought used to occur to me of how the best and most elastic portion of my life had been spent in almost uninterrupted solitude in the deserts and jungles, and I began to mourn over it, as everything that comes not again is mourned over. I dare say you have smiled at some of the passages in my letters, in which I have touched on the best days of my life as if I were a sexagenarian; but then you know not India. Willis has a pretty passage to the point where he says, " Oh, lost days of minority or thereabouts! oh primal manhood! oh golden time! when we have let go all but the enthusiasm of the boy and seized hold of all but the selfishness of the man! Why can we not bottle up thy hours like the wine of a better vintage, and enjoy them in the parched world-weariness of age! In the tardy honeymoon of a bachelor, with what joy of Paradise should we bring up from the cellars of the past a bumper of that sunny Hippocrene!" The only difference is that in my case I have nothing to bottle up but the milk and water of my hobbledehoy days, and this may turn sour. I would far rather strike the next ten years from my life than have to live the last ten over again; and what a cheerless life must a man's have been when he can form such a wish! An acquaintance at Hansi the other day happening to stumble on the passage, asked me what Hippocrene was, and I told him brandy and water, with which, as he is rather partial to the beverage, he remained perfectly satisfied. I am still in tents, grilling and melting away like a piece of fat bacon, and all the consolation I get from my friends, who would faint at the idea of being exposed to the sun and hot winds in a bare plain in April, is " Oh! you can afford to lose a little." I hope to get housed by the 1st of next month, but shall stay only a short time at Hissar, as I intend to take up my quarters in a bungalow on the borders of my district until the close of the rains, or rather until the close of the sickly season at Hansi. The bungalow has only one room, but discomforts are a trifle compared with the Hansi fever, which I shall get to a certainty if I stay at head-quarters. The secret of "keeping moving" is one that the Hansi folks either don't know or won't practice, and the consequence is that the fever has settled upon them like an incubus and destroyed their health permanently. One poor fellow went off the other day with the loss of his eyesight, another with a dreadful dysentery, another with a liver complaint, another with a diseased spleen, and so on,—all the effects of the fever. Withal, now that I have accommodated myself to the district, I would not return to Sahuswan if the offer were made me—I am not fond of changes, and I like my duties and situation here much better than I expected. This wild race of people, in this unfrequented and almost unknown part of the world, know me of old, and we get on well together.

April 24th—

Nothing is talked of but the near approach of the plague, and I have been called upon to establish a cordon of posts on the frontier of my district, and to set on foot quarantine, all which is literally impossible in an open country, and I have told the Government so, recommending them to establish an inner cordon to arrest the plague before it gets across the Jumna, instead of attempting the mad experiment of a cordon on a tract of 150 miles in length. If they adopt my proposition my district will be shut out from the line of posts, and be regarded as an infected one, and treated accordingly, so that with plague and fever the prospect before me for the ensuing hot weather is not the pleasantest imaginable.

April 26th—

I have been looking over some of your letters of the early part of 1836. What touching extracts could be made from the volumes of your letters in my possession! It is for this I keep them. Let me transcribe one or two passages from your May letter, written on the occasion of your last visit to Bath and its haunted scenes. They are very beautiful, and raise the moisture to my eyes.

" We entered our fly at half-past six, and took our way to another haunt of our past days—to Weston. We went to that beautiful lane which leads to the Bristol road and to Sigmund the dentist's cottage. We sat on the stile; and then returning, went quite to the end of Weston village, where we got out and walked nearly an hour in some of our beloved fields of later date than your time, called by us 'The Happy Valley.' We saw the sun set, and mused on worldly removals and separations, and uncertainties and anxieties—then resumed our fly, and ended in our favourite haunt in the park, paying it also a last farewell."

Again,—

" In the morning Emma and I got into a fly and went all round the Upper Crescent, up Lansdown, looking on Winifred House to the left with the nursery window in view where you all used to live. Then we turned to the right, into that beautiful lane leading to Charlcomb, by the same old farm-house, to the gate leading into the Church Field. Then we left our convenient little vehicle and walked to the churchyard, sat on its wall, sat on the timbers by the saw-pit, gathered a veronica and hawthorn, which Emma put into her pocket Testament to-day, and which is going out to you in the next letter, if it does not become dust by the way; yet if it become dust, it will be almost holy dust. The morning was lovely—the sun shone, but no shadow—there was a delicate, sympathetic gloom in its softness—a sort of farewell tint—for surely with my children I shall never more walk there, nor, indeed, ever again at all. I turned at the gate and looked back, and a crowd of deep but varied feelings rushed to my heart. Emma's childhood met her at every gate and stile—and our hearts were full!"

And so is mine at this moment, full even to bursting, and my eyes are full too, and my spectacles are dimmed with moisture. Never did I read anything more exquisitely touching, and yet so simple—the true language of the heart. Mine sinks when I revert to these scenes, as if I had already taken my last look at them. Oh, India! India! . . . . .

May 3rd—

I have been sorting to-day my old letters and papers, and I found a curious medley of them. Some of your letters and Ellen's of 1827 and 1828 I have read again, and very sweet and beautiful I found them; some of the chits that used to pass between McKenzie and myself when we were both Writers studying in Loudon Buildings; the last tokens of deceased friends; the correspondence of others my seniors during the first three or four years of my Indian career; a bundle of papers, consisting of notes that passed between Trevelyan, Sir Edward, and myself during the investigation at Delhi; letters nine years old; letters written by natives in defiance of the King's English, soliciting service; and a mass of other indescribables I have been routing over, and recalling at the same time old days and old scenes. For the last five years I have received few, if any, letters worth keeping—your's and my friends at home of course excepted. My former correspondents have either died or been scattered, and none of the Hippocrene that Willis talks of has been left to give them a flavour. Yours, dearest Mother, are like the widow's cruise, and the draught after nine years is as fresh as it was then.

May 4th—

I have had another read at yours and dear Ellen's letters of 1828, 1829, in their chronological order. They have set me wandering again in the regions of the past. Why should I disturb the visions?

It seems to me as if I had passed over too hastily at the time the deep recurring affection of Ellen's letters,—so warm, so cheerful, so *à propos*. They and yours combined give me a complete picture of your domestic life eight years ago. It ought to be set in a frame of gold. And then your quaint fun made me laugh again heartily, as when you tell me very seriously and consolingly that you are sure it will please me to hear that " Mr. Gough's pigs" (meaning Fred and Joe) are becoming quite well-mannered and refined, and that Charley Babington was studying eleven hours a-day for honors, and " how he must have contracted his brow and twisted his nose about like a rabbit;" and, again, the concise notice of Mr. Heckford's dwarf's decease, " Mr. Heckford's dwarf is just dead—should think his soul was as disgusting as his body!" Oh, there is a mine of deep feelings and tender expressions in these letters that must not perish; they have ever their refrain by mine. There was an unlucky expression used by some one of you sometime ago, in which mine were spoken of as *sentimental*. God knows there is too much of the dull, cold, barren reality of life in a dreary sojourn of eight years in the jungles to admit of any ground-work for sentiment. There can be no strained feeling in such a situation beyond the natural effect of nature. Oh, that dreadful, dreary spell of eight years, cheerless and companionless, and unbroken, save by short intervals of boisterous amusement! My dear, dear Mother, you never can realize anything of the kind. Mine has been an existence during that period beyond the sphere of yours; a separate world in itself, and most certainly very far from a happy one. You cannot enter fully into the high-wrought feelings of the sojourner in the wilderness, which are all the stronger from being only occasionally drawn forth. But enough of this. What have I, a great fat man, to do with sentiment, if you will call it by that name. I wish you wouldn't, for it sticks in my gizzard, and I am afraid to write what may be looked upon in that light as fustian. Again I exclaim, oh, India! India! My heart is bitter against it sometimes, and at no period more so than when I revert to your old letters, which show me what I have lost, never to be recalled, never to be enjoyed again—never, never!

May 5th—

I met the other day by chance with a little book called the "Seven Temptations," by Mary Howitt, published three or four years ago. It is not poetry, but merely sweet and tender thoughts and expressions put into unpretending rhyme; yet the simple pathos of many of the passages pleased me much, as I think they would you. The " poor scholar" is lying sick and dying in his room at evening,

attended by a little boy, the only one out of the class of his scholars
who had remained by his sick master. Him, too, he sends away to
his play, after addressing him in a few simple and touching lines of
advice, and then lays himself down on his bed, faint and wearied, in
expectation of his end. The tempter enters, assails him, is baffled,
and the "poor scholar" is once more left alone to die. He kneels
beside his "pallet-bed" and prays :—

> *Schol.*—Almighty God, look down
>   Upon Thy feeble servant. Strengthen him;
>   Give him the victor's crown,
>   And let not faith be dim !
>   Oh ! how unworthy of Thy grace—
>   How poor, how needy ; stained with sin !
>   How can I enter in
>   Thy kingdom, and behold Thy face ?
>   Except Thou hadst redeemed me, I had gone
>   Without sustaining knowledge to the grave.
>   For this I bless Thee—oh ! Thou gracious One—
>   And Thou wilt surely save.
>   I bless Thee for the life which Thou hast crowned
>   With never-ending good ;
>   For pleasures that were found,
>   Like wayside flowers, in quiet solitude.
>   I bless Thee for the love that watched o'er me
>   Through the weak years of infancy ;
>   That has been, like Thine everlasting truth,
>   The guide, the guardian angel of my youth.
>   Oh ! Thou that didst the mother's heart bestow,
>   Sustain it in its woe :
>   For mourning give it joy, and praise for heaviness.
>   [*He falls back—his mother enters hurriedly.*]
> *Mother.*—Alas, my son ! and am I come too late ?
>   *   *   *   *   *   *   *

This is scarcely poetry,—but be it what it may, it is very simple,
and touching, and soothing; and I can fancy your sweet-toned and
feeling voice reading it aloud with true pathos. What a crowd of
exquisite female writers have sprung up in England within this
century, and how different from the *bas bleu* women of literature of
the times of Johnson ! They have written, too, as women should
only write, on the feelings and affections; in short, on what they
understand better than men, instead of entering the lists with them,
and babbling about literature and the *belles lettres.* Mary Howitt is
the most sweet, and natural, and true of all, and I have met occasionally with many beautiful things from her pen in the shape of ballads,
descriptive touches, &c., &c.

But I must leave poetry, and go to my Cutcherry, to be suffocated
with the heat, and noise, and bad smells, instead of taking a ramble
by some brook at home, with the book in my hand, and reading its
quiet and gliding versification by the side of the quiet and gliding
stream, its flowing accompaniment.

Hissar,
June 8th, 1837.

My dear, dear Mother,

     I wrote you a very cross letter last month, and I have since been reading, again, a number of your late letters, by way of completing the series of the family correspondence since 1828, which I have gone through lately. My softer feelings have revived under their influence, and my heart smites me for penning a line calculated to cause pain to your tenderest and most loving of hearts. Beautiful, indeed, are your letters,—most beautiful! Surely such letters were never written before by a mother to her child. Surely such tenderness was never poured forth so abundantly with so poor a return. How often have I wished I could recompense it by a similar outpouring of the heart before you, which you have so frequently and earnestly longed for; but my affections, my dear mother, if deep, are hidden, and I cannot unlock the heart and bring it forth to the day like those who have been living in your bosom for the last ten years, in the constant interchange of family love. A call upon me for the display of my feelings only leads me to repress their expression still more, and hence the lifeless replies which you receive, in return for your chronicles of affection. It is my nature, and ever was so, and I cannot help it as long as I remain in this chilling, deadening country, which has long ago rubbed the gloss off my wings by its unsocial influences. I am ready enough, as in my last letter, to expatiate upon what I like or dislike, at any cost, but my hand is powerless to apply the balm. Not so my heart yet; it is as warm as ever, and the sweet tone of your letters has already revenged itself on it for the impatience of my temper, under advice or rebuke. In this respect I can never change; and if you do not receive the outward signs of my affection so frequently from me as from my brothers, do not attribute the omission to any other cause but this peculiarity of disposition. If I cannot write so fully and glowingly as you wish, I can *speak,* and if we ever meet again my voice shall not be silent or constrained. Bear, then, awhile, with any occasional pettishness, and leave me nothing to grumble about, by removing the cause, which I have so unsparingly pointed out. India has left its mark upon me already. Do you think that a young man, brought in contact with fraud, and vice and crime every day of his life, and excluded from all friendly intercourse with his fellow countrymen for nearly ten years, can improve? I fear not. His character unavoidably hardens; its asperities become more prominent; its good qualities more hidden than before. He becomes, by degrees, suspicious, reserved, imperious, and it is well if his heart does not harden, too. A life in the jungles has many drawbacks, and is the last I should recommend to my son. I must copy another extract from your August letter, written at the time of your departure from Bath. How well I can enter into your feelings on the occasion. The extracts are not given so much for yourself as for your children:—

"The evening I left 32, Park Street, about half-past six, as I descended the stairs I stopped at each tier, and, surveying the empty, melancholy rooms, I sighed, but thanked God for the many, many blessings vouchsafed to me and mine during a lapse of seven years, and praying that a like blessing might attend our going into another residence as had in our sojourn in that ; and, though many sources of interest could not occur again to me, yet one deeply joyous one might to our next, which 32, Park Street, never knew. I then took an affectionate farewell of old Cookey, and, shutting the hall-door on me, which rung as it closed, I hurried down the street. I did not weep, for I was in a street, but my heart was desolate, and the evening was melancholy, windy and cloudy. The dust, blown by the wind into eddies at the corner of the street, seemed to gather round me as if to insult the houseless and the companionless."

Again,—

"I left Miss Pilot's friendly home on the 18th June, at ten in the morning, in a fly, and passed Mrs. Oates's and Winifred House gates, and all the well known scenes of thirty years, on the very day thirty years on which I first put my foot into those grounds and that house ! How very extraordinary ! The day was lovely,— an English summer-day, in its brightness,—which made every object I was bidding adieu to doubly painful. In the very streets of Bath I could call up some tender reminiscences of those so dear to me, some to the grave gone down,—others scattered, and lost to me ! The beautiful new road soothed me, but my mind was sorrowful, and my heart lonely, and I wept much and prayed more. I am glad the struggle is past, and that Bath is now behind me. Very pleasant have its scenes been to me for thirty years."

Very beautiful, and sweet, and touching, are those expressions of your feelings, my dearest Mother. I can enter into them well, and I have felt for you when reading them, as deeply and tenderly as your heart could desire.

June 26th—

On tumbling about my drawer of papers the other day, I met with a bundle of the school letters of " Mr. Gough's pigs" (Fred and Joe), written to you in 1828. They are full of stories about stoats and weasels, and goats, and four-footed animals of every kind,—rabbits in particular. The history of the rabbits is kept up through a number of letters, and it appears that you had made a remark on the apparent cruelty in keeping wild animals in cages, for in a letter of Fred's I find the following :—" You greatly mistake our keeping rabbits, for all the rabbits we had got were all born in boxes, so that they do not know what liberty is just like canaries, for we had an old rabbit, and we used to put her out in a large orchard, but she never went away, for she always came back to her box again, and it was the same with most of our rabbits." There is then a pause in the stories in the next letters, until one or two months afterwards, when I find the following pithy piece of news in one of them :—" Mr. Gough wants me to be a clergyman very much. We have killed all our rabbits now, and ate them in pies." A very satisfactory and comfortable way, this, of reconciling one's stomach and conscience. So much for the buoyant days of one's childhood. No one regrets those days, or would wish to live them over again ; but we revert to them fondly when we find that the dew and the freshness of the early morn of one's life are gone for ever.

I am thinking of taking a month's leave of absence next month, and taking a trip to Delhi,—or rather, to my old quarters, at the Cootub, where I spent so pleasant a two months with Trevelyan and Jim Blake, six years ago. I am attached to the spot. I went there for a day in December last, with the senior member of the Sudder Board, and John Thornton, of Clapham, an old Charterhouse contemporary, and found it much improved, and beautiful. It is certainly a striking spot, and a very fair specimen of Indian romantic scenery. I wish I had the patience to sketch in water colours. I should have liked well to have carried about with me some of the scenes of my Delhi life, which I might have reverted to in after years, like Sir Thomas Munro did to the lovely secluded spot, where he lived for some time, amongst the ghauts. My movements, however, now depend wholly on the rains, which have commenced late and unsatisfactorily. If we have anything of a drought I shall be tied to the spot; but I hope for the best. A month at the Cootub would give me new life and vigour, and enable me to stand the brunt of the sickly season here, at the close of the rains. I had better not, however, form plans. How many have I concerted, at different times, to pay a second visit to the Himalayas, which I may now, probably, never see again. But business and duty invariably intervened to disappoint me. Ellen tells me, in her last letter, that they were meditating a second tour to the lakes, with Fred and Joe. How I envy them.

I am sorry, my dear Mother, I cannot bow to your reproof about my use of the word "cant" as applicable to the practice of imputing every accident that may happen to those not within our own pale to a judgment of Providence. The religious world at home have begun to adopt a language of their own, and this is one of their pet phrases. The mind is narrowed by being confined to intercourse with those of one's own class and profession, and notions are fostered and adhered to which will not bear the test of reason or Scripture, amongst which I reckon the above. How different from these were the views of Mortlock, and how carefully he steered clear of everything that approached "cant" in his walk and profession. The same may be said of all religious persons who have been in India, where one loses the narrowness of vision which clings to people on all subjects, more or less, at home.

July 3rd—

Well, six months of the year are already over, and the pleasantest half of it is to come. All well, as yet; no sickness, either amongst my people or elsewhere, though, if this terrible weather continues, much may be looked for. How well do the emphatic words of Scripture describe it—"And the heaven that is over thy head shall be brass, and the earth that is under thee shall be iron, and the Lord shall make the rain of thy land powder and dust." Such is precisely the appearance of things in these burning wastes, in the absence of the periodical rains, which have now been delayed three weeks beyond their usual time, nearly. A noble dog which I have, of the Newfoundland breed, is lying by me, panting and gasping, and I fear the weather will kill him. But it is time that I should close this very uninteresting letter. The July heats of London must be bad enough, and in the confinement, or rather the sense of it, you will be able to realize the misery of one's imprisonment within the house, in this country, for six months of the year.

COOTUB,

September 7th, 1837.

Dearest Mother,

Behold me once more at the Cootub, my old haunt in former times, the spot of our excursions and pic-nics from Delhi. My companions in those days are all either dead or scattered, and I am the only one left in this part of the country of the many who were connected officially with Sir Edward Colebrooke. The tombs and old buildings here are truly tenantless now. I am far too substantial to act the ghost, but having been disappointed in a small party, which I had endeavoured to assemble here for a few days, I wander disconsolate enough amongst the ruins, and find the place too dull for the month's residence I had intended to make here, so that I shall return to Delhi or Hissar a week or ten days earlier. I wrote a short note to-day to Trevelyan, asking him if he had utterly forgot old friends and old times, which had been re-called vividly to my mind by my visit here. I will give you his reply when received. In the mean time I have a young man staying with me who had come out from Delhi for a change of air. He only left England last September, and is looking forward with dismay to the period of his service in this country, which I have been using my best arguments to dispel. His company is quite a relief in the utter solitude of the place. I am lucky in getting away from Sahuswan at the time I did; there has been an utter failure of crops in that part of the country, which has of course brought on a famine, and the starving population are rushing headlong into every crime; I hear of nothing but plundering and burning and wounding and killing in my old district; the villagers have risen en masse and are attacking their neighbours, and the Magistrate is fairly set at defiance. In an adjoining district to Sahuswan the joint Magistrate was wounded lately in the execution of his duty, and everything appears to be in utter confusion. No doubt this will all be put down in time, but my successor's seat must be at present a thorny one. Disease too has trod in the footsteps of famine, and the cholera is killing its hundreds daily. Luckily we on this side of the Jumna have been exempt as yet from any disorders of this kind; the drought has been a severe one here and in the Hissar district, but the soil being lighter the little rain we have had has told more here than in the more clayey soils. My district at all events has, I hope, escaped the horrors of famine in the present year, and I may consider myself fortunate in escaping the scenes of distress and annoyance which I hear of elsewhere.

September 27th—

In that odd but clever book, "The Doctor," I met with the following passage this morning: "Of all things in this immortal pilgrimage one of the most joyful is the returning home after an absence which has been long enough to make the heart yearn with hope and not sicken with it, and then to find when you arrive there that all is well. But the most purely painful of all painful things is to visit, after a long, long interval of time, the place which was once our home; the most purely painful, because it is unmixed with fear, anxiety, disappointment, or any other emotion but what belongs to the sense of time and change, then pressing upon us with its whole unalleviated weight." Such would be my feelings on revisiting Bath and its old scenes. There have been no changes in my family since I was last there to call forth regret or sorrow; the contrast would be purely personal. It is not until my return home that I shall be able to form any idea of what time and change have wrought on myself. I may fancy myself to be the same, but when did twelve years ever pass over a man's head and not leave him far different in most things from what he was in the outset? "The Doctor" speaks to the point on this: "Ten years, if they bring with them only their ordinary portion of evil and of good, cannot pass over anyone's head without leaving their moral as well as physical traces, especially if they have been years of active and intellectual life." And again, "Think of the changes that any ten years in the course of human life produce in body and in mind and in the face, which is in a certain degree the index of both. From thirty to forty is the decade during which the least outward and visible alteration takes place, and yet how perceptible is it during that stage in every countenance that is composed of good flesh and blood—ten years!!" In one of the briefest but most exquisite love-stories I ever met with, which is introduced in the book, the author says, speaking of the young lover, "Young as he was at their separation, his character had taken its stamp during those peaceful years, and the impression which it then received was indelible. Hitherto hope had never been to him so delightful as memory. His thoughts wandered back into the past more frequently than they took flight into the future," &c., &c. What is here said of the lover may be equally applied to the Indian. And here are some exquisite verses, which almost make one young again :—

> Love ? I will tell thee what it is to love !
> It is to build with human thoughts a shrine,
> Where Hope sits brooding like a beauteous dove,
> Where time seems young, and life a thing divine.
> All tastes, all pleasures, all desires combine
> To consecrate this sanctuary of bliss.
> Above, the stars in shroudless beauty shine ;
> Around, the streams their flowery margins kiss,
> And if there's *heaven* on earth, that *heaven* is surely this.

> Yes, this is love, the steadfast and the true,
> The immortal glory which hath never set,
> The best, the brightest boon the heart e'er knew ;
> Of all life's sweets the very sweetest yet !
> Oh ! who but can recall the eve they met
> To breathe in some green walk their first young vow,
> While summer flowers with moonlight dews were wet,
> And winds sighed soft around the mountain's brow,
> And all was *rapture then*—which is but *memory* now !

However, these are fitter for a young lady's album than for a letter written by a man of fifteen stone, of the sober age of eight-and-twenty. They will show you at all events that ten years have not destroyed my taste for these things ; and to that taste I owe much—much more perhaps than I am myself aware of, for it has been my companion in the jungles and preserved my mind from degenerating. I do not believe that a solitary life ever led to the improvement of the mind, and I question whether mine has made any advance for the last seven years ; still it is something that it has not retrograded, and that the tastes and pursuits of my early years are as strong as ever. Let this then be my excuse for the introduction of verses about love in an English letter. I wonder whether I shall be ever sensible of the reality.

"The Doctor" exclaims against the practice of young clergymen always preaching their own sermons, and recommends them to have recourse to those of the older divines, and he utters a malediction against all unnecessary extempore displays—and in this I agree with him. People in England nowadays seem to think that it is a great step gained when their friends, be their abilities what they may, make their first attempt at it ; and hence what rambling, loose and un-meaning discourses are frequently delivered from the pulpit ! In this Henry Mortlock signally failed ; I never could carry away with me any part of his discourses, and following him was as difficult as riding a steeple-chase. There are few men who possess the composure and order of mind necessary for extempore sermons ; and of what use is an impressive or energetic manner when the matter is all the time slipping through one's fingers? Yet this is one of those vulgar errors that people cling to, despite of their own constant experience to the contrary. The common people understand and delight in the homely but plain phraseology and similes and metaphors of the old writers, and the object of a young clergyman should be to interest his hearers first and to make them listen readily to him, instead of starting up at once as a Boanerges. But I have no room left for a dissertation on this subject.

CAMP ON THE CUGGAR,

December 5th, 1837.

Dearest Mother,

I despatched my November letter three days ago. A note to Hannah Williams was inclosed. I have since marched to the banks, or rather the bed, of a stream which pours down here from the hills in the rainy season, and after passing the northern boundary of my district loses itself in the sands to the westward. It is now dry. The country near it is rich and fertile, but a complete waste. It only came into our hands—as I think I told you in my April letter—this year, and I am hard at work now endeavouring to repeople the deserted villages, which have been uninhabited since the two years of famine in 1780—81. During the last six months, I have induced settlers to occupy about fifty of them. Much still remains to be done; but the tract is now in a fair way to prosper. You will see the Cuggar in any map of India, so you may fancy my whereabouts. I was gladdened yesterday by the receipt of your two letters of June and July. Give my salaam to Fred and Joe, to whom I will write shortly. They ought to write me an account of their tour on their return. Why, if their trip comprises Egypt, they might just as well have extended it to Hindoostan and Hissar. I hope they will enjoy themselves, and be able to effect their meditated trip to the Pyramids, and the wonders of Dendera and Thebes. Egypt will give them a very good idea of an eastern country, for the features of all are the same; and the Nile, with the country around it, is a counterpart of the Ganges, Jumna, Indus, and other large rivers here, whilst the Desert will enable them to realize the beauties of Hissar. It is for this similarity that I should not care a fig to see any more of the East, where everything is such a novelty to travellers from Europe; and to Palestine I would rather not go. Lord Byron, in his visit to Rome, very justly says that the pleasure which the imagination derives from a visit to spots noted in history is more an *after*-feeling, and the scenes that must now be associated with Jerusalem and its environs, would not only destroy the deep and thrilling interest of a visit to them, but would rise up after-wards in the mind and debase the pictures previously framed by one's imagination,—pictures framed in childhood, and carried down with us to the present time. Fancy the brook Kedron, a kind of sewer for the abominations of the city, which I believe it is now! I shall be much mistaken if Fred does not experience this feeling, which will be unpleasant from its permanency, if he prosecutes his tour there. I am certain that he will find his impressions far less deep and vivid than he could have supposed possible. Your last letter is redolent of the spring, and Ayott fields, and hedge-rows. " O rus, quando ego te aspiciam !" What a novelty to me will be an English sunset and twilight. There are no such things in this country, for the great round sun sinking behind the sand-hills does not deserve the name of a sunset.

December 18*th*—

As the time draws nearer for my return, I often think seriously whether England will be palatable to me after my years of wild inde-pendence in the jungles, and sometimes I doubt it. The up-country station is even distasteful to me, and I feel, when at Delhi or else-where, like a bird in a cage. What, then, will be my feelings when shackled with the thousand restraints of England! Besides, some things appear incidentally in your letters which puzzle me. Ellen, on the occasion of a few friends visiting her at Ayott, expresses her hopes that she may not be led into any *inconsistency*. I don't recollect any-thing of this kind at Mr. Mortlock's. There was no effort, or fixed rule, of behaviour there, but mirth and unconstrained conversation; and, when the family assembled in the evening, there was no preach-ing *at* any of them, or expounding *at* anybody. Then, again, when any of the ladies visiting there happened to mention any preacher of piety or eminence, they did not call him "that *dear* man," with a peculiar emphasis on the "*dear*," or spoke of him in terms only fit to be used by a newly-married woman to her husband. The raptures into which Miss —— falls, in one of her letters to you, about a young Irish preacher, and the strength of her expressions, would, if read by a stranger to the parties, sound positively indecent—quite Song of Solomon-ish. Weak-headed women are the persons who cover religion with a garb of ridicule, and afford abundance of handles to the laughers ; and though Miss —— is not of that stamp, they abound in Bath above every other place, until a religious phraseology, and dress and habits, even in the most trifling matters, appear to have been adopted. Why, when I go home, all this will make me curb and snort like Mazeppa's wild charger. And then, again, two years of absolute idleness ! The first six months will be sufficient to exhaust the power of my curiosity ; but I fear I am looking forwards too presumptuously to the future. Let me suppose it all pleasure, till I feel the pain.

CAMP,
February 3rd, 1838.

Dearest Mother,

I despatched yesterday a short letter to you enclosing a duplicate of a bill of exchange. It will go by the steamer from Bombay at the close of the month, and will reach you long before this does. Mr. Macaulay, about whom you wrote to me some years ago, has returned to England unregretted by a single individual. He stayed altogether three years in this country, and, with the exception of his official duties, he has done nothing for India or for the people. Expectation was on tiptoe on his arrival from the reputation which he carried with him of splendid talents and active zeal, but he has grievously disappointed everyone, and, from the little interest he appears to have taken in the country, he could only have come out with the intention of saving as much of his pay as possible, and returning to England with some thousand pounds in pocket. So much for your men of profession ! Trevelyan has gone home with him.

I am again in tents, and shall have to remain under canvass until the middle of March, or longer, probably. I am desirous to get into the house again as soon as possible, for the heat is such, the atmosphere having now remained so long uncooled by rain, that I find it unpleasant even in the present season ; besides, I dread the March storms, which will be furious from the heated state of the atmosphere, and it is far from pleasant to be expecting every minute the downfall of one's tent and tent-poles upon one. Thousands are perishing from famine in different parts of the Upper Provinces. Here, most fortunately, we are better off, but if no rain falls in the course of two or three months we shall be as bad, and, indeed, infinitely worse, than any of the other districts. God avert the horrors of a famine! At present the minds of all are in a state of painful expectancy. Lord Auckland and suite arrive at Delhi in a few days. He will not come here this season; and if he wanted to, I would not let him. A large camp like his would create a fictitious famine immediately in this out-of-the-way place.

February 24th—

Half the inhabitants of my district have emigrated, and the rest will soon follow if we have not rain. The ground is quite pulverized from the last six months' uninterrupted drought, and we are treated every day with clouds of sand and dust, which move across the country like pillars,—a kind of mimic whirlwind or, rather, waterspout. I very nearly had my tent lifted up bodily by one of them yesterday. What with the dusty heavens, dusty atmosphere and ground, we breathe dust and eat dust from morning to night. I greatly fear that the next season will be a failure, too, for a drought so general as this has been, embracing the whole of the Upper Provinces and Central India, has seldom, if ever, terminated in a single year. What will become of us all? everyone is asking. What I ask is, what will become of the people? It almost seems as if these dreadful visitations were intended by Providence to allay the miseries arising from a redundant population in countries where the inhabitants have no means of emigrating. The Upper Provinces are (the cities and towns excepted) more thickly peopled than any part of the world, and the soil taxed to the uttermost to sustain them; yet their local attachments are so strong that nothing can prevail on them to move to other parts of the country less thickly inhabited.

February 28th—

I had such a ride amongst the sand-hills on the outskirts of the Great Desert a day or two ago! I started at sunrise with half-a-dozen horsemen, each having a leathern bottle of water at his saddle-bow (water not being procurable for miles in some part of the tract), rode sixteen or seventeen miles to the spot where my business lay, spent several hours on horseback in the sun, and rode back again so as to arrive at my tents by dinner-time. The road led the whole way over sand-hills, rising and falling like the waves of the sea, and my horse at every step came over his fetlocks. I don't think there was an acre of level ground the whole way. A most fatiguing day's work it was, and I feel the effects of it still in my joints and loins. I am at present in the country of my wild subjects, the Bhuttees, a pastoral race, who migrated from the countries west of the Indus and settled in this tract one hundred years ago. They are all professed plunderers, like the Arabs whom you read of, and hate cultivating like poison. Their tribe, which is confined to my district, was disposed to give me trouble a few months ago, but, by severity in the first instance and a gradual relaxing of the reins afterwards, I have got them into capital order for nearly the first time for the last twenty years.

March 1st—

I am very glad to get into the house again, though with the prospect of six or seven months' confinement to it, unless I take a trip to the hills, for it is probable that I shall not take my furlough this year, though most certainly next. My reasons I will give you as soon as I come to a determination on the point. At present I am wavering and undecided, and, consequently, ill at ease. I am afraid, after the active occupation to which I have been accustomed for the last eight or nine years, I should feel listless and uneasy as ever as the novelty of England has worn away; that I should be looking forward to the further spell of ten years instead of enjoying the present. This, you may say, would apply to my furlough whether I take it now or a year hence equally; and so it does, but there is some indefinable feeling at work within me which makes me hang back from my furlough instead of looking eagerly forward to it as I used to do when it was distant. How I shall settle the question with myself I scarcely know, but at present the probabilities are against my return at the end of this year. On the score of my public duties it is very desirable that I should remain another year, for the drought this year has prevented my undertaking any of the duties for which I was specially sent here; and although others may think light of what is expected of them and be glad to shirk a troublesome charge under a pretext of taking their furlough, I am not a lad of that mettle. My letters are getting very short, and very stupid, "mere shreds and patches," but I have nothing to enliven me, not even books, for I now rarely see a recent publication.

Dearest Mother,

I received three days ago a letter from the private secretary to the Governor-General as follows :—

"My dear Sir,—I am directed by the Right Honorable the Governor-General to inquire whether you would desire to be considered a candidate for the situation of Officiating Civil and Sessions Judge for the Etawah district. The acting appointment is likely to last for a long period, &c., &c."

Etawah is a town on the Jumna below Agra—you will see it on the map. The situation of Civil and Sessions Judge answers to that of a Judge of Assize at home. He hears all criminal cases which the Magistrate is not competent to pass sentence on, viz., all cases of serious offences; they are committed to him for trial, and his power extends to fourteen years' imprisonment. He has also civil jurisdiction, in which he is assisted by subordinate native courts of law. You will see from this that the office is one of great responsibility, and in point of rank and dignity it is far above my present one of Magistrate and Collector. The duty is entirely judicial and criminal, and has nothing to do with the executive branch of the service, viz., the police or revenue. I mentioned to you in my former letters that two or three of my contemporaries, or rather I should say of my seniors by only six months, had risen to the rank of Magistrate and Collector before me, but to none of my contemporaries, nor to any of my seniors by six months or a year, has the offer of so high and responsible an appointment yet been made. Again, there is a maxim which I have always borne in mind, That a step gained is a step retained. So far, so good. On the other hand, I am extremely unwilling to leave my present charge and district, which I have got into very good order, and which gives me little trouble. I like the people and their character; I have many natives under me in public situations, whom I have employed from amongst the more respectable of my native acquaintances in my former district, Sahuswan, and who have served me well and honestly here. I do not like the idea of leaving them in the power of my successor, whoever he may be, who may pursue, as is too often the case, a totally different line of conduct towards them. I am averse, too, to these speedy changes from district to district, and, besides, a considerable part of the duty which

I was sent here to perform by the Sudder Board, and which I was obliged to postpone owing to the drought, is still incomplete. Again, in point of emolument I shall not be a gainer, for my officiating allowances will barely cover the additional expenses to which I shall be put in different ways, as they will not probably exceed 500 rupees per mensem. A famine, too, is raging in that part severer than in any other district in the Upper Provinces, and it is consequently more unhealthy even than Hansi. The increase of crime has borne pace with the distress prevailing, and the work in the Judge's department is, I hear, quite appalling from its quantity. Last of all, the situation is merely an *acting* one, and after holding it a few months the return of the man who holds the Government appointment may turn me adrift again. All these pros and cons I deliberated with myself for a day and night. Should I accept it or no? But the grand clencher for the affirmative was, "Do not reject promotion in whatever shape offered;" and there was also a feeling of pride or vanity, call it what you will, at having got the start of every one else. So I wrote and said I would undertake the duties if the situation were conferred upon me, and here the matter rests. I wonder where Lord Auckland could have heard of me; I suppose something favourable was told him of me when he was at Delhi lately. My heart is very heavy at the prospect of my removal to a new part of the country. Ties form themselves in my mind to the people and district under my charge almost imperceptibly, and I do not feel their strength until the time arrives to break them. And then what an utter dissevering of them the nature of our service produces! It is not likely that I shall ever return to Hansi, for even if the return of the Judge to Etawah displaces me, it is probable that I shall be employed as Magistrate and Collector in some other larger and more important charge. The three saddest moments of my life in this country have been my first removal from Delhi to Hissar in 1830, my subsequent one from Delhi to Sahuswan in 1832, and my last from Sahuswan here. Every one here, native and European, regrets the prospect of my departure, and certainly my feelings at present are not those of a man expecting his promotion. I shall be able to let you know what becomes of me before I close this letter, which must be a short one.

March 23rd—

No news yet of my appointment, and I am in a very unpleasant state of doubt in consequence. I can't help wishing that I may not have to go after all. I suppose I shall hear in the course of a week. I hope, if I am to go, that the order will arrive quickly, so as to admit of my joining my appointment before the extremity of the heat in May. Etawah must be a good 200 miles from Delhi and 300 from here, and if the weather permit I shall march there from Delhi. I shall sell off all my traps (they are few and of little value) here and merely carry with me such things as may be absolutely necessary. The remainder of my books I am also parting with,—my old companions and fellow-voyagers,—as the expense of their conveyance to such a distance would be tremendous. Altogether, I feel so unsettled and uncomfortable that I am afraid I shall omit sending my usual letter this month.

April 1st—

O ambition! ambition! I received a letter from a friend yesterday, in which he mentions that another civilian, three years my senior, had been offered the very appointment which the private secretary wrote me about, and had accepted it. So down go my castles. It is true the secretary's letter does not amount to a direct offer, as it merely asks me whether I wished to be considered a *candidate* for it, but such questions are usually considered to imply that one may have it if one wished. I have not yet heard from the secretary, but I entertain no expectations now of being appointed, nor do I regret it much, except that it is not pleasant to be baulked. In a pecuniary point of view I am better off here, for I find that the appointment would only have given me 400 rupees per mensem extra, which would have been more than absorbed by extra expenses; and I was, and still am, unwilling to move, but the honour would have been something. I don't know whether the secretary intends to write to me or not an explanation. I shall take care for the future how I trust these offers, which are like Macbeth's fiends, "that keep the word of promise to our ear and break it to our hope." The fault, perhaps, was mine, in being too sanguine, although I always supposed that there was an *if* in the case. I had already sold off some of my things, wine, beer, &c., in expectation of my departure, at a loss, but no matter. I suppose I shall be fixed at my present situation until the time comes for my furlough.

April 3rd—

No news from the secretary yet, but I hear that the appointment has already been filled up; at all events, I have now made up my mind to stay here until my furlough. I think Lord Auckland or his secretary has acted rather unpolitely in not letting me know the result, which they ought to have done in common civility. Lord Auckland and his suite will pass through this district in a few months. The only thing I regret is that I sold off my things so precipitately, as I shall now have to replace them, besides looking foolish into the bargain. Never mind; I have just remitted 2,400 rupees to Calcutta, which I could not have done if I had been ordered off to Etawah.

April 4th—

I have heard nothing further from the private secretary. The accounts from the part of the country where Etawah is situated are dreadful, and I may consider myself fortunate in not having to go there. Hundreds perishing with famine daily; the river Jumna choked with putrefying corpses, which the stream cannot carry down; cholera, as a necessary consequence of this misery, broken out, and extending its ravages to Europeans—all this exhibits a scene which can only be witnessed in this country in a season like the present. Happy Europe knows them not. Even in this part of the country, which is so much better off than any other part of the Upper Provinces, the people are beginning to sell their children, and you can purchase a child for a few rupees. The sale and purchase of children is a common practice in a famine in this country. The children are brought up in the harams of the better class of natives; they are looked upon as slaves, but are kindly treated, and are married off to others in the same situation when of age. The parents, when pressed with want, have the less compunction in selling their children, which they do more to save their lives than their own. The next two and a half months will, I fear, witness many dreadful scenes arising from famine.

HISSAR,
April 12th, 1838.

Dearest Mother,

I told you in my last letter, which I despatched by the steamer, that I had received a letter from the private secretary to Lord Auckland asking me if I wished to be considered a candidate for the situation of Officiating Civil and Sessions Judge at a place called Etawah, below Agra, to which, after many pros and cons, I had replied in the affirmative. I was kept in suspense afterwards for a full month, and my letter was, in consequence, filled with my doubts and uncertainties, in which state I still remained when I despatched it. Well, this morning another letter came, which I opened anxiously, for I had at last come to the determination not to go, even if the appointment were distinctly offered me; which, from what I had heard, I had little chance of,—a similar proposal for the same appointment having been made, as I had learnt, to a man three years my senior. Take the letter:—

" My dear Sir,—I am desired by the Governor-General to inform you, with reference to my former letter on the Acting Judgeship at Etawah, that his lordship has had it in his power to raise you in the grade of Magistrate and Collector by adding 250 rupees a month to your present salary. The official announcement of this increase, which his lordship has been happy in authorizing in recognition of your merits and services, will immediately reach you. Having been able to promote you in your present office, his lordship thinks it best for the public service, as he trusts that it will be most agreeable to you, that you should not be transferred to another appointment and district. Another arrangement has, consequently, been made for the vacancy at Etawah. Believe me, &c., &c."

Now, if I had my free choice of anything that I best liked in the service, next to a permanent appointment of Judge—which I could not, in reason, expect to attain for some years to come—it would have been a rise in my present situation; but, so far from anticipating or even dreaming of such an event was I, that I was perfectly astonished at the contents of the letter, which, I need hardly say, gratified me extremely. 25*l.* a month to my present pay makes it really handsome. I like the district, the duties, and the people, and I dislike beyond measure the prospect of a change to a place like Etawah, situated in the very centre of the famine and disease which is, at the present time, depopulating the country.

Here, then, I shall remain until I take my furlough; and I think, from what you have heard of me for the last four years, that you will admit that an out-of-the-way station does not necessarily render a man forgotten or liable to be passed over in favour of more glib and oily suitors. I never wrote a line to Lord Auckland's secretary, and yet, you see, I have got more than I ever aspired to; certainly more than any man of my rank in the service has yet attained to— so hurrah! hurrah! hurrah! three times three! I am delighted beyond measure at not having to leave my present district, and, in point of emolument, I get within 150 rupees per mensem what I should have received had I gone to Etawah. In short, I look upon it as a lucky windfall. It was fortunate I was not such a spoon as to decline the offer first made, as I might have waited, in that case, long enough, perhaps, for another opportunity. Had it been repeated, or, rather, made at all—for the first was not an *offer*, merely a question—I was so sick with waiting for a reply, and with the prospect of having to move at this season of the year, that I should certainly have refused.

April 20th—

Here am I, in my nine-and-twentieth year. I am close upon my meridian, if an Indian's meridian can be fixed at thirty. I fear the average of Indian lives would give a much earlier date. Ten years ago the world was opening on me, and I was full of excitement and enthusiasm. I feel quite an old man now, in comparison; and my mental acquirements in the interim—what have they been? Few, I fear, and scanty; nothing, in short—reader as I have been—to place me on a level with my more fortunate contemporaries at home. In the knowledge that becomes a gentleman I cannot but consider myself superior to three-fourths of those whom I meet, but it is not active or practical knowledge, that would enable a man to appear as a man of general information in England.

My letters have become very short and uninteresting; but what can I communicate to you from a place like this, where one's mind is unrefreshed by news or books? In short, I wonder what I used to fill my letters with seven or eight years ago. Ten years make some difference in a man, and the effusions of one's pen, which I may have poured out in the fullness of my heart at that period, very soon subside when we get on the wrong side of twenty-five. Pity we cannot retain the freshness of our feelings as we advance in years!

Why continue toiling amongst sands and deserts, I sometimes ask myself, when the road to England is open, and the first spell of one's exile has passed? But there is a sort of doggedness of purpose in me which prompts me to prolong the first period of my residence in this country for one or two years longer, so as to curtail one's after stay. What may be my ultimate resolve I know not, but it is certain that I shall not take my furlough this year.

Farewell, dearest mother, and give my affections to all. My heart is as steady and warm as ever to all of you. Heaven knows there is nothing in this country that can sully the brightness of one's family love.

HISSAR,

July 15th, 1838.

Dearest Mother,

I received four days ago your January letter, and to-day your letter despatched the 9th May, giving the news of Emma's safe confinement—the former *viâ* the Cape, the latter by steam, a fair specimen of the vast advantages of the steam route over the ships. I trust that nothing will induce you to alter for the old route again. Your letters reach me perfectly uninjured ; in fact, letters from England to this country are never opened or fumigated ; and if mine are, what's the harm provided they be legible; and whether legible or not, at all events you know that all is well months sooner than you otherwise would. The steam route, too, is as safe and much more sure than the other. My first letter sent by steam was that of February, the receipt of which is acknowledged in your present one. Since then I have written regularly by the same route, and shall continue to do so. If any of my previous letters have miscarried, which they appear to have done, the fault lies with the old route. Never fear my not taking the necessary precautions to insure the safer despatch of my letters.

As Emma intends to have twenty children at least, it would be needless for me to offer my congratulations intermediately. By waiting until the number is complete, and then lumping my good wishes, much tautology and waste of paper may be saved. I am glad the last is a girl. A large family of boys is a great calamity, and the proportion of one boy to three girls in the expected twenty is the utmost I can allow her. I am rejoiced too to hear that she has adopted a firm system with her children. Many in their own fondness and affection for their first child see no harm in a little over-indulgence, which they never intend to extend to their future ones ; but they forget that on that first child everything depends, and that the others will ever be guided more by his or her example than by the precepts of the parents. Pray convey to her the assurances of my love and affection to her and hers.

And now, my dear Mother, I will give you, as concisely as I can, the reasons which induce me to prolong my stay in this country. You may ask, why did they not occur to you before? and may be led to suppose that they have been got up for the occasion. To this I reply, that as long as my furlough was distant it presented itself in none but favourable colours. Now, however, objections start forward, and on the result of the determination I see too surely that the whole course of my future life must depend. No wonder, then, that I pause. First and foremost: After nine years' residence in India I find myself in a situation where I can lay by £1,400 or £1,500 per annum, and which is a stepping-stone to something better. Why should I, in the first commencement of my good fortune, relinquish its advantages, and absent myself from the sphere of promotion for three long years, carrying home with me a sum which will be absorbed in the expenses of my marriage and its consequents, and leave me to begin the world again at thirty-three with fifteen years of my life spent in vain? Is not this throwing away the fruits of the last ten years, which have just begun to show themselves? Secondly: If I marry in England I shall return to this country with eleven more long years of exile before me. My children will have to be sent home, and my wife's health failing her, she will follow them, leaving me in this country tied to the stake of exile and wretchedness made doubly bitter. This is almost invariably the fate of those who marry during their furlough. It is all very fine to talk about wedded love, a bosom companion, and so on; but I see in the prospect much to counterbalance matrimony undertaken under these circumstances, and I could quote scores of instances to support my position. Thirdly: As I hope to have as good a chance of marrying three or four years hence as now, I would rather not lose my independence before I can help it. Fourthly: An undistinguishable throng of hopes and fears and fancies of all kinds, trifling by themselves, but of weight in the aggregate, leads me to postpone my furlough until circumstances give me the bent for England, which it has not just at present, simply from the temporary revulsion of feeling and design produced by hesitation on a point which, before I examined it, I had always led myself to look upon as settled. Fifthly: I observe that few, if any, of my contemporaries, or those in the service immediately my seniors, who we look upon as promising men, have availed or intend to avail themselves of their furlough just at present, which I can only ascribe to their being sensible that it will be prejudicial to their interests. John Thornton is one instance in point. Though regularly homesick before, he has also postponed his furlough, which he would have been entitled to at the end of the year, and yet there is no want of deep affection in that family. It is strange, but it is the fact, that none but the indifferent, or the "bad bargains" as we call them, take their furlough nowadays at the exact time. In short, my dear Mother, I have no intention whatever to take my furlough this year. If my plans change for the next, I shall have ample time to let you know beforehand. I have arrived at that time of life when my views and plans must be made to depend not so much on my individual likings, or on what other people do or do not do, but on the rational and sober conviction of the line of my interest. If this be not regarded now, when will the time come to attend to it? You act rather imprudently, my dear Mother, in urging my instant return in the strong terms used in your late letter, and you would regret your earnestness if you were to see me haunted by doubtings, regret, or discontent, the invariable consequence to me of any measure into which I may have been forced prematurely, or against my will, after the first burst of excitement had subsided. You are well aware that my delay arises not from want of affection, or any entanglements in this country. Let then my liking overpower my sense of interest, which may be easily and soon brought about by circumstances; let me veer round again quietly and gradually of my own accord, and I may be amongst you in 1840. My present idea is—for it is not yet a plan— to take my furlough as soon as I get together 10,000*l.* of my savings; this, in my present allowances, I could effect by the close of 1841, so as to proceed to England in that year. Then, if you please, it might be *possible* for me,—*possible* mind, to fix in England for the rest of my life, NEVER to return to this odious country, which, if I were to hasten home now, would be totally and wholly out of the question. Think of this calmly, and answer me in the same mood.

HISSAR,
September 2nd, 1838.

Dearest Mother,

Nothing is talked of here but war—war—war! A force of between 15,000 and 20,000 will march next month to the Indus, and the weak and distracted country of Persia will, in a short time, be the only interval of separation between the Russians and ourselves. It is vain to speculate on the results. For my own part, I do not dread external foes; our dangers lie in the vast mass of people whom we have subjected to our rule in this country, and who would gladly rise and shake off the yoke of the "feringees" as soon as any reverses afford them a prospect of succeeding. Our rule is not popular, neither are we, individually speaking; we have neglected the many opportunities presented us of improvement and civilization, and bowed the *mass* to the dust, and kept them there by extortionate taxation. Few think this in England; and how should they, when so many in this country, who can see with their own eyes and judge for themselves if they choose, continue in the gross delusion that our supremacy is a blessing to the natives, and appreciated by them as such. I, who have lived in the jungles and amongst them for eight years, know otherwise. We are now in the situation anticipated by some of the shrewdest of our Indian politicians long ago; we must advance, and the further we advance the weaker we shall become. If we ever have to stand on the defensive against an external enemy, from that moment our Indian empire will melt away, or rather be broken to atoms by our internal foes; in short, our present situation is a subject of anxious consideration to all who are qualified to form an opinion on it. Had I no other motive for delaying my furlough, I could not reconcile to myself the idea of idling away three years at a time when my future means of subsistence and prospects in life were at hazard 15,000 miles off. Colonel Skinner, with his corps of horse, will accompany the force; a part of which,—bad luck to it!—will pass through my district, the nearest of any others in the Upper Provinces, to the future scene of operations, and give me, I dare say, a great deal of trouble. I am cutting a road for them through the dense jungles to the westward, and shall, probably, accompany them, by way of society, as far as Bhutneer, which you will see on the map to the westward, after which they will come on the desert, and how they are to get over it I cannot divine. There will be excitement enough, at all events, during their march in my territory. They will move about the 1st of November. It will be a fine thing for the army, who were stagnating both in spirit and promotions, and, so far, Alfred Williams will be lucky, as a force also marches to the westward of the Indus from Bombay. The active and stirring amongst the junior officers will now have a good opportunity of bringing themselves forwards.

CAMP,
September 28th, 1838.

Dearest Mother,

Once more in tents! I am encamped on the banks of the Cuggar, forty miles from Hissar. The Cuggar is a stream dependent on the periodical rains which finds its way from the Himalayas to this otherwise waterless country, where it spreads itself out into pools until it is gradually absorbed. The wild-fowl are careering over the water close to my tent, and I rise before dawn to-morrow morning for some shooting, and hope to bring home a bagful of the delicious teal and wild-duck, which will be distributed amongst my servants. For myself, I am on strict regimen, to which I intend to adhere. All fish, flesh and fowl eaten by us are lawful to the Mussulmans, provided a knife be passed across the throat before the animal is dead, and almost all my Hindoo servants, one or two excepted, have no objection to eat game. So much for the mistaken notions prevalent in England of the Hindoos' horror of flesh,—one of those vulgar errors, as old as the hills, which seem destined never to be corrected. The weather is still hot, but the change from the house is a delightful one, and I could almost say, with a little alteration from the beginning of the third canto of " Childe Harold,"—

" Once more upon the desert—yet once more—
And my heart bounds within me like a steed
That knows its rider."

I went to Hansi when I left Hissar to bid good-bye to Colonel Skinner, who accompanies the force preparing for the war. He is a man of a singular character; singular, I mean, for simplicity and nobleness of heart and shrewdness of intellect,—a rare union of opposite qualities! He has been a soldier from his boyhood, and his life has been a strange one, full of moving incidents in flood and field. I spent two days with him, and parted from him with regret, for I have known him for the last ten years, and many mutual good offices and acts of kindness have passed between us. War is the universal topic now-a-days. The result it is impossible to guess, for the field of action and the combatants are new. The next three years will be full of anxious events to those acquainted with the country, and the quiet times of the last ten or eleven years will be known no more. A part of the force passes through a portion of my district next month en route to the rendezvous of the army on the Sutledge. My district, being the most westerly, will be the nearest of all in the Upper Provinces to the scene of action, though still far enough off, so never fear. Our rule in this country will be over the moment we have to fight a foreign enemy on Indian soil.

CAMP ON THE CUGGAR,

November 16th, 1838.

Dearest Mother,

I received two days ago your very interesting letter of July. I had supposed that you had relinquished all idea of the tour, never imagining that it could have been undertaken and finished in so short a time. Your letter gave me a severe heart-ache from longing. What would I not have given to have been with you at Netley and Bedstone ! Very soothing, and yet very saddening, must have been your visit to both those places. I recollect well the Craven Arms and the Stretton Hills; yes, and Dorrington, too, and its gingerbread; and I could travel with you over the greater part of your tour, a few places excepted. What a happy thought it was, and how well carried into execution, and happily ended ! I was in a state of childish pleasure and surprise whilst reading your letter, and the second perusal has not dulled the feeling.

My old friend, Colonel Skinner, has just marched past my camp at the head of his regiment of horse, 1,000 strong, en route from Hansi to join the army assembled at Ferozepoor, destined to act against Cabul. I joined his camp from this place, and accompanied him two marches on his way. His absence will be felt as a loss by all here, native and European, and by none more than myself, for he was truly open-hearted and hospitable, and it was a pleasure to visit him for a day or two. What the result of the expedition will be it would be difficult to say. An army of 15,000 is now assembled on the Sutledge, 150 miles from this, and they march to the westward in the beginning of next month. I fear we shall have unquiet times. I have received orders to raise a body of horse 100 strong, fully equipped and officered (with natives of course), to supply the place of the detachments of Colonel Skinner's corps, who have been withdrawn for service in the field, and I am busy now in the enlistment, measuring troop horses, selecting troopers, choosing officers, &c., &c. Quite a new duty this for me, as you may suppose, but I nevertheless hope to raise a smart body of men who will fight when required. Fifty-five I have raised already, and expect to complete the number in a few days. I shall have them drilled well, and exercised with the sword and match-lock. My father, I suppose you know, was a captain, if not a colonel, in the Calcutta Militia, in Lord Wellesley's time. Besides this troop I have another of 100 strong, for police and revenue duties, so that I now command 200 horsemen. Does not that sound fine ! Lord Auckland, our Governor-General, comes to Hansi, they say, in January; I want nothing from him, so I should not be sorry if he kept away, as the visits of these big-wigs always occasion much trouble. The weather is really bitterly cold. I shiver all over in the morning, and hug the stove in the evening. The 300 or 400 souls in my camp look very miserable early in the morning before the sun is high enough to warm them; besides, this is the fast month with the Mahometans; they fast from all food and drink of any kind during the day, and are at prayers half the night, and certainly their powers of endurance are most exemplary.

Business of various kinds still detains me on the banks of the Cuggar, and I do not expect to be able to return to Hissar until Christmas. The country here is still one vast jungle, and the few inhabitants in the scattered villages are the greatest thieves and rascals I have ever had to deal with, but I ride them with a tight curb, and they find restiveness bad policy in the end.

I have been reading some extracts of Wilberforce's Life, by his sons. I breakfasted with him at Bath, with Miss Pilot, in the winter of 1826, and was much fascinated with his conversation and manners. I have also skipped over a very different sort of work, Mrs. Trollope's "Vicar of Wrexhill," which inspires disgust I admit, but of a very different kind from that designed by the author; the disgust is at her coarse and unfeminine mind, of which the book is as condemnatory as anything can well be. Still the book may be useful in its way, and there are many and very many things too in the externals of the evangelical party which call for reform. The vulgar parody of some of these in Mrs. Trollope's book may serve as a beacon. Wilberforce was of *no* party; piety and philanthropy were beautifully united in his character.

December 8th—

This moment your letter of September 29th has been put into my hand. It gives me the details of Ellen and Emma's tour, and, like your last one of July, has tugged sorely at my heart-strings. No, I don't think I shall be able to resist your call next year, if my life is spared till then. Both your July letter, and now Ellen's letter from the Lakes, have stirred up my heart from its depths, and I cannot help asking myself if the pure and unmixed enjoyment of such scenes and companionship, as Ellen so admirably describes, should be bartered for "orient pearls and barbaric gold,"—far less for the weary laying up of pound on pound with a view to that futurity which may never be mine? Ellen's letters show her disposition and character beautifully, and they deserve to be shown beautifully. I will not disguise from her that both, originally excellent, have wonderfully improved within the last eleven years, at least to my perception. She was then " an eagle towering in the pride of place"—now she is full of the sweet household charities, and will go far to realize to my mind, I think, when we meet, the union of piety and cheerfulness which fascinated me so much in the Mortlock family. I shall say the same for her husband; in short, the group she presents to the eye in her letters is a very charming one, and has done more than anything else to draw my heart towards her and hers with a warmer affection than it, perhaps, ever yet felt, or, at least, would acknowledge.

CAMP,

January 15th, 1839.

Dearest Mother,

I received, yesterday, your welcome letter, despatched on the 26th October. The most interesting event in it, by far, is my dear brother's ordination. May he prosper in the path he has chosen. He seems to have entered upon it with high, and pure, and holy feelings. May they accompany him in his peaceful career! I can hardly term a change from your hearth-side to the ministerial duties of an English village a " launching upon the world," as you do; yet, in one sense, it will strictly prove so to him. From a quiet student he has become a " fisher of men;" from a solitary individual he has been suddenly converted into the guide of old and young. Nailsea and Bourlton, each in its own degree, presents as extensive a field for prudence, self-command, and the other virtues of mere human conduct, as the regions subjected to the control of civilians in this country, and certainly a more trying one. I wish not Fred to be a Boanerges, as you do: these are women's ideas of the first qualities of a young preacher. If I were in his place, I should feel my way for one or two years, quietly and firmly; study the characters of my leading parishioners, and the characteristics of the parish generally; and, above all, guard against zeal, however exalted and high in itself, over-stepping the bounds of discretion— I mean worldly discretion, with reference to the little world of every parish. But I touched on this subject before in a former letter. Fred will, I doubt not, discharge beautifully the duties of his calling. He stands in no need of hints from me, nor shall I venture to offer any, except as a make-weight to the incomplete notions of the qualities necessary for a minister common amongst those who only see him in the pulpit, and cannot follow him into parish details and parish management. The last is the true arena of a clergyman, in which he has to fight with "the wild beasts of Ephesus," in the shape of the low selfishness and venal passions of the vulgar. No, no, no—the less of a Boanerges the better.

I can well enter into Fred's feelings of loneliness on his first occupation of his lodgings in Bourlton after his ordination. I well recollect the utter desolation of heart which overwhelmed me for the first two or three days of my first arrival in Calcutta. As a schoolboy, I never realized my return to school until the hackney-coach had set me down in Charterhouse Square, and the doors had closed upon me. It was the same with me on my departure from England: I never felt that I had indeed left it for a new world until the boat landed me at the Calcutta ghaut. Bitter were my feelings for those two or three first days; but youth, and the excitement of fresh studies, soon overcame them, and for some time after all was *couleur de rose*. We lose these feelings in after-life, and recur to their existence formerly as a test of youth, with its April gleams and shadows.

Fred's correspondence will be most interesting, and I look forward to it with great pleasure and interest.

January 21st—

Lord Auckland and suite visit my district after all. They will arrive at my frontier to-morrow, and I am in hasty march to meet them. I came eighteen miles to-day; and eighteen miles to-morrow will carry me to their camp, when I shall have to wait upon his lordship and chief secretary, and also call upon the Misses Eden—Lord A.'s sisters. I wish them all at the bottom of the sea, and my wish will, I doubt not, be in part fulfilled, as the Cuggar River, which is the boundary of my dominions, has been much swollen by late rains, and there is only one ferry-boat, and that a small one, so that if they escape a ducking personally, their traps will get a beautiful wetting. The weather, too, just at present, is bitterly cold, colder than I ever recollect it in India—that damp cold, which penetrates to one's very liver. I was so benumbed on arriving here this morning, at ten o'clock a.m., that I had a fire lighted on the plain in front of my tent, into which I almost walked, and by which I sat warming myself for two hours, to the great amusement of the villagers. Another wretched, long, cold march to-morrow, too! Lord A.'s visit to Hansi is merely to while away time until the season comes for returning to the hills; and as the arrival of a large, over-grown camp in a thinly peopled tract like this causes infinite trouble and annoyance to all, without exception, I am the more annoyed at the caprice shown in the visit. All I can do, however, is to grumble, which I do famously, at being put so horridly out of the way by the interruption. I have nothing to ask of his lordship; am well satisfied with my present pay, duties, and district, and care not a fig for the whole kit of them. If promotion comes in its proper time, all well and good; I certainly shall not decline it; but I am certain of one thing, that a third, or, at all events, a fourth, more can be laid by monthly at places like Sahuswan and Hissar,—and that, too, without an effort of economy,—than anywhere else, even at an advanced rate of salary. But I will tell you, in a day or two, all about my visit to Lord A., &c., &c., &c.

January 22nd—

Well, on arriving at the Cuggar stream this morning, fully expecting to find his lordship encamped here, I found that the stream had risen suddenly several feet, so as to be no longer fordable. The Governor-General has, in consequence, been obliged to remain where he is, and wait until the flood subsides, which it may not do for two or three days. Some of the baggage had crossed, and cannot now get back again, so that the camp is in a pretty mess; all which I enjoy extremely. I am fairly sick of this work, and as cross as a bear with a sore head.

January 27th—

Such a business as there has been in crossing the Cuggar! only two or three boats to be had, and a camp—consisting of not less than 10,000 men, with all their immense baggage—to cross in them. I never saw such a scene of confusion: the noise and row was beyond everything. After two or three days' hard work, the advance guard crossed; and Lord Auckland came over on the 25th, with the Misses Eden—his sisters. I was in waiting on the bank to receive them, and paid my respects to his lordship, and a visit to the Misses Eden in the course of the day. In the evening I dined with them, and dine there again this evening, and every day as long as I remain with the camp. It is very stiff and starch-neckclothed sort of work; but, having no decent excuse, I cannot shrink. The Misses Eden are clever, sensible women, and his lordship seems a good sort of man, but nothing striking, either in manner or appearance. They will not leave my district for the next week—deuce take them all. The trouble they give is quite inconceivable, and no thanks for it either. This is the way with great people.

CAMP, HANSI,
February 2nd, 1839.

Dearest Mother,

I have got rid of the Governor-General and his party at last, and well pleased am I at my freedom. I did not see much of them, after all. There was most miserable weather during the last week of their stay in my district, and the whole camp suffered not a little inconvenience, at which I could not help chuckling. I hate to be put out of my way, and the degree of constraint which even the society of an Indian out-station imposes is irksome. This comes of living in the jungles. I consulted Lord Auckland's physician. He looked wise, and told me my liver was affected; which I could have told him a year and a half ago. He seemed to think the original cause of the derangement to be the liver, whereas I *know* it to be the stomach, which has, of course, affected the liver in its turn. I really find it quite useless to apply to the doctors. A man who eats his pound of beef-steak and drinks a bottle of wine a day cannot possibly prescribe for a stomach too weak to digest the simplest food. This is all very unpleasant to a man who, if any one did, enjoyed his dinner, both solids and liquids, but always in moderate quantity. But we cannot have everything, and the inclosed remittance, which makes up a total sum of 1,850*l.*, more or less, remitted in the course of this year (I mean from the savings of 1838), may be looked upon as a make-weight to a little dyspepsia.

Late news from England is of a very threatening complexion. Everything seems to point to war. I trust it will be averted. The result of the expedition to the eastward of the Indus here is still very doubtful. The troops, a well appointed force, but a mere handful, have not yet got half-way, and nothing can be more uncertain than the extent of assistance or resistance they may meet with on their arrival at Cabul. Matters here are very critical. I know not whether they are looked upon in that light in England. In the mean time, what wonderful doings in the way of railroads and steamers are taking place at home, and what a perfectly new face will the country present as soon as, far and near, civilized and rustic town and village are brought together by the improved internal communication in progress in the course of a few years! This is, indeed, the age of movement and improvement, and we are making gigantic strides onwards. You, I see, still view everything in the gloomiest colours, and make out that we are rushing to revolution, whereas we are escaping it. I fear I am the only Whig amongst you. I had some hopes of Fred, but I see that he has been bitten, too, with Toryism.

Here comes my dinner. Faugh! My stomach turns at it, almost. A dish of rice and split pulse, cooked dry, with a little curry spice mixed, and four cakes of unleavened bread, like what the Egyptians—I mean the Israelites—cooked, by Moses' order, for their flight from Egypt. ("God help him," the old lady will say, "'e doesn't know which of them it was, I'll be bound!") Odd enough, that unleavened bread should agree better with me than raised bread. One would not think so to look at it, far less to taste it. But this is one of the caprices of the stomach. "Nothing else, khansaman?" "Master always eats this; what more should there be?" I suppose my khansaman, reasoning like a true native, imagined I ate it from choice. Sometimes the pulse is cooked separately, with a few leaves of pottage (sāg), the very same that Esau sold his birthright for, and this is much more palatable, as the natives cook it very nicely; but I do not find it so digestible in that shape. You used to call me, and with some justice, fond of my belly, and I presume it is this very fondness which leads me to humour and excuse it, now that it is weak, by submitting, for month after month, to a diet which would have disgusted every one else long ere this, but which is the only one that suits it. But the exquisite mess is cooling all this time, and I must fall too. Here goes!

HISSAR,

May 17th, 1839.

Dearest Mother,

This morning I received your letter despatched from Ayott on the 16th March. This is, indeed, fast travelling! I am glad to find you all well and prosperous. I wish I had a little of the cold you are complaining of. News by the same opportunity has been brought up to the 27th March. There will be considerable interruption, I am afraid, in the overland route for the next three months, but the steamers which are being built at home will set all things right on their arrival. The movements of our army have thrown open the navigation of the Indus at last, and I see by the papers that regular passage boats for merchandise, travellers, &c., will leave Ferozepoor, on the Sutledge to the north of Hissar, every fifteen days for the future, en route down the stream to Scinde. This is a grand thing for us Western Province people. I have only to march from Hissar, about 200 miles due west, to Buhawalpoor, to meet the boats; and by embarking on them, changing boats once in the Scinde country, and re-embarking for Bombay at Kurachee, the harbour at the mouth of the Indus, I might be at Bombay without the least trouble within less than two months, stoppages included, from the day I started from Hissar. Only think what an advantage this presents to a man tracing his steps homewards,—compared to the dreadfully long and fatiguing overland journey of 1,000 miles, and three months' duration,—hence to Bombay across Central India! Merchandise from Europe will also soon find its way up here by the same channel, and a wonderful extension of trade and improvement may be expected from throwing open the north Indus, which has remained closed to all for the last 200 years. The political situation of the several States in Europe and America, just at present, fills all of us here with deep interest. I do most fervently trust that there may be no war to throw us all back in the gigantic strides to improvement which are now being made. I wish we were well rid of the Canadas; as a free and independent State, which they ought to be, they will be infinitely more beneficial to us than they can ever be as a colony. What wonderful steps are being made, too, for colonization in Australia! And the wonders of steam! It is a very interesting time altogether, and instead of groaning over anticipated evils, I look forward hopefully, as far as England is concerned, to the future. But who can tell the fate of India?

And where can the parallel of our situation here be found in the past annals of the world ?

May 26th—

I have been looking over the album in which I got you all to write my favourite pieces of poetry before I left you at Lyme. It tells the tale of other years most eloquently to me. India seems to have chilled suddenly my fondness for extracts, for I only find two short ones added, and these in 1828, to the copies of my friends at home. The rest of the book is a blank, and is likely to remain so,—a type of the effect of India on tastes and feelings, ardent as mine then were. The reperusal of them, after a long interval, almost brought the tears into my eyes. I could almost appropriate to myself Mrs. Heman's lines in her " Voice of Spring."

> " But ye ! ye are changed since ye met me last;
>
> Ye smile ! but your smile hath a dimness yet,
> Oh ! what have ye looked on since last we met ?"

Changed, indeed, since the time, twelve years ago, when Ellen copied out these lines at Lyme, a day or two before I left you ! Where has all the enthusiasm of that period gone to ? What a joyless, passion-less blank has the interval been ! And I am now on the top of the hill without anything to remind me of what my youth and early manhood were beyond these boyish transcripts. Well, I suppose I must console myself as I best can, with my 12,000*l.* as a make-weight in the scale.

HISSAR,

July 8th, 1839.

Dearest Mother,

I have just received your letter of the 25th March. The last is the first month I have fairly left without a letter to you for some years past. Several of my letters in the interior appear to have miscarried; you will know how many by the number you have minus, twelve in each year since 1835-36. Yours are fortunately much luckier than mine, for I really do not think I have failed to receive one even of yours during the last twelve years,—not, at least, to my recollection. I have the series in bundles, one for each year, quite complete, with the exception of three written at the time of Ellen's marriage, which I lost with my other papers in a box stolen in 1831 at Delhi. They will prove highly interesting as a family chronicle to my brothers and sisters some years hence, if they escape the white ants, from which I do my best to preserve them.

I am reading now, for the third or fourth time, a most entertaining work, which, well known and old as it is, I do not think anyone of you has ever taken up, viz., "Boswell's Life of Johnson" (Croker's edition,—a sad medley, but the completest that has yet been published). He was Tory enough, in all conscience, almost a Jacobite, but his notions on Church Government and Toleration, &c., &c., put to shame the melancholy bigotry of the greater part of the religious world at home even in these comparatively enlightened days. What an excellent book it would be to be read aloud to a family party. Boswell is the prince of biographers, and, at the same time, the silliest of men. His book is the most amusing and instructive one that ever was written.

I have looked out the piece of poetry quoted in your last letter, in the end of one of the two scrap-books once belonging to you, which are as fresh as when they left England. You say you have forgotten it. Here it is, then, on the very last page of the book :—

Epitaph on an Old Lady buried in Hendon Churchyard.

Reader ! she wandered all this desert through
In search of Happiness, nor found repose
Till she had reached the borders of the Waste.
Full many a flower that blossomed in her path
She stopt to gather, and the fruit she pluck'd
From many a tempting bough; *all* but
The Rose of Sharon and the Tree of Life.
This shed its fragrance to the gale, and spread
Its blushing beauties; *that* its healing leaves
Display'd, and Fruit immortal ;—all in vain !
She neither tasted nor admired, and found
All that she chose and tasted fair but false.
The flow'rs, no sooner gather'd than they faded,
The fruits enchanting—dust and bitterness,
And all the world a wilderness of Care.
Wearied, dispirited, and at the close
Of this eventful Course, she sought the plant
Which oft her heedless haste o'erlook'd, and proved
Its sovereign virtues underneath its shade
Outstretched, drew from her wounded feet the thorns,
Shed the last tear, breath'd the last sigh, and here
The Aged Pilgrim rests in trembling Hope.

This must have been copied out after your widowhood. A number of the poems are copied out in a hand I do not recognize and have not seen elsewhere. The contributors are few, but of those few the hands of all but two which copied out the extracts are now mouldering in the grave. I seldom open the volumes but with mixed feelings. If I live to return, you will receive them back; if not, they will be sent you with my other papers. Little did they think when they were bound by the old bookbinder who lived in one of the Abbey Closes at Bath, and whom you picked out for his cheapness, that they would take a voyage to India, and have to bear an exile of many long, weary years,—twelve, all but a fortnight or so wanting. I feel old in mind; solitude does me no good, but my habits are not now to be broken through. Nothing, my dear Mother, shall persuade me to return to this country when I have once left it. I have proposed to myself the plan of my future life; the disposal of it rests with a higher Power than man. I should be a happy man in England; my reading is incessant and untiring, my wants are few indeed, and my habits easily fixed. But this is premature. Three or four years hence I may begin to think of these things. I am different from most men, so do not argue from them to me, for I do not admit the chain of reasoning. I would not change with my brothers, if I were to begin life again and had the option, but I think them fortunate in not having to wear out their hearts and coin the refuse for gold. I nauseate general society, and I meet with no one whom I could make a special companion of—and so passes life. Yet better is it that I am alone. I cannot tie my happiness to the frail health of a frail woman, for marriage is indeed a leaning on a reed, which will pierce one's hand, to those forced to serve their time in India. Farewell, dearest Mother; I think there is much in your eldest son, if you could see him, that you would like,—much perhaps that you would blame, but his faults and recommendations are his own, not superinduced by others or external circumstances.

Old Runjeet Singh is dead, but all quiet. He was made a great deal too much of by Lord Auckland, and was a crafty old fox. I dislike the Sikhs as a nation, and have had a great deal to do with them in my day.

HISSAR,

September 7th, 1839.

Dearest Mother,

I despatched a letter to you by the last mail three weeks ago or less, and am in daily expectation of the receipt of your June letter, the steamers to Bombay being much more regular than those from it. I have nothing to communicate now, but a steamer is advertised for the early part of next month, and I must not let it go without a few lines. It is rather gratuitous in us Indians to complain of heat, but I never suffered so much from it as within the last two months. This district seems to have been cursed with drought, the seasons for three years in succession having proved most unfavourable. At this, which ought to be the greenest period of the year, not a particle of vegetation is visible, and the vile clammy heat is enough to smother one. "Merry it is for those in the good green woods" of old England. Here a man must sit in a corner, and spin for his subsistence, like a spider, out of his entrails, for it is at their cost that we scrape our pounds and pence together. My life for the last ten years has been that of one who lives on the future—for the first four or five years on the thoughts of furlough and a return, and for the last on the views enforced by prudence. "Hope deferred maketh the heart sick," but I doubt whether Solomon himself ever calculated on one, and that the only one, deferred from youth to middle age.

September 14th—

No June or July mail yet from England, but we are looking out for it daily. The army is on its way back from Cabul, having accomplished the object of the expedition. Tom Seaton, I see by the papers, joined a convoy which crossed the desert between the Indus and the passes of the mountains into Afghanistan, at the worst season of the year, when the route is not practicable, and is never traversed by the people of the country. They were exposed to the simoom, and numbers, both European and native, with the convoy perished. Seaton escaped with the loss of his skin, which peeled off under the effects of the dreadful heat, and must have joined his regiment at Cabul by this time. The army has undergone great privations and difficulties, but surmounted them all gallantly.

India is unquiet at present, and there seems every chance of a war with Birmah and Nepaul; I hope the Rajpoot States to the south of and adjoining my district will not be troublesome.

The heat is still overpowering, and the drought continues.

Having no Assistant under me at present, I shall have much on my hands for the several ensuing months, which I heartily wish were over. The zeal which once inspired me has long ago oozed out of the ends of my fingers, like Bob Acres' valour. Even if I were promoted, an increase of 250 rupees per mensem is all that I can look forward to now for years and years to come, but in that case I should be fixed at some large station, and my expenses would increase proportionally. In short, the Civil Service is not half what it was ten years ago.

The army was placed in a very ticklish position between Candahar and Cabul. Had there been a delay of one or two days in storming the fortress of Ghuzni, a great part of Afghanistan would have poured on the army; and had there been a check or failure, not only would the retreat or advance of the army have been cut off, but there would instantly have been a terrible stir throughout India and Birmah. Nepaul and the Native States would have been up and arrayed against us in a twinkling. Much, very much, hung upon the result of the attack, and most fortunate it has been that it succeeded. It was a gallant and cleverly managed affair altogether, and there is no little *éclat* in taking by a *coup de main* a fortress which sent forth the first invader of Hindostan 800 years ago, and which has borne so historical a name for centuries. Lord Auckland has been lucky in this expedition, enormous as the cost of it has been. There would have been a great outcry if it had failed, and its success, by the acknowledgment of all, has been much more owing to fortunate chances than to management.

CAMP,

March 1st, 1840.

Dearest Mother,

The December overland mail arrived a day or two ago, bringing both your October and November letters up to the date of the 21st December.

What will you do when Fred marries? for this event, I think, may be prognosticated, may it not? I do not like the idea of your living quite by yourself in the country. Will not a quiet house or lodgings at Bath be, after all, the goal of your wanderings? I think you are gravitating to it by degrees, and the thought pleases me.

If I live to return, you shall have my arm to the many spots around, so pregnant with recollections of the past; and we could contemplate beforehand, with a soothing feeling, peaceful Weston churchyard as your last,—but I trust distant,—resting-place from your labours of love to all of us.

So Monier Williams has got a writership. The mode in which it was conferred is a singular one, and Hannah's luck is great. He will, of course, go to Bombay, if he can; although the field in that Presidency is a confined one for civilians. Hannah Williams and her children are surely ornaments to our Brown family. I admire her self-poised, well-directed mind, and am glad to hear of the success of her elder sons in their professions. Fred, I see, has fairly launched into his parish business. He must not attempt too much at first, but he needs not my cautions, and probably would be rather indignant at my thinking myself called upon to offer any; the retort courteous to a meddling Indian at home being generally, "Stick by your niggers."

By-the-bye, you should have told me of Jessie C———, if you ever entertained the wish of my marrying her; and a very little would have brought me home, after she had once fixed my thoughts. I feel most disinclined to play the part of Hannah More's Cælebs in person. The double motive of embracing you all again, and of a wife, the approved of you all beforehand, supposing my fancy jumped with yours, would overcome at once all my prudential reasonings. Of the feeling which prompts some men to take a pride in selecting for themselves exclusively the object of their choice, I have none. It appears to me to be just as manly, and much more wise, to allow one's attention in the first instance to be directed by one's friends, and if the object of *their* preference, on the first idea being started, strike his, *then* to run the chances of a wooing, than to leave one's direction to chance. All men who have spent the life in the jungles I have, for so extended a period of years, become, as a matter of course, extremely susceptible when again thrown into female society; and I am not such an ass as to pretend to an exemption from the rule at any future time. English women in this country I am steeled against, but predisposed as I should be beforehand in favour of those at home, if left to myself I might take a wrong direction, and end my doubts of having done so, when too late, by a distressing certainty. Set the compass first, and if it chooses to veer afterwards, let it. As for my ideas of a wife, they are—an equable temper, an affectionate heart, an unspoiled mind, age not exceeding twenty-five, a decent sum of money, and a lovable person. "Very modest indeed, sir!" you will exclaim; but surely there are hundreds such in England, if one could only find them, who would not refuse to link their fate with a man of steady heart and open feelings—all the good qualities I can venture to assume to myself.

I have said nothing of what you would justly place first—the "one thing needful,"—needful no less for me than for her, being well assured that, to be approved by you, this would be the first point looked to. But I *have* referred to it in my desired quality of what I call an "unspoiled mind,"—unspoiled no less by religious sentiments carried to excess in outward observances, than by an over-refined or defective education. Religion outwardly exhibited in a young person, to the degree which characterizes the female religious society of young and old at Bath and such places, would nauseate instead of attracting; and one should be cautious before selecting from what is called a religious family *par excellence*, for, unfortunately, religious parents—people, I mean, like Bickersteth and others of the same grade—good and pious as they may be themselves, do *not* succeed in bringing up their families well. This is an ill-natured remark, but has been proved in hundreds of instances; they *over-do*, and spoil all. I am serious in all I have written above, which contains the pith of all I have to say on the subject of matrimony, as far as I am concerned. What say you to it all?

March 8th—

The weather is getting hottish, and I shall not be sorry to get into a house again. I have had abundance of marching about this cold weather, and have prevented one or two attacks of dyspepsia in consequence. I must keep up my morning foot exercise as well as I can during the next hot weather months, for I find it essential to my health; and if I can only manage to keep clear of it until the end of 1842, I doubt not I shall soon shake it off in England. By that time I trust to have completed my minimum of 20,000*l*., and then, Hey for England! Three years hence, and I hope to be amongst you. May the feet of Time move quickly, and his hand be light on your head in the interim! If I return, I shall have only seven years more of servitude in India, and whether I return or not, I shall be independent and my own master. To me the end of 1842 appears close at hand. In this country we measure time by events and not by days. In 1843, I shall be four-and-thirty—a grave age. But I must not anticipate too much. At all events, I do not think I shall disappoint you a second time. I feel so certain that a return to England now would, after the first novelty was over, be attended with doubtings and prudential regrets whilst there, that I have been forced to give up all idea of it. Hitherto everything has tended to confirm me in my opinion of the prudence of not having taken my furlough when it fell due.

March 14th—

To-morrow, as the natives would phrase it, the fortunate camp of my benignity will make an auspicious entrance into Hissar. In other words, I shall get under shelter again at last, after all my marching and running about. I shall have been absent from Hissar in all five and a-half months. I got so deadly sick of the place during my confinement there in the hot weather,—so disgusted with its unsightly ruins and miserable barrenness,—that I never go near it in the course of my marching, and, in fact, this year went a detour of several miles to get out of its way. The society (wretched misnomer!) there, too, —consisting of a dyspeptic, old-womanish fool of a major, a vulgar cockney veterinary surgeon, with a good-natured but oafish medical man,—is felt by me as a nuisance rather than a pleasure, and I should be much more suitably situated, if alone; mixing with them is a dreadful bore. Hansi I have avoided, too, for some months past, as I have some very important interests of Colonel Skinner's to settle between him and the Government, in my official capacity; and he is so hospitable and attentive generally, that it is difficult to keep one's mind from an almost imperceptible bias in his favour, produced by visitings and intercourse intermediately. If he is satisfied with my decision ultimately, well and good; if not, I am on the safe side. So you see that I am more solitary here than I was even at Sahuswan.

_____

HISSAR,

March 26*th*, 1840.

Dearest Mother,

Your very interesting January letter reached me yesterday. If an exclamation of surprise at the first, succeeded by a deep interest, and yet a perverse disinclination to put an end to the suspense by skipping at once to the end of the letter,—if a throbbing of the heart at passages and words which seemed to indicate an unfavourable issue, and a smile of real and heartfelt pleasure at the close, are proofs of brotherly feeling, Fred has had them all from me. Fred has chosen well, and he has been lucky in his acceptance. I envy him, and at his age; and, let me tell you, a few years between twenty-five and thirty,—the stage between early and mature manhood,—form a clearly marked period in one's life, as you may have traced in me, from my letters alone. My heart, too, could have knelt, as his has done, before its idol; but the shrine was vacant, and I fear that the gloss of one's feelings, at that time, is not easily recoverable in after-life. I envy him, but with a feeling of depression at my own lot, unshared, as it has been, for nearly thirteen years, by a single spoken word of interest or affection from any living being. How different from what his has been, and will be! I am rejoiced at his early marriage, and his future wife I seem to know as well as if I had been acquainted with her for years. Considering that Fred's attachment dates so far back as three years, you have been very sly in keeping me out of the secret so long, for, with the exception of an occasional notice of one "Bright-eyes" I was left to guess whom. You had let nothing drop from your pen that would give me a hint, even, at what was likely to happen. In your present letter, too, you have kept up the interest admirably, and with the skill of a novelist, interspersing the nursery and parish details like the breaks in a story. Truly, you have taken me completely by surprise, and the idea of the white-faced boy whom I left at Charmouth, so engrossed with the glories of coachey and the guard as to be inattentive to my parting nods, being a married man shortly, and an accepted suitor, now tickles me amazingly. I don't know when I ever realized the enjoyment of your delightfully long letters so much as on this occasion. I wish I could make you a better return.

March 28th—

Some opinions or expressions of mine, in my October letter, have called forth, my dear Mother, a theological attack on them of some length in your present letter. Instead of arguing, or explaining, I will copy out some lines, which I met with the other day. They are written by some one in this country, and I send them without note or comment.

CHRISTIAN WARFARE.

Soldier, go, but not to claim
   Mouldering spoils of earth-born treasure;
Not to build a vaunting name,
   Not to dwell in tents of pleasure;
Dream not that the way is smooth,
   Hope not that the thorns are roses;
Turn no wishful eye of youth
   Where the sunny beam reposes.
Thou hast sterner work to do,—
   Hosts to cut thy passage through;
Close behind the gulphs are burning,
   Forward! there is no returning.

Soldier, rest, but not for thee
   Spreads the world her downy pillow;
On the rock thy couch must be,
   While around thee chafes the billow;
Thine must be a watchful sleep,
   Wearier than another's waking;
Such a charge as thou dost keep
   Brooks no moment of forsaking.
Sleep as on the battle-field,
   Girded—grasping sword and shield;
Those thou canst not name nor number
   Steal upon thy broken slumber.

Soldier, rise,—the war is done:
   Lo! the hosts of hell are flying;
'Twas the sword the battle won—
   Jesus vanquished them by dying.
Pass the stream, before thee lies
   All the conquer'd land of glory;
Hark! what songs of rapture rise,
   These proclaim the victor's story.

Soldier, lay thy weapons down;
   Quit the sword, and take the crown;
Triumph! all thy foes are banish'd,—
   Death is slain, and earth has vanish'd.

April 3rd—

Ellen and John appear to be making their way slowly, but surely, amongst the hearts of their wealthy parishioners. And how could it be otherwise? and when did a cheerful demeanour, kind heart, and unobtrusive piety ever fail, in the end, in capturing all within the sphere of their influence! I believe them to be more powerful as instruments for their Master's service than a thousand sermons. How often are we poor mortals won to the doctrine through affection or esteem for the deliverer of it! It is the golden chain spoken of by Dryden, in his character of a good pastor, as let down by him to " draw his audience upward to the sky."

I am afraid Ellen's Italian boy, Michi, will turn out a *mauvais sujet*. But we Indians are over suspicious, and callous into the bargain,— and no wonder. The prominent points in the native character, with which we are unavoidably brought in contact, are their crimes, in our magisterial capacity, and their frauds in our revenue one. The European character in this country affords no relief to the dark picture every day presented, and our hearts gradually shut themselves in from all feelings of compassion, from a stern sense of duty, until they become as hard as the nether mill-stone. India is a bad school in every point of view, and no one can pass through its ordeal without deterioration. Happy those who have freshness of heart enough to feel for their houseless Michis.

Hissar,

May 1st, 1840.

Dearest Mother,

The mail starts on the 20th from Bombay, so I must not lose time. My extracts and poetry will arrive very appositely. I was thinking to-day what a contrast is presented in the life of myself and my brothers,—I mean the daily routine of existence, the details which make up the sum total. To be half-dragged off one's couch by one's bearers before earliest dawn,—to go stumbling along in the grey twilight, half asleep, with feet like lead and ankles doubling under me at every step,—to have to accomplish that most odious of all tasks, a given distance within a given time, three measured miles on foot before sunrise,—to return with a sensation of thirst as if I had swallowed Mount Etna,—to sit down to a cup of tea at eight o'clock with no appetite even for a piece of bread,—then to be entertained with the daily police reports of my district,—then to go into the court room, the thermometer varying from 80 to 100 degrees, with the natives jawing, jabbering and stinking about one,—then to dinner (shocking misnomer) of everlasting pork or mutton, with a sensation of faintness at the pit of one's stomach which I cannot describe,—then at sunset a public audience to the people outside the house, in the hot unrefreshing air, when I am obliged—at least, *I* consider myself in duty obliged—to sit, like the elders of old, in the gate of the city, listening to verbal complaints and petitions,—these constitute my life, and have done so for many a year back. How different from your jollifications and love-makings! These cut off a full third of the thread allotted to man, as they have done hitherto in the case of every member of the Brown family who has been in India. But I have the will to endure and the energy to carry me through in the views dictated by prudence.

HISSAR,

June 27th, 1840.

Dearest Mother,

We have all been expecting the overland mail for some days past, and shall probably have to wait some days longer before we get it; so, as the mail for England leaves this part of the country about the 12th proximo, I will commence my brief monthly letter. I have been passing several days with Colonel Skinner at Hansi, and have been feasted and made much of to my heart's content. I met there what is quite a novelty in Upper India, viz., an old lady, his sister, and a very agreeable one, too, whom I have made quite in love with me,—the only conquest I could ever boast of. She made me stay several days, which I passed pleasantly enough, but was glad at the same time to get back to Hissar, as high living very soon puts me out of sorts.

I met the other day with a book, "Valerius; a Roman Story," which I had not seen since I was at the Charterhouse seventeen years ago. With what deep and vivid interest I read it then; and now, even on turning over its leaves, I could recall the excited feelings which attended my first perusal of it. How well I remembered stealing with it, hid in my breeches, up to the dormitory—a forbidden place in the day—and lying with it amongst the dust and dirt full length under one of the beds to escape observation, the only quiet spot I could find to enjoy it in. Also how the dirty housemaid spied me out one day, and squeaked aloud her alarm, taking me for a burglar at the least, and how I bolted like mad down to the hall just in time to escape the hue and cry. Meeting with a book after the interval of many years, which we have read in former times under very different circumstances, is like meeting with an old friend. I was afraid to read "Valerius" again too attentively, lest I might meet with something that might break the charm, but it appears to me equal, if not superior, to Bulwer's "Pompeii," which you took such delight in. As the story turns on the fate of the Christians at Rome in the time of Trajan, and is moreover written with truthfulness, very different from the forced style of the man of the world, Bulwer, I think it would please you much. It is to be met with, I fancy, in every circulating library at home. That library at Charterhouse was a great blessing to all of us, but the time I spent there was anything but pleasant, and even the retrospect affords nothing to dwell on. After all, boyhood in itself has no attractions, either in possession or otherwise, and instead of wishing with Wordsworth that "I could recall that golden time again," I should not care if it had never existed.

July 2nd—

This morning I received your letter dated the 7th April, or rather despatched on that date. Certainly, if I know anything of the characters of my brothers and sisters I am indebted for that knowledge to you, and, I may say, I know them as well as if I had never left England. Fred's, perhaps, is the only one of which I might feel a little uncertain, as he has not the same salient points which the others possess,—at least, I have not traced them; not, and I say this with cap in hand, that I would presume to insinuate anything in his disfavour, as compared with the other three, only his profile has not the same clearness to my mental perceptions, which may be as much owing to my dulness of vision as to circumstances which have not admitted of an equal display of character through the medium of correspondence. Over Joe I feel disposed to exercise to the full all the rights of an elder brother, seeing that I well recollect him, as if it were but yesterday, attempting his first jump on the grass-plot of poor, dear, old Winifred, in the presence of an admiring group, over three pieces of stick placed gallows-fashion about three inches high from the ground. As I write this, the day recurs to me vividly : a beautiful July afternoon, when he was about two and a-half years old and I a schoolboy of eleven,—the horses, with William Wordsworth, which were to convey me to Dr. Knight's, the holidays being over, standing all ready before the door. I can even recall the feelings of the moment, which were condensed at the moment into a vehement wish that I could be, too, a happy child of his age, caressed by all, with no school or pedagogue in immediate prospect. To tell the truth, every letter which I receive from you gives a violent shock to my intention of postponing my furlough two or three years longer. For an hour or two after perusal I am as weak as water, and plans begin to form themselves in my head, but in a short time prudential and other motives intervene, and I have again to fling myself, like one of the Titans of old, on Indian earth and acknowledge that the load of Etna itself cannot be greater than the force of circumstances. I long to meet my brothers and sisters, and to conciliate, if possible, their affection and esteem. I ardently desire to hold you in my embrace once more. My God ! you may talk about hope deferred, but you never can experience the sharp twitches occurring now and then in the course of a protracted dream of ten years of expectation, —and this not limited merely to a reunion with you all, but to the chief end and aim of all men's affections. Yet I am in cooler moments as firm as a rock, notwithstanding that the circumstances detailed in my last letter are likely to detain me in India until the end of 1844, if not later.

July 6th—

I do indeed trust that our dear old friend, Miss Pilot, will be spared to us yet awhile. I should grieve with a pang of real sorrow over her death, but I would fain believe that this is still an event far distant. If the chain has not yet snapped which binds her mounting spirit to this world, assure her of my unceasing affection. I have ever felt towards her, and feel still, as if she were in the place of a second mother, and although my pen has been silent, the warmth of her own feelings will have often, I feel sure, secured me against any imputation of silence of heart in anything that may concern her. The face of her saintly mother beams on me with all the holy placidity of its expression of old, whenever I turn my eyes back to the mists of former days, and sorry indeed should I be to find no memorial of the Pilots at Bath, if I ever live to revisit it again. Her life has been indeed an useful one; may it be prolonged yet for many years!

Hissar,

September 4th, 1840.

Dearest Mother,

I have been waiting for the July mail to begin my letter, but this time it has been ten or twelve days beyond its usual time. At last, this morning, I received your May letter, despatched the 3rd June. You are still too early in sending off your letters, as the mail brings newspapers up to the 6th July, and a letter of three months' date is quite stale nowadays. You must mistake the date of the monthly despatch. Whether stale in date or not, the letter was a delightful one. I was two good hours, I protest, reading it, lingering over its details like a lover over his mistress's first letter. It breathes, too, of spring,—dear delicious English spring,—and it has made my heart ache to the core. It amounts almost to cruelty to send such details to a man in this treeless, waterless desert of inclement sky and ungenial soil. India is a harsh stepdame. Talk not of her benefits! The life she gives is best described by the poet,—

> " All life is but a wandering to find home,
>   When we are gone, we're there."

A weary looking forwards or a dull, dead acquiescence in existence,— a total absence of everything that can minister to the tastes, sentiments, rational desires, affections or passions! I really wonder sometimes at the firmness of will that keeps me here; but independence is, as a worldly blessing, an inestimable one; and hard as these deprivations are to bear at the time, it will weigh them all down hereafter. Most acutely did I enjoy the springs of 1825—27,—the only ones, I may say, I ever passed at home,—for to a schoolboy all four seasons are pretty much alike. A new world had opened to me, and, in my enthusiasm, I could have fallen down and worshipped it. Those mild, dewy days in April, when the air is genial, the wind hushed, the sun hidden, and the earth literally bursting forth into verdure before your eyes, how intensely I enjoyed them! My very soul is bowed down at the prospect of two or three more years in this barren land, but my resolution is steady—steady. In the meantime, the vivid and exquisite delight, pourtrayed in your letters, tugs hard at my heartstrings. Oh, that this long sleep were over!

September 6th—

This great distaste for India, or rather this keen sense of the deprivations which it entails, has been the growth of the last three years, and no wonder. At Sahuswan, we had our recreations and small society, such as it was ; but here, or at Hansi, there is not, and has not been, one that I care to associate with, and there is nothing to divert my mind from the sense of present discomforts. If it were worth my while to change, I would not stay here a day longer, but even promotion, which will come uncalled for, if it comes at all, would give me no substantial advantage.

September 10th—

Your letter is quite vocal with thrushes and nightingales, " and all the finches of the grove," and I really believe the birds sing nowhere as they do in England ; certainly in no other country in the world is there such an attempered spring. The only birds I have much acquaintance with here are the common house-sparrows, and they are as great a nuisance as the mosquitos. Vain is the attempt to snooze half-an-hour or so after sunrise. The bed being laid out in the verandah, the sleeper is awakened a dozen times by their vile shrieking notes, and the flutter of their rascally wings close to his nose, whilst he is serenaded in front by half-a-dozen crows, whose endless " caw, caw," murders sleep. What a pet they have put me in ! Early rising is a great effort in this country, but the impossibility of snoozing comfortably reconciles me to it. It is the practice of most Indians to sleep under a punka in the hot weather, but I prefer the verandah to the heated air of the house.

So Emma goes to France this year. I wonder at her taste. France, even in the days of my enthusiasm, I viewed only as the thoroughfare to Switzerland. Now I care not if I never see either ; the misery of having to twist my mouth about in my attempts to pronounce French would be more than an offset to any pleasure its scenery could afford, which is mighty little after all, except in some parts of Normandy and the distant provinces. Italy I do want to see ; Naples, Rome, the museum at Florence, Verona, Venice and Genoa, I must contrive to pay a visit to on my return from this country, if possible ; for, once in England, I should find some difficulty in making up my mind to leave it for Italy, which would be almost as if a man were to proceed halfway to India during his furlough, and back again. No ! Devonshire Wales, Derbyshire, Yorkshire, and, perhaps, the Lakes and Scotland again, will form the limits of my excursions. Any grandeur which the scenery of Switzerland may have, has been extinguished to my mind by the Himalayas, and as for its picturesque beauties, I can find these in England. Neither scenery nor people, but places would be my object in Italy. Perhaps I might honour the Rhine, but am not sure. But it is too early, as yet, to form plans for futurity. Two long, long years are still before me—longer will they be to me than any I have ever spent.

September 12th—

The blindness of the religious world at home, or rather of their representatives at Exeter Hall, on some subjects, quite astonishes me. All efforts to repress the slave trade have failed, and not merely failed, they have increased its horrors tenfold. How is this to be met? Oh, says the Exeter Hall meeting, by the introduction of Christianity into Africa! In other words, the Christianity, which is quite powerless as a motive of conduct with the, comparatively speaking, enlightened slave dealer, is to be all efficient with the benighted African. Unfortunately the principles of supply and demand, whether in commodities or human beings, have prevailed, and will prevail, over any restrictions that religion or the excise laws would impose on the feelings or actions of men. Lessen the demand for slave labour by encouraging the production of the same articles of consumption by the free labour of the East,—which can furnish them at a much smaller cost,—and a vital blow will be struck at the slave trade from which it will not soon recover. But no—this will not do for people in England; they argue and act as if the world were governed by a theocracy with direct commands and interpositions as in the days of the Jews. Human aids and means, causes and effects, are alike disregarded. All admit that the time of miracles has ceased since the third century; but few take into account that the raising of Lazarus from the dead would be a scarcely less astonishing instance of miraculous power than the conversion of a common African or Hindoo to vital Christianity. Its scheme and doctrines are literally unintelligible to them, and their intellects require to be raised before the truths of our religion are expounded to them. Dryden's Life of Xavier, the Spanish missionary, proves that, under certain circumstances, it is not difficult to induce the heathen to adopt the external forms: but what trace has been left of his labours? If the thousands and tens of thousands flung away by the well-meaning people in England every year had only been devoted to establishing schools and extending instruction in this country, how different would the result have been! An educated native, whose mind has once been opened, immediately rejects in his heart the idolatry of his fathers. This, experience has proved in in-numerable instances. I do not mean to say that he is converted, or converts himself to Christianity. On the contrary, he almost always flies off into the opposite extreme, and becomes either a Deist or what may be called a freethinker; but even this is a great step gained. He *cannot* return to his former paganism,—of that we may be quite certain; and then is the time for the missionary to step in. A great deal has been talked in England of the Kistnagurh Christians. It is all delusion, conceived by a few on the spot, and caught up and pro-pagated by the fervid minds of the religious world at home. I do not think that there was ever a man of any intelligence in this country who spoke favourably of the prospects of any extension of Christianity here under the present system; but I will not trouble you with any more of my thoughts on the subject. I am no admirer of the Exeter Hall meetings, or of the spirit in which many of them are conducted, but on the slave question they proved themselves destitute of common sense.

HISSAR,
September 25th, 1840.

Dearest Mother,

     Your letter, despatched the 7th July, reached me this morning. Very happy am I to hear of your having got over your indisposition, which alarmed me the less as I confidently contemplate your living many years longer. Sixty years will bring its infirmities with it without doubt, and may connect the termination of life with the commencement of old age; but your winter is a mild one—no foggy November, nor dull December; but genial January—frosty, but cheerful. For his own life who can answer; but, if mine is spared, I entertain a conviction that I shall embrace you again, and, old as you may be, entice you amongst the fields and lanes, the larks and hedge-row birds, "yellow king-cups" and "daffodils,

> That come before the swallow dares, and take
> The winds of March with beauty."

To me there is nothing unpleasing in the thoughts of your gentle descent down the hill of life into the vale of years, for your mind is as young—aye, younger—than it was thirteen years ago. Age may prove a second childhood, in one sense, to some; but that is a childhood of the intellect. I would rather say that age ought to be a second childhood to be a happy and genial one; a time when, after the turmoil of life is past and at a distance, the mind has leisure to revert to the peaceful tastes and pleasures of early life,—a time of heart's ease and tranquil enjoyment of the present without forgetfulness of the future. What say you to my moralizings?

Thank Ellen for her share in your letter.

Ellen is in an error as to my taste for dove-like women. A dove-like heart, if you please; but if it extends to the person and manners, it would but turn out mawkish in the end. Marriage, like most things, requires some salt to preserve it from insipidity, and for this something more piquant is needed than the neutral quality of a mere passive softness of disposition. Sweetness of temper is a sine quâ non to a man's happiness—I mean his passive happiness—but the real zest of marriage will be found, I suspect, in a woman's looking up to and loving her husband, and in the husband's admiration and love of his wife. I have put "love," you see, the last in both cases, as the durable love of wedded life is a consequence of their mutual regard. As for love in its common sense, I am far beyond that—smile as you may—having passed, by many a long year, the era assigned by Shakespeare for the lover—

> "Sighing like furnace, with a woful ballad
> Made to his mistress' eyebrow."

The love which is the child of esteem is all that I now hope or wish for. In my own case, I cannot agree with you to the full extent of what you say about money being, comparatively speaking, so unimportant in the scale. A man who, with an income of 600*l.* or less, marries a penniless girl, has to commence life again to all intents and purposes; and what a life! No, no. I may come out to this country again, and live independent and like a gentleman, whilst my wife's money and my own are nursing at home; but I cannot again enter upon the up-hill work of scraping and saving. It is a perfectly different case with a man in England, who can live moderately, and who, along with his wife, can enjoy home instead of being condemned to perpetual exile. I repeat, I cannot begin life again at the age of thirty-five. My life during the last four years has been one of simple endurance of existence; so will the next two years be. The money scraped together during this time is valued by me, not so much as money, but as bearing the stamp on every rupee thus collected of bodily ailments and mental deprivations; so that every 100*l.* in money presents a hundred pounds' worth of dyspepsia, and far, far more than its own intrinsic value, in so many days and weeks cut out of the best part of one's life, and flung, unheeded and unmarked, to the past. Consequently it is a store which, having been purchased by the best of my years and time, and at the cost of everything that deserves the name of pleasure in this work-day world, must be tended accordingly, and not be frittered away in marriage expenses, and house-keeping after marriage.

In the meantime, who can describe the heat of this place? I never recollect such a season. For the last ten years I have always been under canvass in the first week in October, but this year the season is such a dreadful one that I fairly shrink from the exposure. The sickness exceeds anything I ever witnessed. I have been laid up with three attacks of fever, and am still far from well. Detestable hole! detestable climate! detestable country!

October 8th—

I scarcely know how I shall endure this country for two years longer. It is now nearly three years sinc I knew what it was to eat my single meal with any appetite, or, when I had the appetite by any chance, could venture to indulge it. Such are the pleasures of money-getting in India. Fortunately I have a fund of passive endurance, which has been tried on some occasions more severely than you think for, and on this I must repose in the interim. The past two years have floated swiftly, the next two will necessarily be protracted by that hope deferred that maketh the heart sick; but the prison doors will open at last, and then for the song of the emancipated captive! The best plan is not to look forwards at all; at least, not for the next year and half, and to bind up the loins of resolution with the girdle of patience, as the Persians say.

October 12th—

Your Nailsea primrose must be repaid by some lines which I found in "Blackwood's Magazine"—

> That flower—that flower! oh, pluck that flower for me!
> There in the running stream
> Its silvery clusters gleam:
> Oh! give it me.
> The same! the very same! I knew it well,
> Last seen so long ago. Oh! simple flower,
> That sight of thee should waken up this hour
> Thoughts more than tongue can tell!

But the whole is too long for this short letter, which I must send off for the October mail.

Time has mended my taste for poetry, but it exists as strong as ever, only in another direction. How I doated, ten years ago, over the "kind-hearted" plays of Beaumont and Fletcher, and the exquisite melody of many of the passages of Ford; but I was enthusiastic in all things then. These hideous, barren plains are enough to drive all poetry from one's soul.

Business again prevents my meditated trip to the hills this season, and next it will be hardly worth while going. I should have been glad to have got away for a month or so. Truly the enjoyments of Indians might be contained in a nut-shell, and that a rotten one.

I met the following passage the other day in turning over my books. Whether it is true or not those who are qualified must decide. "There are many 'intensifiers' to the passion of love; such as pride, jealousy, poetry (money, sometimes), and idleness; but if the experience of one who has studied the art of love in an 'Evangelical' country is worth a para, there is nothing within the bend of the rainbow that deepens the tender passion like religion. I speak it not irreverently. The human being that loves us throws the value of its existence into the crucible, and it can do no more. Love's best alchemy can only turn into affection what is in the heart. The vain, the proud, the poetical, the selfish, the weak, can and do fling their vanity, pride, poetry, selfishness, and weakness into a first passion; but these are earthly elements, and there is an antagonism in their natures that is for ever striving to resolve them back to their original earth. But religion is of the soul as well as the heart—the mind as well as the affections; and when it mingles in love, it is the infusion of an immortal essence into an unworthy and else perishable mixture."

Camp,

December 29th, 1840.

Dearest Mother,

Your welcome letters of September and October reached me a day or two ago, after an interval of two months, occasioned by the suspension of communication with Europe, *viâ* Egypt. A civilian from a neighbouring district was on a visit to me at the time, but I managed to pack him off to the jungles on a day's shooting, with a gun in his hand and a basket of prog at his tail; and the day being a holiday, I sat down and had a fine read at them, from ten o'clock a.m. to near four, for no less a time was taken in getting leisurely through their ample details.

Ellen's letters from "the North" are admirable, and afforded me much amusement, with many a hearty chuckle. I would fain flatter myself that my commendations of that part of England have had some effect in influencing their choice of a tour in that direction. Whether or no, it appears to have been a happy and joyous one.

Your tours tug hard at my heart-strings, harder certainly this time than in any former year. The contrasts between your most ordinary every-day life, exclusive of family pleasures and cheering excursions, become so strong day by day that I really begin to doubt whether I shall have courage to endure until the end of 1842, when I place beside them the most monotonous, most cheerless existence of mine.

My above-mentioned visitor's was the first white face I had seen for two whole months of tiresome marches backwards and forwards over these barren plains, and I am so totally indifferent to the mis-called society of the only two places in my district which affords even a shadow of such—viz., Hansi and Hissar—that I care not, as far as these two places are concerned, if my next year be as solitary as the preceding one. I minded not such matters as long as my health and spirits continued good, but I have endured enough during the last three years to have sent any other three men whimpering to England; and of late my liver, which had before merely acted indirectly on my stomach and its digestive powers, has been so troublesome on its own account that I begin fairly to hesitate about my future plans. True, if I leave India at the close of 1841 I shall be short of the sum I had previously determined to lay aside as a store for the future, but money must not be balanced against the health I have lately been losing. Dyspepsia and its attendant discomforts, if not miseries, I have borne manfully; but this constant stinging in the side, which neither abstinence, exercise, nor physic relieves me from, is not to be trifled with. I have not by any means yet altered my plans, but I feel that my equilibrium has been disturbed. I am gravitating towards England, and the next six months will determine me for or against. Your last two letters have merely given a fresh impulse to the change, which prudence had begun to point out to me.

January 6th, 1841—

You must not take me at my word in what I have above written. The pendulum is oscillating, but the clock has not struck. Whenever it does, you will not fail to hear. Now that I have broken the ice of the last entire year remaining, I begin to pluck up fresh heart. Only let me get to the close of 1841 well, and the next nine months will be soon over.

Your account of our dear family friend, Miss Pilot, is painful. The bowl, I fear, is breaking at the cistern, and I anticipate the worst in the next letter I receive from you. Her sisters, I think, are all still alive; but thus it is in the world as Wordsworth beautifully says:

> The good die first,
> Whilst those whose hearts are dry as summer's dust,
> Burn to the socket.

Her death will shatter one of the strongest links which bind me to past times in connection with future anticipations. I have all along entertained a lively hope of seeing those dear old friends again, but it has left me utterly now.

January 14th—

I shall have to make a miserable return for your two copious letters this month, for I have nothing to add on my own account, and the time for the mail has arrived. I have just been to meet my lord and master, the senior member of the Board of Revenue—half-way to Delhi—to give him an account of my four years' stewardship, he having procured my appointment on public grounds to this district.

January 16th—

Your European politics give me great uneasiness. We have played into the hands of Russia most effectually; and, independently of laying Mehemet Ali at the foot of the Porte, which is little else than Russia in disguise, ready for the swoop which the latter must and will make at the fitting opportunity on Constantinople and all that belongs to it, we have blindly carried through the object which Russia has ever had at heart since 1830—the detaching England from French goodwill and alliance of interests. If England and France can only be brought to quarrel, Russia well knows that a clear stage will be left her in the interim to do what she pleases upon; so we carry through the schemes of Russia both ways, and at the same time have the brunt and expense of the outbreak with our nearest neighbour and best friend. I hate to think, far more to write, of such blundering; but the French are more to blame than we are, or, at least, as much. For their own special interests they were insincere at first, and we were rude and uncivil in our proceedings afterwards. John Bull has always burnt his fingers in foreign politics. What we gain by our arms we lose by our diplomacy—a remark 200 years old, and a true one. The ministers deserve to lose their places for such mischievous measures—not for the Tories, but for others amongst the Whigs; and lose them they would if the people's indifference or sluggishness were less.

Hissar,
May 21st, 1841.

Dearest Mother,

Five months of this year have passed, and if I were only at the close of it I should be thinking in some earnest of England, for, say or write what I may on the feeling of the moment, I suspect I shall not be long in turning my face homewards when I have once completed my minimum of 20,000*l.* I suppose you are now at Ayott, all amongst the sweets of a spring in the country. I have almost forgotten what lilacs and laburnums are like. A faint sort of recollection does exist of the violets and cowslips, but that is all. I suppose I shall like them all the better when I see them again. How delicious was dear old Winifred in the month when we left it for ever, and how I enjoyed myself in the mere pleasure of animal existence, lying with my book on the grass near the arbour, as if there were no such things to come as India, and 20,000*l.*, and the liver complaint. Depend upon it, England is the only country in the world in which we can form an idea of what spring really is. No wonder they did it such "observaunce" in the olden time. Farewell, dearest Mother.

** His health completely failed him in the autumn of 1841. He was obliged to flee from the Plains of Hissar to the Hills, and thence by dawk to Calcutta, where he embarked for England. He recovered his health on the voyage, and, viâ Cairo and Alexandria, arrived in England, and met his assembled family at Ayott Rectory on his mother's 62nd birthday.

LONDON:
PRINTED BY C. F. ROWORTH, BREAM'S BUILDINGS, CHANCERY LANE.

For EU product safety concerns, contact us at Calle de José Abascal, 56–1º,
28003 Madrid, Spain or eugpsr@cambridge.org.